11693

CA 95623
118
ian Education Alliance, Inc,

D0383865

PROFILES IN WISDOM

PROFILES IN WISDOM

NATIVE ELDERS SPEAK ABOUT THE EARTH

STEVEN McFADDEN

BEAR & COMPANY
PUBLISHING
SANTA FE, NEW MEXICO

LIBRARY OF CONGRESS CATALOGING-IN-PUBLICATION DATA
McFadden, Steven S.H., 1948-
    Profiles in wisdom : native elders speak about the Earth / by
Steven S.H. McFadden.
        p.   cm.
    ISBN 0-939680-71-8
    1. New Age movement—North America. 2. Indians of North
America—Philosophy. 3. Indians of North America—Mythology.
4. Nature—Religious aspects. 5. Earth—Religious aspects.
BP605.N48M374 1991
299'.7—dc20   90-49873
                                                              CIP

Text copyright © 1991 by Steven S.H. McFadden
Illustration copyright © 1991 by Angela C. Werneke

All rights reserved. No part of this book may be reproduced by any means or in
any form whatsoever without written permission from the publisher, except for
brief quotations embodied in literary articles or reviews.

Bear & Company, Inc.
Santa Fe, NM 87504-2860

Cover & interior design: Angela C. Werneke
Author photo: Carolyn Mercer-McFadden
Editing: Gail Vivino
Typography: Casa Sin Nombre, Ltd.
Printed in the United States of America by R.R. Donnelley

9 8 7 6 5 4 3

To the wise ones,
the elders who hold and keep bright the light
of the one true tradition,
no matter the color of their skin
or the name of their religion—
I honor you.
And also to the generations who follow,
that you may remember and honor those
who have gone before you.

Photo Credits

Photos of Grandfather William Commanda, AmyLee, Willaru Huayta, Hunbatz Men, and J. T. Garrett by Steven S.H. McFadden. Photos of Lorraine Canoe and Tom Porter by Tina Sunday. Dhyani Ywahoo photo by Pamela Cabell-Whiting © 1986; used by permission, all rights reserved. Eunice Baumann-Nelson photo by Brian Higgins, NP Studios. Photo of don José Matsuwa, doña Josefa Medrano, and Brant Secunda courtesy of Dance of the Deer Foundation. Grandmother Twylah Nitsch photo by Stephen Schoff © 1987. Medicine Story photo by Don Himsel, *The Telegraph*. Sun Bear photo courtesy of the Bear Tribe. Oh Shinnah photo by Michael Silverwise. Slow Turtle photo by Eric Radack © 1985.

⫷⫷⫷ CONTENTS ⫸⫸⫸

⟪⟪⟪ ACKNOWLEDGMENTS ⟫⟫⟫

*F*or sharing their time, their stories, and their wisdom, I thank all of the elders who contributed so generously to this book. For inspiration and guidance, I thank Margo Schmidt, Carolyn Mercer-McFadden, Fred Cutcheon, Anderson Hewitt, Marilyn Perkins, Bill Watkinson, Grandmother Dorothy Commanda, Oswald White Bear and Naomi Fredericks, Uncle Jack, and Grandmother Julie. For technical support along the path, I thank Julie Arpin and Karen Payne. For making this book not only possible but also an act of beauty, I thank all my skillful sisters and brothers at Bear & Company.

⟪⟪⟪ INTRODUCTION ⟫⟫⟫

*I*n 1983, after three days and nights of praying and fasting on a mountain-top, I snapped a twig with my fingers and had a revelation. I saw that this simple action had changed the world, and that it would never be the same again. I could never put that twig back together the way it had been. This was a small change, but an important change nonetheless. As the sound of the snap reverberated within my mind, I understood how everything I said and did changed the world. What came with the snapping twig was not an abstract idea or a philosophical insight, but a living experience of how all my actions influence creation. Since then, the lesson of this experience has guided my life in a world where, until recently, it seemed as if most people were oblivious to the way their lives inflict deep wounds upon the Earth, the air, and the water.

The realization I came to on this summit is something many Native American people have known throughout their lives: that all things are related, and that each action in the web of life influences everything else. Modern science has finally established this principle with the Superstrings Theory, but many Native Americans received the lesson in childhood as part of their cultural heritage. They have tried to live their lives in accord with it, making sure that, to the extent possible, their actions arise out of respect for the spirit in all creation. Now is a time when all of humanity desperately needs to learn this basic lesson.

No one would argue with the premise that most modern people have lost their connection with the Earth. The distortions and abuses resulting from this lack of connection are plain. Millions of people are finally waking up to notice the obvious: that the human relationship with the natural world is greatly distressed. Some observers call this The Great Awakening. This awakening is good news. But what will it lead to? How will we respond? Where do we go from here? These questions are just coming into focus.

Because they have lived on the Earth with conscious respect for thousands of years, Native American people are the keepers of ancient wisdom that could be of enormous value to people who are wrestling with contemporary environmental and cultural questions. Dozens of books have presented native wisdom from the mythic or historic perspective, but many people have discounted this information as anachronistic—wistful descriptions of a simpler world to which we can never return.

We are not going back to tribal culture, nor should we. This book in no way advocates a return to a romanticized past. It is, rather, a journalist's account of contemporary men and women who are concerned with the modern world. Coloring their concern is a deep reverence for the wisdom tradition of the past, the wisdom tradition that is the gift of their culture to the world. But their focus, and the focus of this book, is on the present and the future.

In our times, we have the privilege and the responsibility of creating a new culture, especially since our modern culture has proved itself unworkable. This is true not just for communists. Capitalism also has many tragic failures, especially evident in its ravaging of the Earth and in the many thousands who have been left hungry and homeless. Equally tragic is the fact that, even among those who are warm and well fed, many thousands lead aimless lives. They do not know why they are here, or what the purposes of their lives are.

Through the eyes of the elders who are profiled in this book, we can look to the roots of wisdom on this land. What do the ancient ones who have been trained in the sacred traditions of this land have to say to us as our existing culture crumbles and we experience the first, tentative birth pangs of a new culture? We cannot simply adopt the Mohawk or Cherokee or Algonquin customs and ceremonies. They are not appropriate. They will not work for us. We must create new forms in response to the living spirit of our times. Yet we can learn much from looking to the spiritual roots of this land, and from listening to the contemporary elders who have access to these roots.

Profiles in Wisdom: Native Elders Speak about the Earth is a collection of true stories about contemporary native elders who are, in various ways, keepers of wisdom. For the purposes of this book, elders are defined as those who have gone beyond midlife and who have demonstrated wisdom in the way they have lived their lives. Two subjects, AmyLee and Willaru Huayta, are just entering midlife; however, as their stories make clear, their circumstances make them worthy of exception.

This book gives the elders an opportunity to relate their diverse teachings about the human relationship with the Earth. Each of the elders has a personal story, character trait, or insight that can help us get in touch with our own innate wisdom. Their teachings are in response to a series of critical questions asked of each of them: What is your personal story? What do you see happening in the world now? What do you see ahead? What specific advice do you offer to those who will listen? What have you come to know about living in balance on the Earth? How could other people apply these lessons?

One cannot make sweeping generalizations about Native Americans. Even at this late date, over 250 Indian languages are spoken in North America, and each language represents a different tradition. There is hardly a homogenous point of view, and this book does not purport to convey any official or even representative view. These profiles constitute only a small sample of some people who are Native American.

Consequently, the elders are presented here as individuals who stand for themselves, not as designated spokespersons for their cultures. While all the elders would surely agree on the need to respect the Earth as our mother, they might well disagree on many other less important points.

Unfortunately, many times throughout history the teachings of native peoples have been distorted or misrepresented. To prevent that from occurring with this effort, each elder was sent a copy of the chapter dealing with his or her story. That way they had an opportunity to check their stories and make corrections. Also, my approach was minimalist. I interviewed the elders, framed their responses for flow and coherence, and generally kept my own commentary to a minimum so that the elders might speak as directly as possible to readers.

In learning the stories of these elders, we must be careful not to place them on pedestals. While they may have amazing or seemingly exotic circumstances in their lives, they are human beings with human failings. Likewise, Native American society, like all society, has a long way to go to perfect itself, and there are many failings and disagreements among its people. For example, not all Native Americans feel their teachings should be shared with the world, especially since the world has proved itself so eager to take their lives and their land. However, certain teachings are common in Indian society, and all of the elders profiled here exemplify these teachings: reverence for the Earth as the basic source of our livelihood; recognition that we are in a spiritual relationship with all of life; and tolerance of other beliefs or attitudes.

Much of the Western world will celebrate the five hundredth anniversary of Columbus's discovery of America on October 12, 1992. That's when he landed on a Caribbean island, met with the natives, and ostensibly proved that the Earth was round, not flat as some Europeans had thought. But for thousands of years before his voyage, many Native Americans, including the Maya, taught that the Earth was but part of a solar system, and that that solar system was but part of an immense spiral galaxy. Columbus was the first of many thousands who attempted to destroy this knowledge, and who engaged in atrocities that cumulatively became a campaign of genocide against the people and culture of this hemisphere—a campaign that continues today in many places. For the most part, our dominant culture has ignored this genocide. We have also ignored the sacred knowledge of the Native Americans, especially their Earth wisdom. Now, when the well-being of the Earth is so gravely threatened, we need to recall and employ these teachings.

The scope of the book is North America, the continent long called Turtle Island by Native Americans. However, the natives of North America have long been in contact with the natives of South America. For that reason, the book includes a spokesperson from South America, Willaru Huayta, who addresses the relationship of the two continents.

Clearly, our collective life on Turtle Island has not yet jelled. We have no whole or wholesome culture. We are still in ferment, still a melting pot. Can this melting pot produce anything worthwhile without being seasoned with the traditional wisdom of the land? I think not. I believe that we are being called to create social and cultural forms imbued with ethics and aesthetics for the twenty-first century and perhaps the millennium. Those forms must be based on an ecologically informed culture with awareness of sacred time and sacred place. Our culture must gratefully and gracefully embrace the rainbow colors and beliefs of humanity. As I hear it, the message of the elders is that this is necessary and possible.

One connecting theme in this book is the belief of most elders that, many times before, civilizations have existed on Earth and then been destroyed, primarily because technology was developed and then used without wisdom. Obviously, we are again in a period when technology dominates life and is generally applied without wisdom. We still have much to learn.

Most of the elders profiled in this book believe that we are now moving into a new epoch of history, a new age. However, their understandings of this transition are different. Some say we are moving from the Third World to the Fourth World; others say the transition is from the Fourth World to the Fifth; and yet others say we are moving from the Fifth to the Sixth. As I listened to the elders speak about this point, their differences began to seem less and less important. While different tribal groups have different systems for reckoning time, most do agree that we are moving into a new time, a time that their ancestors foresaw long ago. In anticipation of the new time, the ancestors offered guidance through prophecies. Many of these prophecies are woven into the text of this book—not to titillate, but to remind us that with common sense and wise action we can avoid the harsh consequences of the Earth changes that the ancient ones foresaw. Most of the elders agree that we are now experiencing some of those Earth changes, as we are living in a time when the Earth is cleansing itself of harmful influences with intensified storms, volcanoes, earthquakes, and other upheavals. Unless we wake up, they caution, the cleansing will become more vigorous.

Years ago when I was a teenager, I read and was deeply inspired by the late president John F. Kennedy's book, *Profiles in Courage*. In that now classic book, President Kennedy explored the quality of courage in the lives and decisions of several political figures. In so doing he brought an abstract quality—courage—to life. In this book I have tried to follow his lead by bringing the quality of wisdom to life through the stories and words of some seventeen people who are keepers of a true wisdom tradition—a tradition desperately needed in this raucous time of transition. If we but ask respectfully and then listen, the native elders of America will have much to teach us.

PROFILES IN WISDOM

ONE

Sounding a Basic Call
to Consciousness

LORRAINE CANOE & TOM PORTER

*T*om Porter is Bear Clan chief in the Longhouse tradition of the Mohawk people. He lives in a simple farmhouse on the St. Regis Indian Reservation alongside the St. Lawrence Seaway in Hogansburg, New York. He is a family man, a father with four children. He is also a teacher—a traditional teacher of the Great Law.

Lorraine Canoe lives a couple of miles down the road, closer to the village. She is of the Wolf Clan, and a grandmother with a fierce maternal instinct to protect what she feels is good. Her Indian name is Kanaratitake, which means Carrying Leaf.

Though they hail from different clans, Tom Porter and Lorraine Canoe are friends, and they are both articulate advocates for the values of the traditional Longhouse way of life. Much of what they have to say, indeed much of the wisdom of their people, constitutes a wake-up call for the rest of humanity.

The point of view that both Tom Porter and Lorraine Canoe express arises from their life experiences as people of the Mohawk tradition. The Mohawks are part of the Haudenosaunee, the Six Nations Confederacy whose tenets served as a model for the Constitution of the United States when it was created by the founders. To appreciate what these modern Native American leaders have to say, it is important to understand something of their tradition.

In 1977, the Six Nations of the Haudenosaunee—widely known as the Iroquois Indians—assembled some of the wisdom of their tradition in three papers that they presented to an agency of the United Nations, the association of Non-Governmental Organizations (NGO). These papers outlined their understanding of world history and their thoughts on the future. They were eventually published together under the title *Basic Call to Consciousness* (Akwesasne Notes, 1978).

Basic Call is a scathing critique of modern life, and for that reason it has proved to be anything but a bestseller. No one is eager for a verbal spanking; and not everyone would agree with what these Native Americans have to say, either. But they do have a valid point of view, and people who are concerned about the survival of life should at least hear them out.

In *Basic Call* we hear the voices of the elders who have lived the longest upon this land. They are the heirs of traditions that maintained balance here for thousands of years before the European settlers arrived. Most of the world's professed traditions are fairly recent. Mohammedanism is about 1,500 years old, Christianity is 2,000 years old, and Judaism is perhaps 2,000 years older than that. However, the native people of America lay claim to a tradition that goes back many, many thousands of years before that.

Consequently, the native viewpoint is derived from a philosophy that, according to the Haudenosaunee, sees native people as having historical roots extending back tens of thousands of years. This is a geological kind of perspective, one that regards modern people as infants, occupying only a short pulse of time in the long span of world history.

Basic Call to Consciousness conveys a perspective that is both forthright and logical, pointing out that Western culture has been horribly exploitative and destructive of the natural world: "Human beings are abusing one another and the planet they live on. The destruction of the natural world is a clear indication of mankind's spiritual poverty. . . . Over 140 species of birds and animals have been utterly destroyed since the Europeans arrived in America, largely because they were seen as unusable [a conservative estimate, even for 1977]. The forests have been leveled, the waters polluted, the native peoples subjected to genocide. . . . Western technology and the people who have employed it have been the most amazingly destructive forces in all of human history. No natural disaster has ever destroyed as much. Not even the Ice Ages counted as many victims."

"Wake up," the book says. Our lives are part of a sacred web in which everything is connected. When we poison the air or the soil with our lifestyles and technologies, even just a little bit, we are poisoning ourselves.

"Today," the Haudenosaunee write, "the species of Man is facing a question of the very survival of the species. The way of life known as Western Civilization is on a death path. . . . Our essential message to the world is a basic call to consciousness. The destruction of the native cultures and people is the same process which has destroyed and is destroying life on this planet. The technologies and social systems which have destroyed the animal and the plant life are also destroying the native people — a clear indicator that human beings are in deep trouble on this planet."

Through this document, Native Americans are essentially calling for righteousness. By this they mean a shared ideology developed by all people using their purest and most unselfish minds. "Righteousness occurs," they write, "when the people put their minds and emotions in flow with the harmony of the universe and the intentions of the Good Mind, or Great Creator. The principles of righteousness demand that all thoughts of prejudice, privilege or superiority be swept away and that recognition be given to the reality that Creation is intended for the benefit of all equally — even the birds and the animals, the trees and insects, as well as the human beings.

"In the beginning, we were told that the human beings who walk about on the Earth have been provided with all of the things necessary for life. We were instructed to carry love for one another, and to show a great respect for all the beings of this Earth. We were shown that our well-being depends on the well-being of the vegetable life, that we are close relatives of the four-legged beings."

The Indians recall that their Original Instructions directed human beings to express respect, affection, and gratitude toward all the elements that create and support life: "We give a greeting and thanksgiving to the many supporters of our own lives — the corn, the beans, the squash, the winds, the sun."

A fundamental tenet of native cosmology places people in a balanced relationship with the Earth. As the elders write in Basic Call, "Our philosophy teaches us to treat the natural world with great care. Our institutions, practices, and technologies were developed with a careful eye to their potential for disturbing the delicate balance we lived in."

They say that whenever we are about to create or buy something — from gene splicing to laundry soap — we should first consider the effect it will have on the next seven generations. Only when we believe our actions and creations will be life supporting over this long span of time should we proceed.

Putting it another way, these elders call upon us to respect not just the rights of other human beings, but the rights of all beings of Creation: "The people who are living on this planet need to break with the narrow concept of human liberation, and begin to see liberation as something which needs to be extended to the whole of the Natural World. What is needed is the liberation of all the things that support life — the air, the waters, the trees — all the things which support the sacred web of life."

The Haudenosaunee elders also address politics in *Basic Call to Consciousness*: "The problems which we are facing today, as a species which inhabits a planet of limited resources, arise not simply out of physical limitations but from political realities. It is a hard fact of life that the misery which exists in the world will be manipulated in the interests of profit. Politics and economics are intricately linked in the West, and social considerations command inferior priorities in the world's capitals."

The elders believe the profit-oriented interests of the worldwide market economy are exactly the interests that have created the present crisis for humanity and that will continue to heighten that crisis. They suggest as an alternative the rekindling of sustainable, locally based cultures. These elders say that the way to begin transforming the present state of affairs is to create and employ liberation technologies that are complementary to liberation theology. Such technologies are those that can be created and used by people in a specific locality; they enhance self-sufficiency and respect for the natural world. Windmills, solar collectors, biomass plants, and organic agriculture are all examples of liberation technologies.

Lorraine Canoe

Lorraine Canoe is a vigorous exponent of many of the ideas articulated in *Basic Call to Consciousness*. She grew up on the windswept St. Regis reservation in northern New York state. As a member of the Wolf Clan, a teaching clan, she was steeped in the philosophy and traditions of the Haudeno-saunee. "I was brought up by women to be self-determined," she says. "When I became introduced to the outside world, I kept that determination. My great-grandmother, my grandmother, my mother, and I—we're four generations of women in this household. The tradition was always there, in terms of being helpful, being involved politically, being there for family members even if it wasn't asked.

"What does the government of United States label the people in Central America? Communists. They call them communists. Now, the way the Iroquois Confederacy works is a communistic way. You share food, you share land—you don't see fences. It's very rare to see a fence. If my neighbor is not feeling good, I can go through the path over there and go and see how she's doing, if she's got tea or whatever. If there's a fence there, I don't know her. How do I help her? It's not that I want her to help me—how do I help her? That's my way. How do you come back to the basics?

"When Louis Henry Morgan wrote his anthropological book, *Living With the Senecas*, he put down the weave of our people, and described how we lived. When his book was published it went into the library. Karl Marx came from Germany and lived in Brooklyn for one year, and he read Morgan's book, and he went back and what did he do? He wrote *The Communist Manifesto*, and it [communism] was put into practice. But what was omitted was the spiritual part. The spiritual part and also the matriarchal impulse of nurturing. And that's why it is disappearing, because of that rejection of those important things that were not put into practice.

"I'm committed to keep the Mohawk government alive, to keep our language alive, because if the language disappears we cannot govern. It is not meant for us to govern in another language, in a foreign language. And if that disappears, we die, just as the Navajo people are saying, 'Help us or we will die.' The Mohawk mind will die.

"As a nation of people, you must have a language. Every country in the world, every nation in the world, has its own language. For me, the tradition of our language is fundamental—the language honors the women. It is a female language. In learning the language, a young person, even an adult, is immersed in the sensibility of respect for the feminine—that and the continuity of our traditions.

"Basically the Mohawks, and the other Iroquois nations, are a matriarchy. The woman carries the lineage; she is an authority or the head of the clan. Your clan is passed down by birth. My brother, he is Wolf Clan because our mother is Wolf Clan. He carries that clan until his death; he can never pass it.

"When you have a little boy, two years old, you look at him and you watch how he behaves, how he relates to his mother, to his sister. If he should make a mistake, there are always the clan members to help him think correctly. To me, all the Wolf Clan—the whole nation of children—are my children. Who will correct this two-year-old boy who may be a leader someday? You watch him as he grows up. He pretty much conducts his life by how he relates. The qualities of leadership are not so much one person taking charge—there's a continuity. To just say I'm going to put you up as a leader and now you have to fend for yourself, there's no such thing. There's always that need to communicate. When the Great Peacemaker came to fix our nations, to create our nations, to give us a train of thought, it wasn't only men, it was women. We can't add to and we can't delete from that law. It's spelled out for us. You try to live it to the best of your abilities. Now the mainstream culture is not respective of the feminine creative impulse at all. You know, you go out and look at the images of women— obviously it's become very sick.

"What could the mainstream culture learn from examining, making an honest examination of, our matriarchal culture? I would begin to answer this way: when two people live together, whether they are married or not, when the woman becomes pregnant she's not pregnant alone. He is also pregnant. How does he conduct himself toward that woman in the state that she's in, this powerful state of creation? Does he realize that he is part of creation with this woman? Does he ignore her? Is he sexually driven to find someone else? How much honor does he have for himself to be disciplined enough to think only of what he is creating or has created?

"While the woman is with child, the man is always to remember that he's in the same state. That respect, and the honor of that child, begins at conception. How does he help her in the home? How does he help in what food they eat together, and in what she's not supposed to eat? How to keep her weight down? He's not only to be thinking of her, he's also to be thinking of this unborn child.

"So the matriarchal tradition begins at the time of conception. When that child is here, whether it's a boy or a girl, who's the first teacher that child is going to? The mother. Who teaches the child how to walk? The mother. The talking, the behavior, all of it falls on the shoulders of the woman. It's very rare for a man to be doing this. It is important for him not to lose consciousness of the feminine world that he comes from. What did his mother teach him? So, that continuity needs to be there when he becomes a grandfather—not to lose that train of thought about the respectability of who creates. And all of that relates to the Earth.

"It's the same way with planting. When you plant, you have a potato that's left from last year, the seeding potato. The seeds that come from that potato are female, because they sprout, so you take something and you break it apart and you put it into the Earth, that seed. And it's female, because it grows the same way the woman is in pregnancy, month after month she grows and develops that child.

"Let's go back to Abigail Adams, the wife of John Adams. If the founders of the United States really understood how the Iroquois Confederacy worked, about the freedom of women to speak in council, to judge, to be head of household, to be the producer of children—had they known all that, the ERA would not have been needed thirty years ago. It would have been understood as part of the fabric of the Constitution.

"Because they didn't know that, they took only some of our confederacy laws to create the Constitution of the United States. How much did they omit? They made a Constitution where there's a separation of church and state. And who separated that church and state? Not the women. They didn't consult the women. Women did not own land, were not entitled to hold land. They were not even entitled to vote because of that hierarchy coming here and beginning two hundred years ago to create a government without the input of women. And because of that—the failure to involve women in the fabric—that weave has been deteriorating. How can you have a perfect fabric weave if the input in there is not from the children and not from the women? Where is it going to end and how much is it worth? It's so fragmented. Who's going to put it back together? Can it be repaired?

"When the thirteen colonies came together to make a government, they told us that they were going to call us their children, that that's the way it works in the United States government. We said, 'No, we're going to travel parallel paths—you in your boat and we'll stay in ours. You don't come and legislate over us, and we don't legislate over you.' But when you take indigenous people, Longhouse people, who learn these things and then face the attraction of the other government, they want to get out of our boat and go into the other because it seems so attractive. When they do that they cross over, which means they have one foot in our boat and another foot in the other. So what is the attraction over there? Always we are attracted to things that are not for us because it's a test, a human test of how strong we are.

"What advice can I offer? I would say be careful of what you eat. You should give thanksgiving that you're seeing daylight every day. You need to practice until you think you have it right for yourself.

"Practice a life of self-determination, of how you want your children and your grandchildren to be brought up—to respect the Earth and its contents. And focus on the children; we are an extension of children. Look at the children. Who are they going to be when they are brought up?

"How many people put their children on a mechanical horse by dropping in a quarter? What kind of reaction do these children have? A mechanical horse at two years old, a fast car when he's twenty. So the process is started when he's little. The same thing with the guns. Toy guns. It's not the gun that kills the people, it's people who kill people. The gun is just a tool, and it's just as easy to use a knife or a club."

Tom Porter

Up the road a mile or two from where Lorraine Canoe lives, Bear Clan chief Tom Porter makes his home on a modest farm. Of himself he will say nothing. "That's not our way," he says, "to set yourself apart and talk about who you are and what you've done. You let your life speak for you. With the Mohawk people, wisdom is how you live and how you interpret what your mother and father, what your grandmothers and grandfathers, have told you about this world—and then how you interpret that into the fact of living everyday.

"All I know is from our own teachings. We were taught by our elders. It's very simple. To the Mohawk people, those that still follow and adhere to the traditions, we have a responsibility in our life. We have a responsibility to the Earth. The Earth is our mother. And that's what all our ceremonies and practices are all about. It's simply giving thanks to all the things that give us life, and looking at all of those different entities that are part of Creation as if they were human beings, because that's what they are. We can't look at it any other way. When the learning stops, we stop. The Moon stops, the gardens of the world stop. If the birds stop their singing, we will become bored and we will die. So there is no mystery involved, there is no magic involved. It is just complete, simple, human logic. Do you want to live in a dirty house, or do you want to live in one that's clean, pure? If you live in a dirty house, that makes infections, it makes headaches, it makes tensions. When our old people had prophecies hundreds of years ago, they said that if you don't do these simple things, then you make your own bed.

"So, until people from the masses can understand that the world for the most part has taken God and put him way in left field, and then taken money and put it in God's place in their lives—until they can realize that, they can't really begin to clean the house. I think there was a big mistake that was made because people separated the religion and the government. That was one of the big mistakes that was made, because when they did that, then they removed the Creator from their life, or at least from half or three-quarters of their life. Decisions that have been made for the last couple of centuries have been decisions made without the presence of a real God. Instead, the decisions in the United States for the last two hundred years have been made from the vision, not of God, but money. The U.S., and whatever other countries there are in the world, follow the same kind of concept, be they capitalist or socialist. Basically, they are the same people. They both removed the living God from their government, from their lives. And if you look at the countries who oppose each other and denounce each other for the most part, what have they produced that is the result of this? Whether it's Russia or the U.S., it's essentially the same. Centuries and centuries ago they removed the living God from their religion and government. They removed the living God from their daily lives.

"What has that removal done to people? It has permitted them to set a special day aside, which is usually a Sunday, to be holy, to be spiritual. Not necessarily in reality, but at least to speak about such things on that particular day. And then once that day is closed, the remaining days of the week they can pretty much do what they want to do and feel good about it, supposedly—or at least have no consciousness of what they're doing.

"In the Western organized religion, they have this teaching—I don't know where this came from—that's fundamentally contrary to nature. I think that it was a manmade law because it says that we are here to subjugate nature. I don't believe that God or any of God's friends made that law up. The law that insists man was created in the image of God, I don't think that's true, I mean not totally true, because I think that the deer and bears and the eagles and the fish have every right to say the same thing with equal legitimacy. Then the Western teachings go on to say that man has dominion over the fish and the birds and the animals. What that is, really, is a false statement. There is no truth in it at all. In fact, the knowledge, or understanding, or wisdom, or whatever you want to call it, of the native people here, it is contrary.

"Our teaching is that man is the least powerful, is the least strong, in the ways of life on the Earth. It is he that is the weakest and the most undisciplined of all creations. Of course, if one believes man is the head dominator over all these things, well, then it's alright to pollute all the rivers and the water, the air and the land. It's alright to kill the buffalo off. It's alright to kill the elephants in Africa for their ivory and money. It's alright to do all those things and it's alright to take the land in this country away from the native people because the native people aren't really humans. They're a subspecies of human.

"In the last thirty years there has been an orchestrated attempt by our religious leaders, in the Indian nations, to once again have a dialogue with the people of the United States. They tried before, but the Europeans were so entrenched in their belief that—they have convinced themselves that—they are the most superior people in the world. And that belief made it impossible for them to listen and to understand such concepts. They were just left to that. If you go through the old documents, there were some European people who began to understand some parts of our teachings and to have an appreciation for the native perspective. You'd see it documented in the old archives of the Jesuit writings. They mentioned certain things, but they didn't know what it really meant. They were intrigued by it, but they didn't know how to apply it. They didn't know how to understand it totally. But if one studies, if one understands the different native peoples' traditions and beliefs, and then one reads those old documents, it makes sense. That's why, in the last thirty years, the religious leaders of the different native nations have actively had meetings, in universities in urban centers, so they could arrive at some kind of a mutual friendship in under-standing and appreciation.

"The hippie movement in the sixties, those people said they were look-ing toward the Indian people as an example, as a ray of truth in their lives. Most of those people in the hippie era, who were the spokesmen or the inspirators of the American youth at that time, had prior contact with dif-ferent Indian nations. They had dialogues with native teachers, and if not personally, face to face, then they were students to some degree of different writings by native people. And that's why in the sixties hundreds of hip-pie people came here to this reservation.

"That movement was, in a way, like a fad. To a large degree it was a fad. It was stylish to do that, you know. But there was a big part of it that was sincere, that was looking for truth, for actual, positive change within their lives. But they were also influenced by the other ingredients that were the negatives of the society of which they were part. They also incorporated the consumerism. And they still had the false god with them: there was the dollar sign. And that's why all of the drugs and corruption came in. So that was the negative part, so that people were not really seeing. If they came to the truth where it lay, they could see it but they could not understand it. Because in our teachings, the drugs or the alcohol are understood to sup-press the positiveness of one's growth, and they distort reality; they are unreliable; they are only a mirage, never the real thing. That's why there was such a big push from the negative forces. So that even if they bumped into the truth, they wouldn't be able to see it for what it was. They wouldn't be able to take ahold of it. And they wouldn't be able to make it a part of them. The drugs and alcohol in our tradition, in our teachings, were meant to be there as a trap so those masses of young people would not be successful.

"The reason the hippies came here in the sixties was that they said to us that their fathers and mothers had lied to them consistently. Their law-makers, who are supposed to be their leaders, have also perpetuated the same lies. The policemen who are supposed to protect them, to bring safety to men, women, and children, have perpetuated the same lies. Knowingly or unknowingly, they have perpetuated the lies. They needed to hear some of the original truths. And so that's why they came to different Indian peo-ple, looking for that. And they wanted to know: Are there any Indian people who still follow the ancient teachings that came from the beginning of the world—the original truths? At first they asked if they could become Mohawks—if they could join the Mohawk religion. Of course we said no, because we're not Catholics, we're not Methodists, we're not Mormons, we're not Jehovah's Witnesses. We don't go around asking people to join us. We're not a cult. So we said, 'No, that's not what we do.' But what we told them is, 'We will tell you some of the knowledge to guide you in your quest for a spiritual life. We will guide you. We're going to give you some water on this journey that you're making. We're going to give you some food to give you some strength, so that you can continue on this journey. But we are not the answer. We are not your gurus. We are not your prophets. And we are not your god. We're only human beings.' See, many of them wanted to put us up on pedestals. So some of the negative things got in the way.

"That exists to an extent in Indian country. I mean, there are some Indians who have seen a chance to make a big profit. So now they charge for ceremonies. There's people walking around saying they studied with this medicine man or that medicine man, and so it's like they've got a diploma. That's a bunch of bull. There's no such thing in Indian country. You don't show your faith, you live it out every day in the way that you speak and the way that you help people. So we don't encourage people to do Indian ceremonies, but we do tell them why we do them and what they are for. Like the Sun Dance. We do that because we're appreciative that the Sun comes every day. We know that if the Sun doesn't come we're dead. There is an East Coast version of the Sun Dance, different from the one out West. We do it differently here—our language is different, our song is different. But it's for the Sun. There's no difference. Our beliefs are based on nature and original truths, nothing else.

"That's what we told the hippie people. If you want to be proud and you want to be thankful for the Sun, then figure out a way to do it. Sit down somewhere and meditate. Think spiritual ways. You want to work as a unit like we are here, but the way you do it, that's up to you. We can meditate together then. And you can say thank you to the Sun in your own way. You don't have to do it like the Mohawks do, from A to Z. Use your own power, your own understanding. We also have a Moon Dance, and a Thunder Dance for the rain. And we say thank you to the power of the rain for putting new water, in the right season, into our lakes, and water in our corn and our grass and our fields. That's what we told the hippies: 'Go sit somewhere and figure out how you want to thank the thunder. Then it will be original, what you do. As long as it's sincere.' There's no big garage sale on native ceremonies. That's all we're saying, the Indian people. We don't have a magic wand. We don't have a great mystique. And we don't have gurus. We're just human beings.

"You can't force original truth down somebody's throat. And you cannot coerce them, and you cannot threaten. Otherwise the truth dies.

"Ultimately, nature will do the teaching. She's doing it now, and when nature teaches a lesson, everybody listens. There's a lot of prophecies that we know that come from the visions of particular people. Some of the old people told us that there's going to be big changes, that the Earth is going to move. I learned this when I was a kid: that the Earth will move; it will rock, and it will cause a great change to occur. They said it would happen in my lifetime. They kept saying that. A lot of them are dead now. They said that I would probably see it, and that they would not. And they're dead now.

"As for advice on this, the old people said just be faithful to our teachings. Respect the Original Instructions and what they said. We were told that when this begins, the elm tree, which is sacred for us, will die from the top down. And then you will know that the change has begun. Next will be the maple tree, which is the leader of all the trees for us. That's starting to happen now.

"Then you'll see a time, they said, when you can't tell the men from the women. That's what we're talking about. Now the women are all wearing pants, so when you see them you can't right away tell the difference. And the fish, they said the fish would go belly up to the Sun. And then another one is our sacred strawberries. They said we will see a time coming when there will be no berries to come on the plant. There will only be a red leaf. That time has not come yet, but the other signs have come in just my lifetime. When I was a kid, nothing was wrong with the elm tree. I told the elders that, but they talked about it all the time and said it would come. And in my lifetime I look and see what has happened to the elm tree. They all became sick and died. And now the maple trees are becoming weak and sick. There was nothing wrong with those either when I was young. And

I don't know when the strawberry is next—when they are going to get sick. But that's when things are really going to change—when the strawberry won't give fruit.

"Our elders and our old chiefs and our spiritual leaders told us what they know about the world in which we live from the ancient times. Those are our guides to us, to tell us what's coming. If you do this, this will be the result. If you do this other action, this will be the result. So we see. We listen to them, we store what they told us to remember, and then we live and see if it is true or not true. And so far it's all true."

⟨⟨⟨ TWO ⟩⟩⟩

Seven Prophets, Seven Fires
GRANDFATHER WILLIAM COMMANDA

In the deepest night the stars watch over me.
Wisdom Keepers of the North, my mind seeks clarity.
I'm on my way,
to the cold and burning winds.
Let the thunder and the lightning carry me.
Lay my thoughts to rest and send me into sleep.
The owl and the buffalo, my dream's crystal magic medicine.

Adapted from "A Song to the Four Directions" by Kate Wolf

On the Native American Medicine Wheel, each of the four cardinal directions has a meaning. The East is generally represented by the eagle, symbolizing the qualities of vision and illumination. The South is often symbolized by the mouse, representing trust, innocence, and growth. The totem of the West is usually the bear, who teaches human beings to have the courage to go within and face what is in the cave of the heart. The North is frequently symbolized by the Snowy Owl and the White Buffalo, both of which serve as reminders of the purity of snow and the qualities of clarity and wisdom. When a native person seeks wisdom, he or she will often look to the North, the direction of dreams and crystals.

Keeper of the Primstaven

William Commanda was born in the North as the year was turning toward winter, on November 11, 1912. He says his mother remembered

Venus as being prominent in the sky at that time. Because of this, she used to call him Ojigwano, the Algonquin word for the bright star of Venus. In memory of this first name, Grandfather Commanda wears a simple yet striking ring on his left hand that displays a silver star on a field of black.

Grandfather Commanda was born and has lived all his life in the North, on the Manawaki Indian Reserve in the Province of Quebec, Canada, in a landscape of rolling, serpentine hills and abundant waters. His house is clean, bright, and beautiful, set close by the edge of Bitobi Lake. He is a canoe-maker and has taught many young people to make canoes. Off and on over the years he also worked for Weyerhauser as a lumber buyer, driving to New Brunswick to select the logs. His speaking voice is easy, gentle, lyrical, and he employs many delightful vocal devices: pauses, rises, and variations in tone. His eyes are marked with peace and understanding.

Grandfather Commanda is the keeper of the Primstaven, a wooden staff that was carved by the Vikings, who began visiting the North American continent as early as A.D. 1100. The carved markings on the staff acknowledge that, though different people have different ways of understanding the truth, there is only one Creator, and all of us, no matter what our beliefs, come from this Creator. Grandfather Commanda elaborates on this point by saying, "That's why when Indian people gather we always say, 'Let us put our minds together and have one mind.' We know that. The Creator created us equal; he created us one man and one woman, and from there we all derive.

"Later, after the Vikings, when the other Europeans got here, we were already millions of inhabitants in this country. But they seem to want to refuse to believe today that we were the first occupants, and that we have the claim of first occupancy. They all say, well, they came four hundred or five hundred years ago, with the 1492 arrival of Christopher Columbus. He didn't arrive to find us. He was trying to get to India but he got lost. We found him. And then he called us Indians, but we are not. When we see a real Indian from India, we know that it's you that are Indian, not me. I am a North American.

"If my mother stands in the United States, I am still a North American. It makes no difference which side of the line. We did not draw the line. It was drawn by greedy people who came here and saw the riches that we have, and they divided my country into two parts. It almost became three countries once, because there were Confederates in the South, and they had banks and printed their own money and had their own government and were fighting against the Union. But they lost the war. And the same thing happened with the French that arrived here. They had to sign away the land in 1863; they made a treaty in France surrendering the land. But how could they surrender a place they did not own? We were here. Today, they just say that all the legal papers they have made up supersede the aboriginal rights we have, and they want to completely eliminate us. They are talking to us now about granting us self-government, which is very misrepresented. I'm seventy-seven years old and I never went to school, but my Creator shows me true visions of what's going to be, what they are planning. I've had visions since the age of twelve. So I don't believe the government. I know their minds; I could read them. I read their hearts."

Just Who Was the Civilized One?

Grandfather Commanda commented, "Algonquin means 'first people,' but that is a name that has been given to us. We are the Mamiwinini, which means 'nomad,' which we are. That's our name. We had that name because we were not settled. We were wanderers, nomads; we hunted and fished and moved about. That's why we claim people from all over, not just those who are now on the reserve. But now the minute you set foot outside the reserve, they say you are not one of the people, and that you cannot fish, or hunt, or trap. They say you pay, or you don't pass. But we won't pay. We don't think it's right.

"We are over fifteen hundred people in this part of the territory now, and we have people in settlements to the North, some of which are not called Indian reserves—but there have always been our people there. Today the government says they do not recognize that these are Indian lands; they say they are Crown lands. Who made them Crown lands? We always battle with the words. They have obtained everything by squatter's rights. What's a squatter? What about the poor man? Is he a squatter man? Does he have a right to rob the banks? Does he have a right to kill for money, or for food? Is that the way a government should rule? Is the might right? When you ask yourself these questions, then you begin to understand the meaning of the word 'right.' You talk about right, then you can talk about left.

"We love our neighbors, and we opened our hands and arms when they came because we knew they were in peril and misery where they came from. They were probably overruled and overtaxed and over-everything they did not like. They were seeking freedom, and we gave it to them. But after they got over here, what did they do? Turn around and stab us in the back with the knife. Then we begin to think. They were supposed, they thought, to civilize us. They came to evangelize. But today, see, all the waters are foul. You see the trees are dying. And you see the animals are sick—you see the fishes with cancers, and they are not edible in a lot of places because they would make you sick if you ate them. And so you begin to ask yourself, 'Just who was the civilized one? Was it us or them?' And it leaves me only one conclusion.

"When I go to speak in schools, I say, in spite of all the things that happened, I never hate these people. That's a word that should not be used. Love is a factor, because love overcomes. And so I never say, not even one time, 'Go back to the country where you came from.' In spite of all that has happened, we try to get along together. But that's not what they are doing. They are still trying to walk over our backs and to get the last drop of blood that we have in our bodies. And they are still not satisfied. Why did one people, because of a different color of skin, have this urge or obsession to try and overrule because somebody else's skin is different? Why does this happen? What kind of blood do they have in their veins? What kind of heart do they have? Is it a red one like mine, or is it black? And you begin to wonder—it must be black because they wouldn't have all these polluting practices, and be doing all these things they are doing. You talk to them and they just walk away and laugh at you.

"Our tradition teaches of a time when these things will change. They will change. Definitely. But before that change, whenever it takes place and we are awakened, we just let the people do what they are doing. They don't seem to listen to nobody. They have forgotten their Creator. It's the money that rules today, even though God in their book tells them you cannot serve two masters. Either you serve God or you serve the money. So who are they serving?

"I ask myself often, and it makes me cry, 'What's going to happen to the grandchildren?' They are just starting to grow. But two-thirds of these people, who are so-called Indians, we are told that two-thirds of these also will go. In what way we don't know. Maybe diseases, or massacres, we don't know. But it has happened in the past.

"One time back in 1987, at a meeting out West, an Ojibway man was telling a funny story about what had happened to the people, and we all began to laugh. There was a white man standing behind us. We didn't know who he was, and he said, 'How can you do that? How can you people laugh the way you are doing, after all we did to you people?' He said, 'I wouldn't be able to laugh like that.' And I said, 'Well, we forgive you people. We forgive you. We don't forget what you did, but the Creator wanted us to forgive, and that's exactly what we do.'

"People are funny. They're funny, then again they are pitiful. A lot of people blame the denominations—blame the Catholics, the Anglicans, the Jesuits, and all these people. These people were also used by the governments. They were pushed to do things, and they did them in order to receive things from the government. But since they were not natives, when they saw all the riches that were here, they went along with the government. Today it would probably be different.

"You and me, we need each other. That's why I told you in the beginning, we never say, 'Go back where you came from.' Never 'go,' but the people who are doing the bad things, what kind of heart do they have? Why are they doing these things? Let's not talk about the past, but the future. Because the past you can't change. They are still doing it today."

The Wampum Belts

In addition to the Primstaven, Grandfather Commanda is the keeper of three historic and prophetic wampum belts. One belt dates from 1400, one from 1600, and one from 1793. There was a fourth belt, he explains, that may have been sold for money when the belts were in the hands of the wrong people. For this belt, Grandfather Commanda still searches.

The belts are objects of great beauty, fashioned from wampum—polished pieces of sea shells. The wampum is skillfully woven into a thick belt of beads. In the case of the Seven Fires belt, the background pattern is a soft, restful purple. In the foreground, in soft white, are the shapes of seven diamonds, representing the Seven Fires of ancient prophecies.

The Seven Fires belt dates from 1400, prior to the arrival of Columbus. Another belt, the one from 1600, speaks of the French and English, who have played a dominant role in the modern history of Canada. "It also speaks about an agreement made between the two," Grandfather Commanda says, "with the nation of Indians standing in between. There's a cross on the belt, which means the Vatican; it represents the Vatican. That cross also represents the priests who blessed the agreement, which said that as long as the Sun will shine, as long as the grass will grow, as long as the rivers will run, these two people promise that their word will never change. The rivers are still running. The Sun is shining. The grass is growing. Where are the white man's words? False. They have been false people, who you cannot fully trust.

"But remember that we never surrendered what you call Quebec. There's no such thing as a treaty. Quebec belongs to the Mamiwinini—that we know. But the government says no. It says it has squatter's rights, and it won't believe in what was agreed upon long ago. But we know what is the truth. And they know, too, even if they won't say."

Grandfather Commanda's great-grandfather was also a holder of the belts. His name was Pagnawati, which means Stick Hit by Thunder, or Thunder Stick. He lived at Lake of Two Mountains and became the holder of the belts in 1822. Pagnawati died in his sleep in 1874, without having named anyone to be the new keeper of the belts. So the belts came into the possession of his son-in-law, who apparently was the wrong man. He did not fully respect the belts. While he held them, he was involved in a series of misadventures, and ultimately he gave them up to an Indian band living in the bush of the far North.

Eventually the belts came into the possession of a native man named Clinton Rickard, who kept them in a sacred way for many years. One night he had a vision in which he was told to return the belts to where they had been before. So in 1968 the belts came to Manawaki, and William Commanda became the keeper of them for all the people.

"In 1968 I was given relics to carry for the people. Not only the Primstaven, which is for the world—that's only part of it—but also the wampum belts for the people. These things, not everybody holds them. I am the holder of these wampums for all the nation. I don't own the belts, but I'm part of them. The belts belong to everyone. I am only the keeper. Anyplace I go, I always tell them, 'These belts are yours. These belong to everybody. They are not mine. I'm only the keeper of the belts.'

"I just came back from the Yukon four days ago [spring 1990]. We had a nine-day meeting up there: three days with just the elders, and then after that some days with the other people who had something to say. And while I was there I read this belt to them, to all the people there—some four hundred people from all parts of Canada.

"I do not have a right to show the belt to just anybody. My people only, because they own the belts as a nation. I'm only the carrier. They tell me, 'You cannot show these to the media, the newspaper, or reporters, or writers of books.' I would have to ask permission of them first, because they own them. But I can tell you about the belts.

"The Seven Fires are times in the life of the people. What the belts say will happen is a purification. And that day, whenever that takes place, two-thirds of the aboriginal people will have faded away, or disappeared, or have been destroyed. That's what we are told. Notice, we are only a handful now. And after that the rightful occupant, who was here first, will take over. But by whose command? There's one Creator. And at that time, all will believe.

"I believe the rightful inhabitants are the Red Nation; that it's not going to be the White Nation. But there will be room for people of all colors: the reds, the yellows, the blacks, and the whites. Because, as I said, there are a lot of good white people.

"For a long time we did not show the belts. At a meeting we had in 1987—the Constitution meeting in Ottawa—I brought the belts to the meeting and we exposed them to the TV for all the world to see, for the first time. We never had allowed anybody to take pictures of these before. But we opened them then. And we try to get along. We've been having meetings among the aboriginal people, like this meeting in the Yukon where I was the other day. That's all we talk about there. We try to get together and explain it to the government. But they only want to talk about the land claims. Always it's the money. You know, it's wrong. And they were even mad when we told them otherwise about things that are really important. They want the millions and millions."

Seven Prophets, Seven Fires

Grandfather Commanda shared the story symbolized by one of the relics. "Let me tell you about the Seven Prophets and the Seven Fires. The wampum belt tells that many years ago seven prophets came to the Anishinabe—the People—who include all of the Algonquin-related peoples: the Micmacs, the Maliseets, the Penobscots, the Ojibway, the Wampanoags, and so forth. At the time the prophets came, the people were living a full and peaceful life. The prophets left seven predictions of the future. Each of those predictions is called a fire, and each fire refers to an era of time. All together they are called the Seven Fires of the Ojibwa."

Grandfather Commanda shared a document describing the lessons of the Seven Fires wampum belt. The document was prepared by representatives of various Algonquin nations. According to the document, the first prophet said that during the First Fire the people would follow the Midewiwin Lodge, the sacred path. They would look for and find a turtle-shaped island that was linked to the purification of the Earth. Many native groups refer to North America as Turtle Island.

As held in the tradition Grandfather Commanda keeps and in the document he shared, "The second prophet told of the Second Fire. He said, 'You will know the Second Fire because the nation will be camped by a large body of water, and the direction of the Sacred Shell will be the host. The Midewiwin Lodge will weaken, but a boy will show the way back to the sacred path.'

"The third prophet told of the Third Fire, a time when the people would move to chosen ground that would be to the west.

"The fourth prophet told of the Fourth Fire, a time when light-skinned people would come to Turtle Island. If they came wearing the face of brotherhood, then there would come a time of wonderful change for generations. They would bring with them new knowledge, and new articles to join with the knowledge of this country. In this way the knowledge could all be joined together to make one mighty nation, and that nation would be joined by two more, so that the four nations would form the mightiest nation of all. We would know this if the light-skinned race came carrying no weapons—if they came bearing only their knowledge and a handshake.

"But another prophet said, 'Beware if the light-skinned race comes wearing the face of death. You must be careful because the face of death and the face of brotherhood look very much alike. If they come carrying a weapon, beware. If they come in suffering, they could fool you. Their hearts may be filled with greed for the riches of this land. If they are indeed your brothers, let them prove it. Do not accept them in total trust. You shall know that the face they wear is the one of death if the rivers run with poison, and fish become unfit to eat. You shall know them by these things.

"It's all spirit, and it's all connected," Grandfather Commanda comments. "If you pollute the water, you are going to see that the things in the water are dead, because the waters have killed it. No more life. And look at the trees. Every time it rains it's supposed to be pure water, not acid rain. The pure water that we used to have a long time ago was good for the trees; it would hang on them in drops."

As of 1990 there were over fourteen hundred dead lakes in Canada, and many of the forests had been visibly weakened by acid rain.

Grandfather Commanda showed photographs of the wampum belts, and then went on sharing the story of the Seven Fires as written in his document. "The fifth prophet said, 'In the time of the Fifth Fire there will come a great struggle that will grip the lives of all native people. At the warning of this fire, there will come among the people one who holds a promise of great joy and salvation. If the people accept this promise of the new way, and abandon the old teachings, then the struggle of the Fifth Fire will be with the people for many generations. The promise that comes will prove to be a false promise, and those who accept this promise will cause the near destruction of the people.'

"The prophet of the Sixth Fire said, 'In the time of the Sixth Fire, it will be evident that the promise of the Fifth Fire came in a false way. Those deceived by this promise will take their children away from the teachings of the elders. Grandsons and granddaughters will turn against the elders. In this way the elders will lose their reason for living. They will lose their purpose in life. At this time a new sickness will come among the people. The balance of many people will be disturbed. The cup of life will almost be spilled. The cup of life will become the cup of grief.

"At the time of these predictions, many people scoffed at the prophets. They then had medicines to keep away sickness. They were healthy and happy. These were the people who chose to stay behind on the great migration of the Anishinabe. These people were the first to have contact with the light-skinned race. They would suffer the most.

"When the Fifth Fire came to pass, a great struggle did indeed grip the lives of all native people. The light-skinned people launched a military attack on Indian people throughout the country, aimed at taking away their land and their independence as a free and sovereign people. It is now felt that the false promise that came at the end of the Fifth Fire was the materials and riches embodied in the way of life of the light-skinned race. Those who abandoned the ancient ways and accepted this new promise were a big factor in causing the near-destruction of the native people of this land.

"When the Sixth Fire came to be, the words of the prophet rang true, as children were taken away from the teachings of the elders. The boarding-school era of 'civilizing' Indian children had begun. The Indian language and religion were taken from the children. The people started dying at an early age. They had lost their will to live and their purpose in living. In the confusing times of the Sixth Fire, it is said that a group of visionaries came among the Anishinabe. They gathered all the priests of the Midewiwin Lodge. They told the priests that the Midewiwin Way was in danger of being destroyed. They gathered all the sacred bundles. They gathered all the scrolls that recorded the ceremonies. All these things were placed in a hollowed-out log from the ironwood tree. Men were lowered over a cliff by long ropes. They dug a hole in the cliff and buried the log where no one would find it. Thus, the teachings of the elders were hidden out of sight, but not out of memory. It was said that when the time came that the Indian People could practice their religion without fear, a little boy would dream where the Ironwood Log, full of sacred bundles and scrolls, was buried. He would lead his people to the place."

At this point in the description of the Seven Fires, Grandfather Commanda paused to make an observation. "This time is coming soon. We are waiting. It won't be long."

He continued sharing the document: "The seventh prophet who came to the people long ago was different. He was young, and he had a strange light in his eyes. He said, 'In the time of the Seventh Fire, new people will emerge. They will retrace their steps to find what was left by the trail. Their steps will take them to the elders, who they will ask to guide them on their journey. But many of the elders will have fallen asleep. They will awaken to this new time with nothing to offer. Some of the elders will be silent out of fear. Some of the elders will be silent because no one will ask anything of them. The new people will have to be careful in how they approach the elders. The task of the new people will not be easy.

" 'But if the new people remain strong in their quest, the water drum of the Midewiwin Lodge [the sacred way] will again sound its voice. There will be a rebirth of the Anishinabe Nation [the People] and a rekindling of old flames. The Sacred Fire will again be lit. It is at this time that the light-skinned race will be given a choice between two roads. If they choose the right road, then the Seventh Fire will light an eighth and final fire, an eternal fire of peace, love, brotherhood, and sisterhood. If the light-skinned race makes the wrong choice of roads, then the destruction that they brought with them in coming to this country will come back to them.'

"Traditional people of Indian nations have interpreted the two roads that face the light-skinned race as the road to technology and the road to spirituality. We feel that the road to technology represents a continuation of the headlong rush to technological development. This is the road that has led modern society to a damaged and seared Earth. Could it be that the road to technology represents a rush to destruction, and that the road to spirituality represents the slower path that the traditional native people have traveled and are now seeking again? The Earth is not scorched on this trail. The grass is still growing there.

"The prophet of the Fourth Fire spoke of a time when two nations would join to make a mighty nation. He was speaking of the coming of the light-skinned race and the face of brotherhood that the light-skinned brother would be wearing. It is obvious from the history of this country that this was not the face worn by the light-skinned race as a whole. That mighty nation spoken of in the Fourth Fire has never been formed. If natural people of the Earth could just wear the face of brotherhood, we might be able to deliver our society from the road to destruction. Could we make the two roads that today represent two clashing worldviews come together to form that mighty nation? Could a nation be formed that is guided by respect for all living things? Are we the new people of the Seventh Fire?"

After contemplating the message of the Seven Prophets, Grandfather Commanda pointed to a photograph of the wampum belt and said, "When you see this belt, and you think of these things, think also of the possibility of lighting an Eighth Fire, which is represented by the center diamond, a double diamond. There are seven fires all the way up to here," he explained, "and then the eighth one. The Seventh Fire is close now. We are facing the choice of the two roads. That's when the double diamond will close in if we choose the right way, and it will represent the time of an Eighth Fire."

All This Came to Pass

Grandfather Commanda has many stories to share, all of them marked by the wisdom of the North. "Let me tell you something that happened even before the coming of the light-skinned race. They were having a ceremony one morning, and one of the grandfathers came over. He had this vision. He said some day, very soon, his vision would become real, and that these colors would come; people who were not here then would come. He said, 'We are known as Red People, the Red Race, but there will be other colors. Just look over there,' he said, 'and you will see a white birch standing over there. And over here, there's a yellow poplar. And then, if you look out there, toward the South, you'll see a black cherry tree standing out there. Those trees represent the people who will come. They are not here yet, but they will come. And there will be a person coming with a long rope and a cross. What he represents is just like the Sun when it comes up brilliant in the East. But after he has been here a few years, then he will start to form a thundercloud in his mind, in his head, and then he's going to forget what the Creator told him and fall away.' And you know, it happened. All this came to pass.

"We have to have one mind for the Four Directions. Until we reach that one mind, we cannot be filled with understanding. We pray a lot of times and make ceremony with tobacco. But, you know, you can get a big crowd around the fire, of say some two hundred people, and some of the people may have a different mind. If that's so, then the prayers, most of the time, are not answered because you have twenty-five different minds. The Creator will not answer until you have just one mind, just like if you have one person.

"And there are the Four Corners of the Earth that we talk about, and the Four Colors of people, and the Four Winds. You see the winds—they are spirits—and they are probably the most dangerous thing there is in the world. It could destroy all the cities and kingdoms, everything, within an hour, if the Creator permits it. Nothing could stop it. Atom bombs and jet planes and all that, they are nothing compared to the Creator. And also waters. There's a lot of power in nature, as we know from the Seven Fires. Fire is visible, but the wind is not. The wind is connected with the North.

"The North is the wisdom direction, the direction of clear mind. Remember that. It's white because it's bright. That's where the snow always exists, twelve months a year. The snow never disappears from the north side of the mountains. It's always on top. The snow is up there year round."

In his life, Grandfather Commanda has been gifted with twelve separate visions. One of them came on August 4, 1988, at 9 a.m. "I saw the Peace Tower in Ottawa, which is the capital of Canada, and the tower was standing just fifty feet from me, with the Canadian flag with the red maple leaf. And the wind was blowing it south because of the way it was placed. And I was lying deep in a trance, sitting toward the East in the morning. Then I began to see it going down—the tower was going down; everything including the flag was all going down, disappearing into the ground. So that was really something. Then in October of 1988 there was an election between incumbent Prime Minister Brian Mulroney and Hal Turner. While they were debating, Mulroney was accused of selling out to the United States with one stroke of the pen when he signed the Free Trade Accord. And it's so. With that one stroke of the pen he sold us out. We are going to become the fifty-first state of the United States.

"Why? Why this vision? Four months before the debate, I saw the tower and the flag disappear. And so I trust my vision that was given to me by the Creator. I believe it will happen. It might not happen in my time, but it's going to happen, I know. Canada has been sold out and is going to become part of the United States."

⟨⟨⟨THREE⟩⟩⟩

Adventures Along the Beauty Road
DHYANI YWAHOO

*A*s Dhyani Ywahoo tells the story, before she arrived on Earth her grandparents were visited by the spirit of Padmasambhava. He instructed them on how to prepare for her birth and early education, and then he departed. Now, Padmasambhava was the holy man who founded Tibetan Buddhism thousands of years ago, so this story transcends your average account of an apparition—especially when you consider that Dhyani is not Tibetan but American Indian, a member of the traditional Etowah Cherokee nation.

In many ways, this prebirth visitation set the stage for Dhyani's life, a life that has focused on creating a healing link between East and West. Dhyani Ywahoo grew into a woman of power and then became a grandmother. She moves and speaks with regal grace, but her heritage is not that of kings and queens; it is of wisdom. She is the twenty-seventh generation of her family to carry forward the sacred Cherokee teachings about quartz crystals and the tones that activate them. She is also an acknowledged master of Tibetan Buddhism, a modern-day bodhisattva. She blends the best of both traditions in a path she calls The Beauty Road.

Throughout her childhood, Dhyani was trained in tribal wisdom by her grandparents and other elders. They taught her to communicate with nature, to respect the sacred web of life, and to live from her heart. "To the average person," she says, "some of my early training would sound kind of cruel. They would take me out to the woods and leave me alone for a whole day and a night. I knew they were nearby, and I wasn't afraid. They would just tell me to stay there and look into the eyes of a deer, to stand there and listen to the wind and look at the stars, listen to what nature was telling me. And I see now that that was really helpful.

"When I was six years old it was time to go to school, they said, so we came to Brooklyn, New York. Being away from my grandmother was really shocking—because it was very easy to be out there in the country, quiet and peaceful; if you wanted something to eat you got it right out of the garden. To be in the city, where you weren't permitted to go outside without an adult traveling with you, was a different world. At night I would hear the Earth crying. And I'd have a nightmare about huge machines making the mountains flat, and big machines walking across the land, and big wires. Later on I saw, when we drove across the country, that they were high-intensity electric lines. And it looked like they were devouring the Earth. The Earth was crying and it made me cry, and I thought I wanted to do something to help. I wanted to ease the suffering of the Earth. In those dreams of the Earth crying, also I would see people around the world. I'd see our native people suffering in the cities. I saw hungry people all over. And I thought it would be good to do something. That was the only way the nightmares stopped—when I made a commitment that I would do everything that I could.

"I find that's not unusual, that most children have a sense of their purpose and their commitment, and they want to do something good. I'm not really unique. I'm a human being, walking here with the same hopes and aspirations for the future generations as any other grandmother who is walking on the Earth. As I have gotten to know many children—and I have raised many of my own and many foster children—I know they all have the desire to do something. Every child has something they feel they can do."

In 1976, when she was a parent herself, Dhyani's path took a curious turn. As she was leaving on a pilgrimage to India, her grandmother called her on the telephone. "She had been dead for a couple of years," Dhyani explains, "but she called me. Well, my husband picked up the phone and he said, 'Oh, oh. This is very long distance.' My husband's hair was standing on end. And she spoke to me in Cherokee, and I just totally melted. She said, 'Remember what we taught you.'"

Her grandmother's admonition to remember her training stood Dhyani in good stead on her pilgrimage, as she endured landslides, monsoons, and serious injuries to members of her traveling party. "I understand now that obscurations will arise and that one needs to have firmness of mind—a certainty that this will be accomplished for the benefit of all. So I kept walking." Ultimately, she attained the summit of a high mountain where she had a profound realization. "I realized that my grandparents' name for me, Dhyani, was the correct name, and that henceforth I would live up to it." The name means both "light" and "a gift for the people."

An Ancient Connection

His Holiness the Drikung Kyabgon, Chetsang Rinpoche, is head of the eight-hundred-year-old Drikung Kagyu lineage of Tibetan Buddhism. He is the thirty-seventh person to carry forward the teachings of his lineage, which includes such sages as Milarepa, Naropa, and Tilopa. When Chetsang Rinpoche was only three, he was recognized as the reincarnated head of this line. He received his vows from the Dalai Lama at the age of five.

Chetsang Rinpoche says that, from the time he was young, he heard about the American Indians and knew that there was a link between them and the people of his land. When the Chinese invaded Tibet in 1959, he was imprisoned and held for twenty years. Finally, he escaped and fled to India, where he was greeted by thousands of rejoicing monks gathered at the Phiying Monastery in Ladakh. There he established his seat in exile.

Chetsang Rinpoche is still a young man. He has a strong face and a keen interest in Western culture. In addition to the classic Buddhist message of kindness and compassion in the face of all, he bears the sacred Phowa Teaching about death and the transference of consciousness to another realm of existence. Early in 1987, after many years of waiting for the right opportunity, he came to America to tour, to teach, and to meet with Dhyani Ywahoo. These two exceptional people became friends, or perhaps it's more accurate to say that they renewed an old friendship, for they believe they have lived many incarnations together in preparation for the work they are doing in this lifetime: helping to forge a cultural and spiritual link between the Tibetan people and the American Indians.

Dhyani explains the connection this way: "Our prophecies tell us to look for our brothers to come from the East wearing red robes and red hats.

Together we would make an offering. This is indeed what the old people prophesied. Always, from childhood, the medicine people have spoken of our Tibetan brothers and sisters—our relatives, who, when we were having ceremonies, we prayed and hoped that they were having ceremonies. And we believe that we were in direct contact mentally with our relatives in Tibet."

Return of the Sun Clan Brother

The connection between the Tibetans and the American Indians is apparently more far-reaching than most Americans have ever imagined. The encounter of Dhyani Ywahoo and Chetsang Rinpoche, for instance, was preceded by a visit in 1979 of the Dalai Lama, the spiritual leader of six million Tibetans. He met first with elders of the Hopi tribe and then with elders of the Iroquois Confederacy. These meetings were historic not just for their cultural import, but also because, according to those who were involved, they were the culmination of ancient prophecies.

A Tibetan prophecy from the ninth century states that "when the iron bird flies, ponies run on wheels, and carts run on lines, the Dharma [Buddhist teachings] will flourish in the land of the Red Man." According to a Hopi prophecy, Pahana, a true spiritual being whose name is derived from salt water, will come from the East at a time when the balance of the Earth is greatly threatened. He will be the Sun Clan brother, and his return will mark the end of a millennium-long ritual. As journalist Marcia Keegan explained in a report on the Dalai Lama's meetings, the name Dalai Lama means "teacher who is an ocean of wisdom."

Keegan also noted some striking correspondences between the two cultures. Geographically, Hopiland is located directly opposite Tibet. In Hopi language, the word Nyima means "Moon"; in Tibetan the same word means "Sun." Conversely, the word Dawa means "Moon" in Tibetan, "Sun" in Hopi. For both peoples, the purpose of their religion is to help maintain the natural harmony of the universe by living in balance with it.

According to Hopi legend, in the beginning of time Hopi land was the center of the world. After a great natural disaster, the people were scattered. So the Hopi feel that their meeting with the Dalai Lama was in part to welcome him home. Earl Pela, a Hopi chieftain, invited the Dalai Lama to visit Hopi country. "In our prophecy," he explained to Keegan "it says that because of great problems coming to many people, we are going to start looking for one another, and we will eventually find each other. We can compare not only our ancient knowledge, but also the problems."

That process of comparing problems and sharing knowledge has continued. The Dalai Lama has met with many other Native American leaders, and so have a number of other learned Tibetan lamas, including Chetsang Rinpoche. With Dhyani Ywahoo, and on his own, Chetsang Rinpoche has traveled to many Indian reservations across America to pay his respects and join in prayer.

This cross-cultural and cross-spiritual exchange has proved reaffirming for both Tibetans and American Indians. According to Dhyani, the Red Race has a particular responsibility to be caretakers of the planet and to teach others about the absolute importance of this. By joining in prayer and ceremony, Tibetans and Indians are reminding many people that, as one Indian song goes, "The Earth is our mother; we must take care of her."

In a Sacred Cave

At the behest of tribal leaders, Dhyani Ywahoo has moved with her family to the northern end of the geologic spine called the Appalachian Mountains, far from her tribe at the southern end of these mountains in the land of crystal caves. Near Bristol, Vermont, deep in a valley of the Green Mountains, she has established the Sunray Meditation Society, an international organization working for world harmony. Students who join the society's Peacekeeper Mission learn from both Native American and Buddhist traditions, for since 1983 Sunray has been an officially acknowledged dharma center.

From her Vermont base, Dhyani sees the East-West connection deepening over time, particularly now that it is occurring on the physical plane. "It's amazing," she says. "We meet many lamas, and we have good relationships with so many great teachers and illustrious spiritual beings. The main abbot for all of the Drikung Kagyu centers in North America [Khenpo Konchog Gyaltsen] has been to visit with us and give teachings at our centers for two or three years. From that we have realized that there's a very deep connection. When we knew His Holiness [Chetsang Rinpoche] was coming, we knew that more of our family was coming. And then actually seeing His Holiness, we know that our relationship is indeed very deep. The causes have been planted in many lifetimes for us to meet in this way."

Chetsang Rinpoche expresses equally strong convictions about the connection: "The first time I met her was special. A strong recognition feeling was there, especially when I came to the place where Dhyani resides. The feeling was so warm. Not only that, that area, I felt, is special, a holy place. In the Buddhist higher teachings, it speaks of a hidden valley. It was that kind of holy place, I felt. And there were different signs.

"While I was in that area I went to a special cave that is close to the area to get a special soil, a clay. In the higher tantra teaching there is a practice where it is necessary to have this clay to use for a ceremony. It is the special kind of place of a female enlightened being. To get into the cave is not easy, kind of dangerous. Anyhow, I did go inside the cave and successfully get down inside and I found the special clay. I didn't know it would be there before. But when I saw it I knew it was the right one."

Dhyani says that the cave is also sacred to Indians. "When we were making a film, we found it by accident. Our chief, the Peace Chief, he went back there and found the red paint [clay], and he was so surprised; he was so happy. We had the sachem from the Wampanoag Nation, Slow Turtle, who was there, and some old Cherokee men, and some Lakota—young and old men—and a Seneca learned, wise lady. When they saw the paint there, we were all so happy. The paint is also important for our ceremonies. Then a double rainbow came out in the sky to say it is very good that we found that place. That the clay would have such importance to both people is very significant."

A Meeting in the Heart

Before coming to America, Chetsang Rinpoche had responded to the invitation of the pope and journeyed to the autumn 1986 meeting of world religious leaders in Assisi, Italy. He explained that while in Europe he had been deeply impressed by the fabulous technology of the West. "It dispels physical discomfort," he said, "but there is a corresponding spiritual debt. The West must develop spiritually to balance the outer developments of material technology. If we cannot balance, then it will be like loading a horse too heavily on one side. The load will fall down and probably take the horse with it. It's very important to connect both East and West. In technology, the West is very advanced, the East is very slow. But at the same time the East has more spiritual understanding, and that is needed in the West."

Dhyani, who is noted for her eloquence, agrees on the importance of this connection: "There is a meeting in the heart of East and West, because the Sun rises and sets on all of us. Wherever you are on this Earth, you can face East or you can face West. Underlying all human division is one truth. All people can trace their roots to the great tree of peace. Everyone wants peace and happiness, fresh water, good food. Every creature wants a safe home to live in. Even the snake and the worm, they are thinking about getting a safe place for their young. And human beings all around the world are thinking about what it is going to be for the next generation, how to make it good. Basically, all people want the same things. But we must set aside the illusion that we are separate or different.

"There's no reason for different religions to fight. People do need different religions because they have different levels of understanding and different life purposes. Each nation has its own way of understanding. But when a person goes beyond nationalism and wants to look at the nature of their mind, then they can see what is needed to be seen. So for human beings now, it is wise to look at the common threads in our religious practices, and to know that we have nothing to argue or fight about."

By way of example, both teachers point to the common ground of Native American wisdom and Tibetan Buddhism: clarity of mind, compassionate care for all beings and for the Earth, right relationships, and generosity. As Dhyani puts it, "Buddhism gives a language that can make the deeply intuitive wisdom of the native teachings very accessible to the Western mind. So it is a good meeting."

The First Step toward Wisdom

In the Etowah Cherokee nation, Dhyani is a chieftainess not only of the Wild Potato Clan, but also of the Whirlwind Clan, which carries knowledge of the movement of the air and the mystery of the spiral. Given this context, it is not surprising that when asked about wisdom she says, "Wisdom is not particularly acquired, it's revealed. Wisdom is within the very fibers of our DNA structure [the spiral of the double helix]. Wisdom is the capacity to adapt and to see things as they are and to be in good relationship, and this resides within the spirals of our heart. Wisdom already exists, and it is only obscured by mistakes in thinking. So, the first step to heal that ignorance is to just notice and look around at what's happening, and to recognize that what's happening to the person over there could be happening to me over here, so let me help, let me help them.

"One of the best ways to reveal inherent wisdom is through action—to care for other people. First, though, you may need to learn to care for yourself. I see that many people really hate their own selves. They feel they are cut off from the Earth, cut off from the Creator. Many people have a high degree of self-hatred, and this causes destructive behavior and harm to others as well. You hear people say, 'If I can't have it, well then no one should have it.' I hear people talk this way quite often, and they think it's their right or that it's appropriate behavior. But it's not appropriate behavior to want to cause more harm. It's better to make peace and to make something good happen so that we can overcome this ignorance of separation and this ignorance that causes harm to other people by seeing them as objects.

"Even the smallest act of generosity can bestow wonder in one's own heart and one's own mind. You think you have nothing to give—well, then you start giving a little bit of the food from your plate, just a pinch, and offer it so that whoever is hungry, maybe they'll have food and they'll find it. So it begins as an idea, maybe even imagination, and then eventually this caring for other people becomes real.

"It's time for the caretakers of the Earth to arise, awaken. In Buddhism, the Lotus Sutra talks about that: 'Caretakers of the Earth awaken and arise and let things be good upon the Earth.' The whole essence of Native American teaching is to know that everything is our relative, and to be caretakers of the Earth and one another.

"Now there many people around the world who are awakening to better caretaking of the Earth, as with the sacred ceremonies of people. Just giving thanks, for instance. When people say grace before their meal, this is giving something back to the plant kingdom so that it can continue to send forth to us, and also it is giving something to the Earth so that she can make new water within her center. When we have community celebrations, when people get together, when they go to church or meditation—whatever their religious practice is—whenever people come together and make an offering, make a prayer, this is giving something to heaven and Earth.

"We all have a relationship to heaven and Earth, and everyone has a spiritual duty, a reason for being here. When people forget to keep their religious observations, it makes the mind less stable because the physical realm, they begin to think, is more important—the car or the house or money is more important. But money is green. It's like corn, beans, or squash. It's meant to help people live and feed them. Sometimes people forget that it's just that simple. It's about taking good care of one another. So when we remember even something as simple as saying grace before eating, this opens something. It enables us to make contact with the clear light within ourselves, whether we call it God, Allah, JuJu, the Mystery, whatever. This creates contact with that, and more good comes from making contact with the Light. We become generous. Like the wind, generosity sets the waves in motion to bring good energy, and it also washes away the illusion that there is not enough. Because really there's enough here for every human being—all, I think they say five billion now—to eat. All it takes is our willingness to send it to one another."

The Native Tradition

According to Dhyani, the native traditions of the Americas are very ancient. She says her lineage, in particular, is thought to be over 100,000 years old. As a representative of this tradition, she has a number of concerns about the faddish popularity of Native American rituals and ceremonies such as the sweatlodge, a sacred steam bath that takes place in a small hut.

"Because of its simplicity and beauty," Dhyani says, "the native tradition looks like something you can easily do yourself. It is the wise person who recognizes that the sweatlodge and the other rituals of the native peoples are very sacred and powerful medicine. Before you would work with a chemistry set—which is what the sweat lodge is, for it purifies you and rearranges your molecules—you would want to have a firm foundation in the philosophy, the wisdom, and to have a direct transmission of the spiritual tradition and the building of the sweatlodge. It's very powerful.

"It's become fashionable in these times for people to imitate Native American ritual and Native American practices. It's also dangerous, not having a good foundation, because the sweatlodge is where worlds begin and end. When someone goes in there without proper preparation, without knowing the proper means of constructing it, without knowing the prayers for even taking the skin off the willow, the prayers for putting the poles in the ground, you take a chance of creating a vortex of hurt, because it's powerful. I don't think anyone would consider creating and imitating the Communion of the Catholic Church, or seek to do ceremonies of the Jewish Temple. They would seek instruction. It's the same thing with Native American rituals."

Dhyani also has concerns about the wisdom of relying strictly upon channeled information. "Just because it seems to come from a spirit doesn't make it any wiser. Do you believe everything you read in the newspaper? Well, the same thing with those so-called channelings. Be aware. Observe. Does it make any sense? Does it bring positive energy? Does it bring benefit to the people? And cohesiveness? Or is it divisive? Evaluate it like that. In our tradition it is thought that to talk with the universe, and to talk with the beings of the universe, is natural. The trees are talking, the wind is talking. The idea of channeling sometimes connotes that a person puts aside their power of thought and observation and choice making, and steps aside so that something other may come through. Better you know yourself really well, and understand the wisdom that arises in your heart, than run around listening to every wind blowing through the trees. Understand your heart and then you'll hear and know all that is. It's kind of dangerous, the idea of channeling this, channeling that.

"According to some of the native prophecies, this would be happening in this final time. And it is a hypnotic subterfuge. The thoughtforms of the past see that they are being dissipated because people no longer think that Russia is all bad and so forth. People are beginning to see our common factors rather than our differences. People are looking for more ways to make peace. So these thoughtforms, which have been fed by aggression and fear and many other attitudes of the untrained mind, as they see that they are no longer being fed, they will try to inspire a little fear, because fear keeps that thoughtform alive. When people are not able to make clear communication with their own mind, then they are always looking somewhere else for information."

The Age of Flowers

As with many native elders, Dhyani looks upon the present as a time of profound cultural and planetary transition, a time when the world is moving into a new cycle of evolution. She says this epoch of transition is something many native peoples have long known would come, just as they accurately foresaw the arrival of Europeans who would not respect their culture or the land.

"Before Cortés actually arrived in the Americas, the people shared a common calendar. It was known that at the end of that era something would happen, so runners came from what's now called Argentina, and also from way up north, and they sent messengers. People would run, and then another runner would go, and another runner, until all had been informed. The message was that times of change were coming: 'Secure your teachings, and secure your medicines and your sacred fireplaces, and leave your cities.' So the cultures that had built large cities began to disperse. That's why a lot of the Central American communities just seemed to disappear. Where did they go? They left because they knew what was coming to be, actually well before the five hundred years. So they dispersed, knowing that to preserve any of their teachings they needed to be one with the Earth, and to be unobtrusive and unobserved. When Cortés came, some people saw the boats coming and thought that it would be the Great Peacemaker returned. But he, of course, proved himself to be a very violent and destructive person, so it is very wise that the ancient Native American councils looked ahead and made those decisions."

Dhyani says many Native Americans share the understanding that as of August 1987 the last dark cycle of the old age, which began with the arrival of Cortés, came to an end, and that since that time we have entered the early, transitional stages of a new age. As understood by many Native Americans, the modern world has been preceded by four other worlds or creations, each lasting about twenty-six thousand years. All the previous worlds were purged or destroyed as they became spiritually corrupt. According to the prophecies of the Native American calendars, our fate, now that we are at the end of one age and the start of another, is in our own hands. As always, we can choose with our free will to act in harmony with Divine Will or to ignore it. If we ignore Divine Will, we may bring on cataclysmic cleansing activities; if we act in harmony with it, we will be at peace with ourselves and with all the creations who share life on the Earth.

Dhyani says, "This age ending has been a time when people have gathered information about building and about inventions to make life better. Now it's time for people to recognize that the inventions are a creation of mind, to put aside such inventions as cause harm, and to bring forth and further develop those activities that benefit all beings and the future generations."

Dhyani teaches that the new cycle, which began in August 1987, can be thought of as an Age of Flowers. "According to the way we are taught, and the seeds that are being planted, the calendar is to manifest peace—an age of peace. It is time for all of us to plant seeds of good relationships that understanding may flower, that peace may flower, that what is needed for the well-being of those who are suffering may flower.

"The elders have asked—this is a large council of elders, so they speak to Central and North American people—that the morning after every Full Moon, at about 10 a.m., we gather flowers and go outside and look to the Sun, to the flowers, and to the heart of the Earth. In so doing, we bring more solar energy and flower wisdom to the Earth, because the new age is the Age of Flowers.

"Flowers give light and joy. They also have a very subtle consciousness. They have a unity of mind. The flower energy is peaceful, and flowers are great medicine. By meditation on flowers we can reduce the inflammation caused by aggressive habits of mind.

"Flowers are the medicine we need for balance and tone. The old people say that when properly prepared—and some of the preparations can take as long as twelve years—flower essences can widen the frequency response of the human mind. They increase our sensitivity. But they need to be prepared with prayer, right offering, and dedication. Flowers can remove the poisons of incorrect thought and stir the body to its fullest health. Flowers move with the Sun; thus they have a certain committed solar consciousness—they know the proper relationship between Earth and spirit. The flowers remind us to look up to the heavens and to actualize the solar energy in our own lives—to speak more clearly and act more clearly.

"Through the movement of flower pollen in the air, we are all being quickened, and that quickening for some is frightening and it also brings a reaction. Just like when someone takes a homeopathic remedy, the first thing that happens is they become a little sicker. But it really is a reflection of the sickness being a little exaggerated, so that the organism can be awakened to heal itself."

One of the reactions to this quickening, Dhyani believes, has been an increase in the number of cases of allergies and allergic reactions, even among people who have been purifying themselves with organic foods. The whole issue of allergy, she says, is really an issue of the planetary system and not the human system. "In some instances the Earth and the people are so out of alignment with one another that anything natural is disturbing to the human body, because for years we've been taking artificial vitamins and the food has been grown with artificial fertilizers. So the natural realms have been made an enemy, and the body and the immune system responds as if it were an enemy. This is a result of years and years of improper drugging of the crops. I also think that's why there's so much of an increase in addictions. The plants are jazzed up and people get into the habit of being jazzed up and then they start looking for more and more stimulants or depressants to continue that cycle."

Dhyani teaches that good diet, proper exercise, and prayer can help us stabilize our lives so that we may offer them in service toward stabilizing life on Earth. "We are moving around the spiral," she says, "coming again to a place of whole civilization, of true planetary consciousness. What we see now are the fever throes, the end of the fever's nightmares as the sickness and poisons leave the system. How much the planet will suffer, how much the people will suffer, is really determined by the consciousness of groups. It is no longer a matter of just individuals finding light within themselves; it's really necessary to establish a network, to rebuild those areas of the Earth's web that have been harmed by unclear thinking.

"According to the teachings of the native elders, and according to the teachings that have come through the Ywahoo lineage, the Earth will not be destroyed by man's armaments and munitions. If the Earth should decide to shake people free, it would be the fire burning, the fire that comes to purify the aggressive tendencies of mind. So humans have a choice to transform that aggression.

"In 1983 the elders told me, 'The tide has turned, Dhyani. There are enough people doing good medicine to prevent the destruction of the

Earth.' Many people are taking the right steps to look at the nature of their own minds, to find stability, to seek good relationships, and to be responsible in word, thought, and action. This is making the difference."

⟨⟨⟨⟨ FOUR ⟩⟩⟩⟩

The Mind of a Scientist, the Heart of a Mystic

EUNICE BAUMANN-NELSON

*D*r. Eunice Baumann-Nelson is a thoughtful social scientist and a distinguished teacher. She has lived abroad, traveled far, and read widely. She was the first Penobscot Indian to win a B.A., an M.A., and a Ph.D. She has taught at the University of California at Davis, Indiana University, Purdue, and the University of Maine. For many years she lived in Peru and Bolivia as an active participant in the Peace Corps and the wife of a Peace Corps staff member. One of her main tasks was in-country, cross-cultural training for the volunteers. In recent years she has also taught at the College of the Atlantic. She is the recipient of an honorary Doctorate of Humane Letters from the University of Maine, and one of three women in Maine to receive the Hartman Award for outstanding achievements.

Now a grandmother, Eunice makes her home on ancestral lands alongside Maine's Penobscot River. She is in her seventies, but considers herself unemployed, not retired. "I would love to teach one or two courses still," she explains, "but not a full load. I love teaching, and over the years I developed a lot of methods that I thought were quite effective, based on sociopsychological understandings." She got her wish and is now teaching a course entitled "Native American Spirituality and Tradition" at the Bangor Theological Seminary.

"I was born right here on Indian Island in Old Town, Maine, right in my parents' home, located at the edge of the Penobscot River, and the midwife was my maternal grandmother. My mother, who was the seventh daughter of a seventh daughter, was what used to be known as a 'medicine person'—that is, one who, among other things, heals and prophesies. She collected and prepared herbs, and also used the laying on of hands in her healings. She read palms, cards, and tea leaves for prophesying. She used to read cards almost every week for my three older sisters who lived out-of-state, and was so accurate that she gradually became frightened, convinced that the devil was working through her. Eventually, she went to the Catholic priest who was here at the time and expressed her fear. He told her to give thanks to God for the wonderful gifts that had been bestowed on her. She could not convince herself of this, however, and stopped the prophesying.

"Don't fall into the illusion of thinking that I was raised a traditional Indian. I was not. That had died out years before I came along. I don't even have my language. Because the Indians in the Northeast have been so acculturated, you'll often hear them repeating things that they read in books written by non-Indians—you know, 'the Indians do this, they believe that, these are their practices.' I hear Indians repeating these things as if they were true of the past, as well as the present. I believe differently mainly because I've really gone into researching the roots."

I Consider Myself a Human Being

Eunice told of her upbringing through several stories. "My family and I were Catholic, due to the fact that the Catholic missionaries came into this area first, and my ancestors took to the French better than they did to the English with their Protestantism. So as I was growing up I attended the parochial school here on the island up to the sixth grade. Then I went over to Old Town to the junior high school and then to high school. We met with a lot of prejudice. I was in a fortunate position in that I was able in childhood to form a very good opinion of myself, which has, of course, to do with self-esteem. I thought that I was an OK person. Anyone else's opinion, that was their problem.

"I have a master's degree in child psychology, and one of the things I learned was that we form our self-image based on what sociology calls the mirror image; that is, we create an image of ourselves, as to who we are and what we're like, from the way people react to us. In other words, the image in front of us is a mirror image made up of the many reflections we get from others through their reactions to us. Now, I was born in a position where I had five older siblings, and I was the baby in the family for four or five years. One of the consequences of that was that much was made of me. I mean, my nickname was "Love." I have an older sister, and sometimes when we're talking on the phone she slips and calls me Love. Getting all this attention and so forth from my siblings, I was able to begin to think that I was a significant being. So when I went to school in Old Town and encountered someone or some group that would say something derogatory, I would just think, 'Well, what's the matter with them? What's wrong with them? I like me.'

"I learned a lot from that, which is why I don't necessarily consider myself Indian or non-Indian or anything else. I consider myself a human being. I'm a socialized human being, and I know that anyone is capable of achieving adequate self-esteem, which of course leads to confidence in yourself. There's not a hell of a lot that you can't accomplish if you set out to accomplish it and have the confidence. And that's all. Every child goes through a process of forming a self-image. That happens all over the world, and it's not specific to any one ethnic group. We all form self-images, and much of our behavior is pretty well determined by how we feel about ourselves."

After high school Eunice went to Portland, Maine, to make her way in the world. She took a job as a house cleaner. "One day I was cleaning under the bed, dusting the mop board. I was on my back, reaching in through all the wires under there, and I got an electric shock. To this day I can close my eyes and see the bed springs. In those days they had metal springs, and the mattress pressed onto that wire contraption, the springs. I can see that to this day, and remember that moment, because I thought, 'What the hell am I doing here?' I knew I was in the wrong place. I knew I needed to get more education and find some kind of career so that I wouldn't be doing this the rest of my life. So I came back home and enrolled late at the high school to fulfill the requirements for college entrance."

An Insatiable Curiosity

After completing her preparatory studies, Eunice enrolled at the University of Maine, where she met the man who became her first husband.

They moved to Ithaca, New York, where he was studying for a Ph.D. at Cornell. In subsequent years she worked at the Vassar library, at the *New York Daily News* library, as the head librarian at the Museum of the American Indian in New York City, and also as head of the art library at Vassar.

"Eventually the marriage came unhinged, and I had to explore ways of preparing myself to make a living. I had long been fascinated with questions of why people are the way they are, and I needed to be economically self-sufficient. So I decided on a career in psychology, more specifically child psychology. I figured I'd be able to help people and do some good in the world, as well as earning a living and being my own boss. I located a program at New York University [NYU], the downtown campus at Washington Square, and enrolled in the childhood development and psychology program. But before I really got very far into my studies, I realized that you can't treat the child in isolation—you need to treat the whole family unit. It's in the family that the child becomes ill enough for a psychologist to be consulted. You have to work with the parents and the siblings and the other influences on the child from the outside, like the in-laws and the grandparents. I talked with the instructors about this, but nobody seemed to think it was as great an idea as I thought. Yet it made such eminent sense to me.

"I realized that parents don't set out to make their child ill deliberately, so that raises the question of what they are doing to the child to make it ill enough for them to seek out psychological help. Then I began to consider the culture and the values that parents have. The first things that hit me were the competition and the materialism. You know, there's this competitive pressure to make enough wealth to buy a Mercedes Benz and all that sort of thing. That was what hit me the most. Well, when I realized that nobody was going to listen to me about treating the family as a unit, then I figured, 'What's the sense of staying in this particular field?' I felt it would not be worth the time and the effort that I would have to spend getting a Ph.D. if I then had to go out into the field and treat just the single child in isolation.

"I did complete my master's in child psychology, however, and I totally intended to become a child psychologist. But by the time I got the piece of paper, I was so turned off to the subject that I began to look elsewhere." Eventually she found a program that suited her at NYU's experimental interdisciplinary Center for Human Relations Studies. The program brought together faculty from every different department: science, sociology, history, comparative religion, child development, philosophy, and so forth. She enrolled to get her Ph.D.

"I had to write a paper to gain entrance to the program. I remember writing that the approach of the academic world was like the six blind men in Aesop's fable. The men were asked to describe an elephant and they each went to a different part and felt what they could. One man went to the tail and felt it. He said the elephant was like a piece of rope. Another man felt a leg and said the elephant was a hard object like a tree, and so it went with each of the blind men. They all had different ideas about what the elephant was really like. Everyone of them had a spark of truth, but no one had the whole picture of what an elephant was like, and I felt that the academic world was like that. They were all touching on some aspect, like political science or biology or whatever, but none of them had a total overview; none were near getting to the whole picture of what, especially, life is really like."

The Theory & Practice of Leadership

While completing the requirements for her doctoral degree, Eunice began to teach. "In the early part of my teaching career at Indiana University and Purdue at Indianapolis, I began to develop doubt. During one Christmas vacation, I worked from about nine in the evening till eight in the morning for about two weeks to figure out where it was I could really make a difference in teaching. I'd studied a lot of things before I got into the magic of self-esteem. The current theories dealing with group leadership, or teaching, or whatever, posited three main types of leadership: authoritarian, democratic, and laissez-faire.

"In the authoritarian model the leader gives all the rules, regulations and orders, and the group has to go along. The second model was democratic, where the leader facilitated a discussion through which members came to make decisions. The idea was that when people were involved in the discussion and the decision, they had invested their time and energy and interest, so they would be fully participating in whatever the group decided upon as a whole. Now, with the laissez-faire approach you just sat there; the leader just sat and let someone else pick up the ball. If someone wanted attention, you didn't have to recognize them, they just spoke out.

And in that way it dispersed the energies of the group to such a point that, usually, utter confusion and chaos resulted. So, naturally, the theorists said that democratic leadership was the best type."

Fascinated by this theory, but also skeptical, Eunice set about writing her doctoral thesis on it. Specifically, she studied a community housing project in Indianapolis where the men had cooperatively built their own homes. Though it was a cooperative venture, the development process was structured along the authoritarian model. There were clearly defined tasks, decisions were made by the architects and technicians, and there was little freedom and choice for the families. When the families settled into the development, though, they swiftly bonded into a closely knit and supportive neighborhood.

"I had to come up with some theoretical explanation of why the growth in neighborliness had taken place in the group; why it was taking place in a situation where the accepted theory of the time said it was impossible. After I did this research, I could see that the leader was the really important element in the group, and that success depended on the way he or she related to the members of the group.

"When I had it worked out, it made me realize that leadership was not a great art. It was something you could learn. I had always heard this expression that 'teachers are born, not made,' and the same for leaders. But that's not true. People can be made into good teachers and leaders through learning self-respect, and learning to respect the others in the group. To me it was a beautifully simple thing: respect the students you are teaching, or the group you are leading, wherever the interaction is taking place. Respect makes the difference. You can be as authoritarian as you want under the circumstances—just show the respect that will make the people accept what you're saying.

"If people don't get respect, they will resent it. Now, this usually happens on a nonverbal or nonconscious plane—the buildup of the resentment, I mean. If people don't get respect on the job, they resent it, but they can't retaliate directly against the boss. Children can't retaliate against their parents. Students can't retaliate against their teachers. So what do they do? They go into what psychiatrists call transference. They transfer their resentment of the leader to the subject material. Students turn against the material they are studying. Children become defiant, and then behind their parents' backs they start smoking or taking drugs or whatever. On a job you get workers goofing off, or you get sloppy work. The retaliation, the frustration that's experienced, since it cannot be directed at the source, the authoritarian figure, is transferred to the subject, the content of whatever the group is involved in.

"Now, one of the things you'll often hear about Native American culture is the importance not just of respecting each person, no matter who they are, but also everything, like the animals and the grass and even the inanimate objects. I mean, you couldn't treat your canoe paddle with disrespect because one time you might be crossing a river above some rapids and your paddle would break on you if you hadn't respected it and laid it down carefully. If you were making a birch bark basket and you didn't respect it, then it might spring a leak while you were gathering maple syrup, and you could lose two weeks of your labor. There was this power that was believed in that was manifest in everything—everything and everyone. You were insulting the whole kit and caboodle if you showed disrespect to any one manifestation of that power. And they were right, you know, the Native Americans were right, and that's been demonstrated now by science in the Superstrings Theory. These superstrings are alive, you know—with memory, with intelligence, and, I suspect, purpose."

A Moral Gyroscope

"When I took my oral exams at the end of school, I was asked, 'Is there anything you can point to that you can attribute to having grown up in the Indian culture?' And, you know, by now there aren't that many differences. We've been in contact with the European civilization for nearly four hundred years, and the materialistic values have had a deep impact on native cultures. As I sat there I couldn't think of anything that I could point to, and it wasn't till about five or six years after I finished my degree that I recognized that there was something, a real difference. It was the type of discipline used by my parents, and by some other Indian parents.

"In the native way there was a system of disciplining children that involved loving ridicule or gentle teasing when a child misbehaved. Such teasing continued into adult life—you know, gentle teasing when someone is reacting childishly or unthinkingly, like throwing a temper tantrum. The teasing is actually a way of showing love to the one who is being teased. As a gyroscope for behavior, this type of discipline inculcates shame, rather than guilt, which is the case in majority society. Having internalized shame, you yourself are the judge of your misdeeds. With guilt, it depends on the judgment of others who may learn of your wrongdoing, which is to say that, as long as no one finds out, a person need not experience any remorse. So, it seems to me one can commit almost any type of misdeed and not be bothered about it unless or until others find out about it. Further, I conjecture that self-judgment constitutes a stronger check on wrongdoing than does the judgment of others.

"So, with the native way it's not whether people find out about what you've done or not. That's not as relevant. Today we have all these laws out there that say if you do this, then it's wrong. So a lot of people go along leading their lives saying, 'Well I won't do this or that because it's against the law.' But that's not nearly as strong as having your source of morality within you, having your morality arise out of an inner perception of what is wrong, ridiculous, or shameful. You are your own judge. Guilt comes from other people knowing that you have done wrong. It doesn't come from yourself. When it does come from yourself, as with shame, then you find you have more control over your actions."

What the Mystics Have Long Known

"As I went on studying, I began to appreciate that the whole structure of society, and especially the structure of the English language, completely dichotomizes the world with its either/or propositions. There's no allowance for paradoxes. Something has to be either animate or inanimate, natural or supernatural, and so forth. Our language shapes our way of understanding the world, and this is the only way we can see it.

"For example, we have no words for me to communicate that you are and are not the same person you were ten years ago. You are, and yet you are not, right? But there's no English word that says that, no word for communicating this basic reality, because the language does not make allowances for paradoxes.

"There are some problems now in physics where, if you had the right orientation in semantics, you would see no problem. There is, after all, a clear connection between physics and mysticism. Even though scientists had been using the Quantum Theory for over sixty years, it wasn't until

1982 that definite proof came from physicists at the Institute of Theoretical and Applied Optics in Paris. However, the findings didn't make many waves in the scientific community because they meant making an either-or choice, namely, (a) that objective reality exists only in the minds of the observers or (b) that faster-than-light communication with the past and the future takes place. The structure of the English language makes it nearly impossible for us to comprehend not only that objective reality is 'real,' at least on the plane at which we humans observe, but also that, at the subatomic level, faster-than-light communication does occur. In short, it is not a matter of choosing either (a) or (b), but a matter of accepting both (a) and (b).

"Even now our physical sciences are getting deeper and deeper into reality and, for instance, they are finding things they can't classify as either an animal or a plant. The organisms have characteristics of each, and the academic systems don't make allowances for this kind of a cross category, a paradox. That's a limitation. Obviously, paradoxes are a big part of reality."

Her Mystical Experience

Perhaps the central event of Eunice's life occurred spontaneously when she was a young woman. "I remember everything except the date. It was sometime in October 1951, and I was beginning my graduate work in New York City. I lived on Eighth Street, between Fifth and Sixth avenues, which is a real busy place with restaurants all over and all kinds of traffic. To get to class at New York University, I had to cross this street and go through Washington Square park.

"This one day I was going to a late afternoon class, and when I stepped off the curb something happened. In the time from when I stepped off the curb to when I got to the other side of the street, this thing happened, and it was as though I had lived all my life with a blindfold on, and it had been ripped away in that instant. Or maybe, it's hard to find words for it, it's as if I had lived in a dark cave all my life and had suddenly come out into bright sunlight. It was instantaneous, and I mean there was no time; I couldn't time it, but it must have been very short by our usual way of reckoning, because by the time I got to the other side of the street it was over. I walked a short block to Washington Square and entered the park. I was cutting across diagonally when I looked up for some reason. All I saw were these dark branches of trees against a blue sky, and it reminded me somewhat of the type of Japanese and Chinese paintings that they do with these outlines of trees. I stopped and thought, 'My, how beautiful, what glory, and it's been around me all my life and I've never seen it.'"

"The experience was ineffable; there are no words for it. I didn't really see anything—it just came to me as quick as a thought. The thing was faster than instantaneous. It occurred while I was still walking. I don't remember what went on the rest of the day or anything, but I kept wondering what it was that had happened while I crossed the street.

"I had been reared a Catholic, and I later found that in the Western world this is called a mystical experience. It has been interpreted by some as a meeting with God, a union with God. I guess I was still under the belief system that had been foisted off on me, but that experience really convinced me there was no such thing as God—at least, I've realized since then that the concept of God that had been presented to me was inaccurate. Years afterward, when I talked to people about this, they would say, 'Oh, you believe in God—you just don't know it.' And I would say, 'No, I don't.' But it's no use to protest to people who put their own interpretations on it. That experience sent me on an intense search to understand what had happened.

"It took me nine years to find more clues regarding what had happened to me crossing the street. Of course, I had this background in child development—how we form the image of ourselves and how we become socialized—so I had that at my fingertips. But nowhere could I find a clue as to where this experience had come from. I concentrated first on psychological works, various schools of psychoanalytic thought, and then comparative religion. When I got into the study of philosophy, I came across a statement that all human experiences, such as the mystical one, had to have their genesis in the organism; they had to have a 'materialistic' basis. I liked that thought, for it had been my guiding principle through my search to understand the experience in Washington Square park.

"In the fall of 1960 I was asked to lead a discussion group on the subject of Zen Buddhism. This was for an adult study group of the Unitarian Church in Indianapolis, and the topic was existentialism. Every member of the group read the same book, and discussion centered around the ideas presented. I read Suzuki's *Zen Buddhism* and hit the jackpot—I recognized my experience in the description of *satori*, or enlightenment. I realized from my anthropological training that the 'mystical experience' and satori were identical—they differed only when it came to verbalizing and explaining the origin and source. In other words, the differences in interpretation reflected the differences in the two cultures—East and West.

"I realized that there was something beyond what they were verbalizing, and what the rest of us were verbalizing. All the Western mystics interpret this experience as a union with God. In the West, God is generally understood as something out there, beyond us—in the heavens or the kingdom, in a domain inhabited by angels. You know the popular concept of what heaven is. Well, that was the picture I got growing up as a Catholic. But when I had my experience I realized that, with my background and training, I was in a position to make a contribution, to add another dimension of understanding, and to show that the experience of satori or enlightenment was identical to the 'mystical union with God.'"

"As I wrote and thought about it, what I finally discovered was this: In our development as an organism, resting within our mother's womb, the heart and the circulatory system are ordinarily developed at about five weeks, and then they start functioning. The heart starts beating and the blood is circulating and so forth. I reasoned that if the circulatory system was developed and functioning at five weeks, then the neural system had to be functioning, too. Now the primary function of the neural system is to imprint experiences and store them as memories. Within the womb there is awareness, so what could those experiences be of the organism within the womb of the mother? Certainly, one of those is that we hear the heartbeat of the mother while we are in the womb. Obviously, we wouldn't have words yet to explain to ourselves what we are experiencing. We have no concept that we are in a place; there's no time. We are imprinting eternity and infinity into our neural system. Very likely a lot of it is imprinted in this primitive part of the brain called the brainstem. So, if you had to describe it, I would say that at that time we are experiencing, in an absolute way, sheer existence, or being. It has no beginning, no duration, no ending, and its main characteristic could be designated as a state of nonseparatedness.

"As I mentioned before, I had been into the study of semantics—the structure of language and the way it is used in culture. Because of that I could make the connection and understand that, after we acquire language, we are unable to verbalize this prenatal experience. As you can see, though, nonseparatedness translates into connectedness, and this first experience of connectedness forms the core of our memory. This core can be likened to the heart of an onion, which is to say that postnatal experiences, except for those of infancy, are accessible for recall that can be verbalized, for, like the layers of an onion, the postnatal experiences surround and 'bury' the core. I speculate that this core memory is a strong, albeit 'unconscious' force in human lives—the quest for connectedness, to reclaim or discover the lost memory of Eden, so to speak.

"So what had happened to me during that experience, when I stepped off the curb on Eighth Street, was a sudden recall of that early, limitless, boundless experience of nonseparatedness. In a sense, I suppose it could be likened to déjà vu—maybe a situation in which you hear a melody or a song, or see a face or some scene, and the memory awakens. Somehow, I believe, something must have triggered it for me, but I have no recollection of what it may have been. All I remember vividly is the knowledge thrust upon me that I was one with all—humans, animals, the Moon, Sun, stars, universe. There was no separation between me and them. At the time, however, I had no way of explaining to myself or anyone else what had happened to me, except that it had brought about the feeling of oneness with all."

All My Relations

"Now, we know that connectedness does exist—that we are, in fact, connected to everything. It was known about, acknowledged, and acted upon by traditional Native Americans. My ancestors knew that we are related to the butterflies, trees, the ocean and rivers, the Sun, animals, plants, other humans, and everything. And actions based on this premise produced real results. My experience had given me an unshakable conviction of my connectedness, and I had developed what to me was a rational explanation as to its ontogenetic source. But was it really 'real'? In what sense were we connected? What, if anything, formed these connections? I still had a lot of questions. Did my conviction of connectedness stem merely from the prenatal memory of nonseparatedness?

"And then, eureka, in the November 1986 issue of the magazine *Discover*, I came across the story of superstrings, a new theory about the nature of ultimate reality. I literally pounced upon this, for, at last, I'd found a physical basis for understanding how we are connected."

The Superstrings Theory was developed in 1984, primarily by physicists John Schwartz and Michael Green, after more than a decade of work. Their theory so captivated the scientific community that it was quickly dubbed TOE, or Theory of Everything.

In brief, the Superstrings Theory supports the work of Albert Einstein by showing that matter and energy are interchangeable and, ultimately, blended into a single unified field—in other words, all matter and all energy are linked. The theorists describe matter as consisting of tiny primordial lengths and loops of something like strings, and they say energy arises from the actions and interactions among these strings. These superstrings connect everything to everything and apparently exist in ten dimensions: our familiar four of length, width, height, and time, plus others that cannot be observed by normal human senses. These additional dimensions operate only on the Planck scale, which in size is to the atom as the atom is to the solar system. If you laid 1,000,000,000,000,000,000,000,000,000,000 (10^{30}) of these superstrings end to end, they would be just one centimeter long. This is a submicroscopic nanoworld, accessible only through mathematics or mysticism.

As the November 1986 issue of *Discover* put it, "The theory has turned physicists into mathematicians, and mathematicians into physicists, and the universe into an entity in which all matter and energy, all forces, all people, planets, stars, cats, dogs quasars, atoms, automobiles, and everything else . . . are the result of the actions and interactions of these infinitesimal strings."

A string vibrating in a particular way might manifest as an electron, a photon, a quark, or any of the other subatomic particles. It is the action and interaction among strings—the colliding, the splitting, the joining, and so forth—that creates the fundamental force from which all other forces of nature flow. Superstrings, thus, are now thought to be the basic stuff of which we and our universe are made, and leading physicists are convinced that superstrings are all, in fact, connected. Essayist Philip Dunne has expressed this emerging understanding of physical reality in a poetic way:

"Our bodies, hearts—and perhaps our minds and souls—are just the harmonics of tiny harps plucked by an unknown musician."

When Grandmother Eunice read and appreciated the Superstrings Theory, it brought an end to her search for the nature of our connectedness. "I knew then that our connectedness really is 'real.' I try to illustrate the point by asking my listeners to imagine themselves under water, with other people nearby. They can see the others and recognize that they are all joined together by that medium we call water. Just so, I say, are we all connected by the submicroscopic medium we are now calling superstrings—the 'solidity' of the water connection on the human scale is matched by that of the strings on the Planckian scale. Whereas we can experience the water medium through our human senses, we can, perhaps, only conceptualize the strings with our minds. We have long accepted the concept of atoms, so I have no problem with accepting the concept of superstrings.

"We've finally arrived at a point where purely rational scientific inquiry confirms what many traditional cultures already sensed—as did mystics through the ages also. Numerous scholars of Native American spirituality have found a belief in what they've termed an 'invisible power,' a strange, mysterious power permeating the universe. Early Euro-Americans concluded that Indians also believed in their Western concept of a God, except in a different guise, and coined the phrase 'Great Spirit.' Today, most Indians use 'God' and 'Great Spirit' interchangeably. After all I've talked about, however, you can see that, aside from the very basic belief in the existence of a mysterious power in the universe, the two belief systems parted company.

"It will probably take quite a few years before this knowledge becomes widespread—before most people realize that there is actually, physically, something here that isn't the empty space we've learned to think of as existing. In other words, 'empty space' or 'emptiness' doesn't exist; only at the human level at which we function will the words have any meaning.

"Delving further into implications of the Superstrings Theory, I came up with the idea that we carry something within us that goes all the way back. I even picked up a Greek term for this: *anamnesis*, meaning 'from the beginnings.' I came to the belief that the key to this lies in our DNA, which we inherit via our genes. After all, we inherit genes from our ancestors, and they from theirs, ad infinitum. It's our DNA that carries memories that go back to creation—*anamnesis*. I used to be skeptical of people's claims of remembering past lives, and of the concepts of 'racial memory' and 'cosmic consciousness.' Because of DNA, however, I can now accept the idea that a person can experience a past life, but it is not his or her own—that is, one that he or she as an individual has lived. Rather, there is a recollection, through DNA, of the life of an ancestor. On the same grounds, I can also accept the idea of racial memory and cosmic consciousness. These may also be partial explanations of what we call intuition and instinct.

"Another realization I came to goes something like this: Given the fact that all people have within them the prenatal memory of connectedness, there is the potential that this memory can be retrieved. Once that core memory comes into consciousness, we almost automatically experience a change in our feelings toward other persons and all of nature. After all, once you've experienced it you know you are one with all of creation. I had the experience, the recollection, and so I know that I have the responsibility of caring for you and all things that exist as I care for myself. I have to behave *as if* everything I do to you and creation, I do to myself. So, it behooves me to act with respect and love."

When the Experience Began to Flower

"Actually, the desire to explore Native American spirituality flowered for me during the 1980s when I was researching the literature for a little book I wrote called *The Wabanaki: An Annotated Bibliography*, published by the American Friends Service Committee, the social action arm of the Quakers. It was about the history of the Northeastern Indians. [The term *Wabanaki* means 'People of the Dawn,' and refers to Northeastern Indians, including the Penobscot.] I read the works of early writers, and it really was an eye opener for me. As I worked, there were times when, after reading about the treatment of my ancestors, I paused to ask myself, 'How come I, a Penobscot Indian, exist today?' But then I began making connections, synthesizing the disparate bits of information with the knowledge from my training and experience, fitting these into a pattern that eventually made sense.

"I had not known much about the history of the Indians in the Northeast, including my group. There were a lot of books, a tremendous amount of writing, because in the old days people used to keep diaries and journals.

For the most part my work was with books that are out of print, but are at least accessible in the state library and at the university. So I began to read the books and evaluate them and annotate them. That sparked my interest in traditional ways. With my anthropological background, I found a lot of things that intrigued me. When I got into the legends and the way they were described in the journals, the way writers tried to explain the religious beliefs, there was enough there to show me that I needed to investigate further.

"The world of the Native American, spiritual and otherwise, is not to be understood by assuming that it can be described easily in the English language, and in religious terms. What we now think of as spirituality was not a religion in the commonly accepted definition of the word. It was their way of life, which is to say that it permeated their lives to such an extent as to be inseparable from everyday living. There were no nature-transcending or theistic concepts. Manitou was not a supreme being, but rather a way of referring to that cosmic, mysterious power existing everywhere in nature—what we now know as cosmic superstrings. One could 'work' with this power through numerous actions, such as rituals, ceremonies, meditation, concentration, chanting, drumming, dancing, games, storytelling, and so forth. And in those ways you could bring about healing, seeing-into-the-future, detecting causes, obtaining directions, dream interpretation, communication to and from a distance, and so on.

"Prayers consisted chiefly of giving thanks to all things for fulfilling the responsibilities with which they had been charged by Creation. Take the Sun, for example. Most Indians seem to have accepted that, as white writers have stated, the Sun was worshiped. I can find no evidence that this was the case, and I believe that the thanks-giving ceremonies to the Sun were misinterpreted by white observers of the sometimes elaborate nature of these rites. The Sun was thanked for providing light and warmth, and, with Mother Earth, for making life possible for the plants, animals, humans, and all life in general—like thanking someone who had done you a favor. Trees were thanked for providing bark, roots, leaves, and so forth, which were used as medicine, lodge poles, canoes, and the rest. Incidentally, creation being conceived as a natural process, as was everything else, there was no specific Creator. Though many present-day Indians refer to a Creator, and a Creator who is male, I know of no Indian language that has a word or words to express this particular concept.

"I am convinced that Indians conceived that their role, the human role in the whole scheme, was to take care of all this, to keep the universe in balance. Don't kill too many beavers because if you kill all the beavers then they won't dam up the stream and then the fish will be affected. You know, they were aware of the connectedness of everything that was. Someone had to keep that in mind and keep seeing the reality of it.

"Just as we humans are charged with taking care of the Earth and keeping the whole universe in mind, just as we have been charged with that responsibility, so have the trees and the rivers, the creatures, and the Sun and the Moon been charged with their responsibilities."

Breaking Out of the Cycle

In recent years, Eunice has led workshops on drumming and shamanism to help people go beyond just the theory of our universal connectedness and actually experience it. In the course of this, she has had many long discussions about the native heritage with the local priest at the Catholic church on Indian Island. "One time I was leading a shamanic workshop in the parish hall, and he was in the kitchen getting something together. I went in there to get some water, and we started talking. So I told him, 'You know all the knowledge of the world—past, present, and future; this process of the shamanic journey lets you plug into that. This is why shamans can prophesy and heal and so forth.' Then he comes back at me; he says, 'Well, you know, God is described as all-knowing.' And we began talking about the parallels in the traditions. You know, like your guardian angel who is conceived of as both a guide and a guard—that would be your power animal in the shamanic tradition. It's the same thing. Many of the beliefs of Catholicism can be translated into the terms of Native American spirituality, and vice versa.

"I think one of the important aspects of our modern, Western-derived culture is that it puts so much emphasis on the material aspects of life. That has led to the exploitation of the Earth and natural resources, and also the exploitation of people, for the sole purpose of getting money to live a kind of life that most people think is the way one should live: with a lot of material possessions and a good income and so forth. But that keeps people so much in the material world that they don't have much opportunity to gain access to the spiritual world.

"Coupled with that, there is little in the churches, which are supposed to be oriented to helping people access the spiritual world. But we know the condition they are in. They've taken on the character of society as a whole, so there aren't many opportunities for us to grow up as traditional people did and touch the spiritual world. There just aren't many aspects of the nonmaterial world held up as valued, as something that is valued and that one should strive to achieve.

"As a result of this, the spiritual journey in the modern world has, essentially, to be a personal journey. Maybe later, where there is more emphasis put on the nonmaterial world, there will be greater opportunities for groups as a whole to acquire some nonmaterialistic values.

"I often look to the matter of the individual self-image that's formed at an early age, the foundations of which I believe are pretty well set by the time one is three years old. If the child hasn't been given spiritual values within the family setting, they have no familiarity with the values that are necessary for the just and peaceful functioning of society. And then they come into the world of language and they're programmed with all these beliefs—that if you have a big income with a big house and a lot of material possessions, you've got it made. They latch onto that belief system—heart, soul, and body. The chances then become slimmer and slimmer that they will be able to access this other world, this nonmaterial world. This is a multifaceted problem, and I think an important aspect of it is this matter of self-esteem. If you can develop an adequate self-image, then you are capable of directing your life, of making your own decision to turn against materialism, and so forth. You have to have confidence in your own ability to be able to go it alone, to go against what the rest of the culture is doing."

⟨⟨⟨⟨ FIVE ⟩⟩⟩⟩

Singing the Shaman's Song
DON JOSE MATSUWA, DONA JOSEFA MEDRANO BRANT SECUNDA

*D*oña Josefa Medrano is like a rock—steady, resolute, deep. At age 96, as she joins in ceremony, her gnarled fingers work incessantly, embroidering beautifully with bright colors while she sits, listening and praying. Her husband, don José Matsuwa, is no rock; even at the advanced age of 110, having come many times close to death, he is electric, crackling energy. The air shimmers around him, and his eyes sparkle with good humor.

Doña Josefa and don José are both singing shamans, healers, and master ceremonial leaders, respected throughout the Huichol territory of the Sierra Madre Mountains of western Mexico. They are coupled for a common flight, partners in a lifelong journey. Together they have served as anchors for their village in changing times, raising a family of thirteen children and seventy-five grandchildren and great grandchildren.

Their adopted grandson, Brant Secunda, describes them lovingly, with a note of poetry: "They walk together down the path, side by side as one heart, as a shaman couple." Together they have sought *nierikayaete*, a common Huichol expression that means "to find or complete the circle of your life." In their language they are called *verodica*, which means "the healing feathered people." Their long lives have been spent working hard upon the Earth to bring forth food and beautiful craft, and also engaging the realm of spirit as shamans who heal and help. But even now, at their advanced ages, with all their good works and all their profound visions, don José says they are like babies before the mysteries of the world.

The Huichol Tradition

These elders can only be understood in the context of the culture they are part of, for their lives and works are closely woven with the lives and works of their people. The Huichol Indians live in the Sierra Madre, protected by the deep canyons and rugged mountains of western Mexico. Because of this physical isolation, they have managed to avoid subjugation by either the Spanish military or Catholic missionaries. They have kept their native customs and ancient shamanic traditions whole.

According to Brant Secunda, who lived among them for many years, the Huichols are the last tribe in America to retain their pre-Columbian traditions alive and intact. He says they are the last indigenous group in North America never to have been conquered. Perhaps because of this, the Huichols harbor no bitterness about the coming of Cortés, Columbus, and the European settlers. "It was just life that other people came," don José says. "The old ones never said anything critical of this. They felt the coming of the Europeans was just part of the life process, and they found it strange that the gringos did not pray."

Currently, about fifteen thousand Huichols live in villages (ranchos) of about a hundred people each. The Huichols have a gentle culture; they like to joke and tease a lot. They get up out of bed in the morning teasing. But they are also a very peaceful people, and have been historically. With an economy based on farming and craft, they believe they are following a path that was given to them by the Creator when the Sun was born; it's a simple path, but a path the Creator said would enable them to find their hearts. Everything they do, they do because they say the gods taught them that way. Their crafts, their handmade clothing, and their ceremonies are all exquisitely beautiful, evidence of a refined ethical and aesthetic sensibility. In their tradition, no craft can be made unless the artisan first has a vision of it.

In a Huichol village, everyone is equal, such as in a council where everyone sits in a circle and talks things out. There is no hierarchy. Men and women have equal rights, although they have different responsibilities and interests.

Right now there is pressure on the Huichols to assimilate into Mexican society, and some are moving to the nearby cities of Tepic and Guadalajara. Although the Mexican government is trying to educate and help the Huichol people, most of them want to remain Indian, which is different from being Mexican. There are also a lot of materialistic pressures on the Huichols. When they visit the towns and cities they begin to see and want what the people in town have. It's going to take a lot of resolve on their part to keep their traditions intact in the modern world. In recognition of the beauty that characterizes their culture, a traditional daily prayer of the Huichol Indians involves remembering—remembering who they are, where they came from, and where they are going.

A Shaman Couple

Don José and his wife, doña Josefa, are living representatives of this tradition, and they embody some of its finer attributes. They live high in the Sierra Madre Mountains in the Mexican state of Nayarit, in a small village called El Colorin. As don José tells the story, when he was very young he felt stupid because everyone was seeing things in the spirit world, but he wasn't. So in his early thirties he began to study the shaman's path. He walked in the mountains and the fields, learning from nature, and for ten years he lived alone in a cave or in the forest, praying and studying in the school of the spirit. When he slept, he says, the deer spirit would come and visit and teach him. Altogether, he says, his shamanic apprenticeship spanned sixty-four years, during which he fasted many times, including one stretch while he was on Vision Quest when he went fifteen days without food and water. When people are skeptical of this story, he reminds them that Jesus fasted in the desert for forty days, so that fifteen days is not so fantastic by comparison.

Now that he is old and wise, don José says that what he knows of life is this: With prayer and good intentions, we make our lives sacred and so come to balance. Referring to the deer, the Huichol symbol for the spirit of the human heart, he says, "You grab the deer's tail and you go."

Don José is noted for the beauty and poetic character of his chants. When younger, he often sang for several days and nights during the course of a single ceremony. While singing, he would remain seated in his *uweni*, or shaman's chair, so that the power he manifested would not be lost.

Throughout his life he also earned wide renown for his ability to heal the sick. In the traditional way of shamans around the world, he sucks objects out of the body and uses his prayer arrows (*muvieri*) to adjust the energy fields in and around the body.

Throughout his life, don José has been full of passion, vitality, playfulness, and also deep concern—not only for his own people, but also for the lack of balance in the larger world. In the early 1980s he visited the United States and told interviewer Joan Halifax, "I see that many people here are so caught up in their own little lives that they are not getting their love up to the Sun, out to the ocean, and into the Earth. When you do ceremonies, sending out your love in the Five Directions—the North, the South, the East, the West, and the Center—brings life force into you. That love brings the rain. As it has been since human history began, people are wrapped up in their little worlds, and they forget the elements; they forget the source of their life. People have forgotten. Most people are just thinking about sex and not leaving prayer offerings. People are always looking for elaborate mysteries to bring the world into balance, but prayer offerings are the most simple, direct way."

Although he is filled with laughter and love, don José is also tough. At the age eighty-five, when most modern people would have been resting in a nursing home, he was working as a miner. One day while he was working deep in a cave, the other miners forgot about him and set off a load of dynamite. The dynamite exploded beside him and took his right arm, but don José soon rebounded to full health. He said he only needs one hand anyway—so he can hold a machete, a cigarette, and his healing feathers.

In addition to his role as shaman and ceremonial leader among the Huichols, don José has been an active farmer. He loved to work in the fields. His life, he says, was to grow corn. Until he reached the age of 107, he grew eight tons of corn every year—enough to fill seven storage houses. And each day he would carry one hundred pounds of firewood on his back as he walked up the mountain on his way home from the cornfields. His elders, he says, taught him that hard work was the way to stay healthy.

When doña Josefa was just fourteen years old, according to the custom of the Huichols don José "stole" her. With her tacit agreement, he carried her off into the night and they married themselves. As is apparent to anyone who sees them together, theirs has been a good match. They are kind and loving companions.

Doña Josefa waited until she was in her early twenties and was the mother of three children before she began to walk the shaman's path, with don José's encouragement. In the Huichol way, women who seek to become shamans undergo the same training as the men. She learned by making pilgrimages to many sacred sites: the caves, mountaintops, and springs near their village. She also learned from a teacher.

Even though don José is the one who has attained the most notoriety for his healing and his magical capacity to lead powerful all-night ceremonies, doña Josefa is the real chief of the village. About shamanism and the mysteries, she says, "Some believe and some don't. Those who believe learn." But, she adds, "It's a lot of work to become a shaman. Suffer a little; then you get something. It's much better to be led or guided than to go alone. More people should think about becoming shamans, because the people need help."

In Search of Adventure

Brant Secunda was born June 30, 1952, in Brooklyn, New York, of Jewish parentage. As he grew, his family moved to northern New Jersey. Then in 1970, the day after his eighteenth birthday, he left to find the Huichol Indians. With a mischievous grin, Brant says that he went to the library in New York and looked up the word *peyote*. The entry said "see Huichols"— so he took the message literally and left to see the Huichol Indians.

"Seriously, though," Brant explains, "by the time I was eighteen I knew I had to leave the East Coast. I was just drawn to Mexico. The first of Carlos Castaneda's books on the Yaqui sorcerer don Juan had come out, and that made a deep impression on me. In a sense, I was a shaman tourist looking for adventure."

In Mexico he met a Huichol schoolteacher who gave him the name of his family village, which was a five-day walk from Ixtlan. After an adventure in Guatemala, Brant returned to Mexico and began walking toward the Huichol land. On the third day, while following a little deer trail, he passed out, completely lost, dehydrated, and exhausted. He lay in a stupor and had a wild vision with circles, deer, and eagles. Then he was awakened by Indians standing over him, laughing and sprinkling water in his face. The old shaman of their village had had a dream about Brant, and had sent the young men out to find him. They brought him back to the village. After a few days, a shaman in another village, don José, also dreamed about him and sent for him. Thus began an apprenticeship that was to last for twelve years.

Don José says that when he found Brant, he felt sorry for him because he didn't know anything. But Brant helped him a lot in the cornfield, and in exchange don José taught him the intricacies of Huichol shamanism, to the extent that one person can teach another.

"My apprenticeship was very hard," Brant explains. "You're going without food and water, staying up all night, walking great distances, spending a lot of time alone, and just learning all the different things, which took a long time. And don José was tough with me. He said I wasn't born an Indian, and he knew I was going to be teaching people, so he wanted me to get it perfect."

As Brant tells it, he spent a lot of time with don José, working side by side with him, growing corn and beans, and just being with him. He had to go on Vision Quests frequently and on many different pilgrimages to places of power. He also had to fast a lot—no food or water for days sometimes—and he spent fourteen months on a fruit diet to develop the capacity to see the energy field, or aura, around people. He also had to learn to talk to the fire and to dream. Then he started learning how to heal and how to lead ceremonies.

Ultimately, Brant did two apprenticeships—one of six years to become a healing shaman, and another of six years to become a singing or ceremonial shaman. He didn't think he was learning anything at first, but he persevered, and don José also held fast to his original vision and continued to teach Brant until he did learn. At the end of the apprenticeships, don José dramatically announced he was leaving Brant in his place to carry on the Huichol tradition, and then he led a ceremony to transfer his power. "It was an all-night ceremony," Brant recalls, "very beautiful. Then at sunrise he took me by the hand, led me around the fire, and sat me down in his shaman's chair. I felt like lightning was going through me. And then he announced he was leaving me with the shaman's belt of his family."

Specifically, don José left Brant in his place to carry on the Huichol tradition and to share the wisdom of that tradition with people all over the world. To accomplish this, in 1979 Brant founded and became director of the Dance of the Deer Foundation in California. Through the foundation, which is based in Soquel, California, Brant teaches, leads pilgrimages, and offers healings all across the United States and in Italy, Germany, Mexico, and elsewhere. His intent is to serve as a bridge person between modern culture and the ancient Huichol culture. He says he has dedicated his life to bringing the tools of shamanism into modern everyday life and to preserving the Huichol traditions. At his seminars, he works people hard, playing the drum with abandon while encouraging participants to dance and sing furiously. This gives them the chance to let go of ordinary concerns and move into the realm of spirit. About 20 percent of the proceeds earned by the Dance of the Deer Foundation goes back to the Huichols.

Intense and serious about the work he does, Brant at the same time exhibits a quick wit and a mercurial sense of humor. Like the Huichols, he is inordinately fond of teasing people, albeit in a gentle way. "The central message of Huichol shamanism," Brant says, "is to love and enjoy life. Huichols aren't perfect—they get as angry or jealous as other people—but they know how to leave it behind. They know the goal is to go beyond feelings of anger or jealousy, to reach beyond for God—for balance and harmony in life. Their lives focus on trying to do things according to the harmony of the laws of nature and of life in general. Their basic message is to spiritualize your life, to make your life as sacred as possible.

"One of the most beautiful things the Huichols taught me was to love the gods. It was a whole other concept for me. I was brought up to love a human being, or pizza or bagels. But to love the gods is a very real emotion for an Indian, very powerful to open your heart and offer your life to the gods. Those are my words. The Huichols say, 'Find your life'—look for your life in the Earth and sky and the life all around you, in what we call the Ancient Ones, or the gods and goddesses. We say that the universe, literally, was created out of the power of love, and so look for that and bring it into your heart in a real way, as part of your regular life. There is a responsibility involved in this, too, to the Earth and sky.

"Don José and I are close companions. We have a grandfather-grandson relationship and are good friends. Don José is the one who told me to begin teaching other people what he had taught me. In 1988, I was teaching in Europe when I got word that don José was very sick and close to death. The message said that he couldn't die in peace until I came. Since the Huichols believe that people can't die in peace if they still want to see somebody, I immediately cancelled my workshop and flew to Mexico. When I got there don José was unconscious. He couldn't even lift his head. So it was doña Josefa and their children who asked me to take my feathers out and try to help him. I had been staring at him for about half an hour when they asked me to do the healing. Over the next five days I did six healings on him. Then I dreamed that he would get better. After I told his family about my dream, he did get better."

To everyone around him, don José had already seemed dead for three hours when Brant arrived, but after the healings he began to regain his strength. He says Brant was the one who healed him, along with another shaman, so he could get better. Using his prayer feathers and the shamanic technique of sucking, Brant took two big stones out of his chest—two crystals. Don José says when he is totally better he will grow corn again.

The Shaman's Path

According to Brant, a shaman's job is to heal, to lead ceremonies, to help people, and to help keep the balance in the world. Traditionally, shamans have done this by entering trance through dreaming, drumming, or chanting, and then by working directly with spirits.

Brant defines shamanism by saying it's about life—honoring all life. "Shamanism is a path of personal development, of family and community service, and for healing of the Earth. It includes and honors all of life, the trees, the rocks, the waters, as well as the animals and other people. With each breath we take, we remember the sacredness of all this. We remember the Earth, and with each step we take we try to bring her power up into our feet.

"Shamanism is an old tradition all over the Earth, a tradition that can take you all the way to God. In the Huichol tradition, love is the foundation of a shaman's power: love for Mother Earth, Father Sky, Grandmother Ocean, and all the people. A sorcerer, on the other hand, is into power; they cast spells and try to cause harm. Their primary concern is personal power, whereas a shaman gives his power away for the benefit of all.

"Shamanism involves healing your self, your circle, and the Earth. Step one is personal healing or transformation, which involves healing our bodies, our hearts, and our spirits. Our bodies have to be strong. We have to be in good condition to walk on Mother Earth and feel our connection with her. You can't feel that connection by sitting all day in a car or on a couch. The next part of personal healing is healing our hearts by becoming more intuitive. Then comes healing our spirits so we experience our connection to all life. When we make this connection, we are living a healing tradition and we are healed. No one tries healing anyone else until after many years of training and healing the self, finding their own healing connection to the Earth.

"Step two is to help heal your circle of family and friends. For healing yourself and your circle, it's best to use preventive medicine so you never get sick. Step three is to extend that healing to everything upon Mother Earth, to perform ceremonies to bring in the balance."

How does one go about becoming a shaman? Doña Josefa says, "We've had to suffer a lot to finish our apprenticeships. Brant did a nine-day Vision Quest. Don José did a fifteen-day Vision Quest, fasting alone in a cave. They had to suffer a lot to learn to become shamans. Lots of deprivation: fasting, and sexual abstinence." She adds that there are many other steps to becoming a shaman, including pilgrimage, participation in ceremonies, dreaming, and prayer.

Brant elaborates on this theme: "To become empowered as a shaman, you have to go where there is power. You gain empowerment by fasting and praying at places of power. In that way you are given a dream or a vision from that place—it's like a contract almost. You give a prayer and an offering to the place of power, and you get to harvest the power of that place. One can only learn from and be empowered by a place of power by going there."

Don José points out that "Moses made pilgrimages to the mountain, and Jesus spent forty days in the desert. All throughout history, people have journeyed to sacred places. This tradition of the pilgrimage needs to be revived, and to embrace all traditions. People need to go to sacred places. Everyone should go to the ocean on pilgrimage at least once a year."

One time-honored way of becoming a Huichol shaman is to go to a place of power such as the ocean, a mountaintop, or a cave, for five years in a row. If you go to a cave, for instance, you make an effort to learn to communicate with the living spirit who resides in it—to dream about the god or goddess, to speak to the cave, and to have a vision from that cave. Then you use that vision in your life.

In the same way that they communicate with the spirit of a place, so Huichol shamans communicate with the spirit of the fire, Tate Wari. Each morning when they wake up, they sit before the fire and tell the dreams they have had that night. And then they make a prayer offering. Brant says this simple technique greatly increases our ability to dream powerful dreams and to remember them. Don José also feels strongly about this practice, and recommends that everyone tell their dreams to the fire every morning, even if it is just a candle flame. And, he says, "People should make a conscious effort to dream of the gods, the ocean, and the Sun by thinking of them when they go to sleep. That will make your dreams more powerful. When you wake up at night, talk to the gods and then go back to sleep. More dreams will come. To really learn, you dream."

Attending ceremonies is another important empowerment. The shaman who leads a ceremony empowers everyone who attends, but an apprentice must attend many ceremonies to receive the full empowerment of the ceremony. As Brant points out, "When you sing at a ceremony, you bring yourself into a state of ecstasy. You literally change your body-and-mind chemistry. You alter your state of consciousness."

The Huichols are the original peyote Indians. Many, but not all, Huichol shamans use this hallucinogenic cactus pod about once a year to enter a deep, dreamlike trance. Before using it, though, they fast and abstain from sex for at least a month. It's an arduous, sixty-day round-trip walk to the land of peyote. Don José has made that long pilgrimage thirteen times in his life. The pilgrims walk in single file for thirty days to peyote land, eating just a little fruit and even fasting from water. The last five days of the peyote pilgrimage they do not even eat fruit. Don José says they do it to have a direct experience of God, and they realize that they can only do this in a good way with peyote if their bodies, minds, and spirits are clear—if they are doing it for a high intention, with a pure motivation.

Even though some people forget or ignore it, Brant says, perhaps the most important shamanic practice is prayer. "People often equate shamanism with having wild visions, but learning how to make a prayer is just as important as receiving visions. The art of prayer is humility versus self-importance. We pray that we won't forget that our life is sacred. Gratitude is a mainstay of the Huichol tradition. They say it takes nine years to learn how to pray. When your turn comes, you don't even think about what you are going to say, you just let the spirit speak through you.

"One way of coping with the busyness of modern life is to make your life and work a prayer. The Huichol people make their farmwork in the cornfields a prayer, and so we should make our work with machines or numbers or words a prayer. We don't pray to God to do everything, though. That's a crutch kind of thing. A prayer is an affirmation of life, it's a good action toward life, it's a wishful thought."

While a shaman's path of learning is long and often arduous, doña Josefa and don José both encourage people to consider becoming shamans. "We have an obligation, a responsibility, to empower our lives. Otherwise it's wasted time. The world needs more shamans," they say, "to make it a better place." Don José says that while it is a lifelong journey, "if you dedicate yourself to the shaman's path, you can learn a lot in just two years." But how can a shaman aspirant be guided and maintain stability as he or she attempts to marry the ancient practices of shamanism with the modern world? "Watch your intention," don José counsels, "that is the most important thing. Pay attention and watch your intentions."

To this, Brant adds a note of caution: "There's a danger in people thinking they know more than they really do. People get tricked by their own egos or sense of self-importance. They think that after they've learned a few things they really know shamanism. Even when they have gone through part of an apprenticeship they often get tricked into thinking they know everything. But there is so much to know. An apprenticeship never ends. Shamans are always learning; they are apprenticed to the gods. Sometimes people forget that and fall away from the path. They think they've finished their apprenticeship, and that they've learned all they need to know. But you never graduate, you just keep learning a little more each day."

The trait of humility, the Huichols emphasize, is important for someone who undertakes the work of a shaman. Brant says sometimes he and don José would be just flying at night, in spiritual ecstasy during ceremony, but then in the morning they would wake up, and don José would look at Brant and say, "Last night we were flying with the gods, but now we're just idiots again. Back to the cornfield!"

Counsel from the Wisdom Keepers

Don José and doña Josefa say they are sharing their wisdom tradition now because "this is what the gods say. We are all children of the Great Spirit. The teachings are for all, not just for Indians. Many native people are bitter now because white people have been so bad to Indians. They say the whites have stolen everything, and now they want to steal our religion. But times are different now. The white people never really wanted to learn before. They thought we were savages. Now they have a different understanding, and they do want to learn. We are all children of God. The tradition is open to anyone who wants to learn. But who really wants to learn?"

Even in speaking of the present, the elders maintain equanimity in their point of view. They say that right now they see both the best and the worst going on in the world, but from their vantage point they see that things are improving. Doña Josefa says she thinks the world is getting better. "We are seeing both the low end and the high end now; we're seeing both in the world. The people have a big desire to learn the old traditions. This is why the world is changing and healing. If people pray and remember the gods and goddesses, the world will be OK. When people forget, then the disasters come."

Adopted grandson Brant echoes this theme. "We're planting seeds. All the ceremonies and prayers are like seeds, and though we may not see the fruits in our own lifetime, they may come in the next generation or the one after that. I really feel things will come out well. But you have to start at the beginning. You have to start with the individual. If someone is acting like an idiot in their everyday life, they can't change, they can't help heal the Earth or anything. So a lot of what I do is to help people bring the power of life, the sacredness of life, into their hearts on an everyday basis, as regular people. Then they can bring that back into their homes, their families, and from there out into the community and then out to the healing of the Earth. So we have to start at the beginning to get the balance back.

"There are two things going on in the world now. On one hand you have dramatic change—people getting very seriously spiritual. A lot of people are dedicating their life now to some spiritual tradition or path. And then on the other hand you have the lowest side—people killing each other in the cities and being totally uncaring, and all the homeless. You have two polarities. We have people who are changing fast, and then you have a lot of people who never even have a glimpse of the spiritual life.

"A lot of the people who are changing are going to help others. That's the key to service, the whole key to it. If we are going to change, we are going to have to serve. Rich people will need to share with poor people; they'll need to share the wealth, not just monetarily speaking, but all kinds of wealth, physical wealth. You are going to have to have people serving, going into small towns and helping out, making their lives useful. In this way our whole society will change, and make it really good.

"Big changes are going to have to happen for there to be total love on the Earth, and for all people, society, to be focused on God—that's going to take a while. In my heart, though, I'm totally positive that it's going to happen. I have a very positive attitude that there's going to be beautiful changes here on Earth. That somehow God is going to help us, the Great Spirit is going to save us. No matter what. When you really study it now, it looks almost hopeless. I mean the waters are polluted, the air is polluted. We're in bad shape. But somehow it's going to come together. Science and spirituality are going to unite. They are going to realize that they have to unite."

Don José offers a final bit of wisdom to the modern world: "Never take a leaf or move a pebble without asking permission. Always ask permission. That maintains the balance and teaches humility. That leaf you want to pluck could be far more important than the little purpose you have in mind. You don't know—so ask permission first. We can't go on this way, with the modern culture. Plants, species, and animals are dying. We need to listen to the spirits and bring them back."

Doña Josefa also offers pointed advice for those who will live into the next century: "Always listen to what the elders say." Her elders said many things to her when she was young, and she did not listen. If she had, she would have become a shaman much earlier. "More shamans would make for a better world," she counsels. "Anyone can become a shaman if they want to, but they must make the effort. They must suffer."

Since the writing of this chapter, don José Matsuwa has passed away. When he awoke on the morning of November 6, 1990, he knew it would be his last day. He called the people of his village together, offered them a final blessing, and then quietly passed into Spirit. He left his healing feathers for Brant Secunda, who arrived two days later to help with the prayers and chanting in a ceremony for don José. In accordance with Huichol custom, they sang their songs to help send his soul to the Sun.

⟨⟨⟨SIX⟩⟩⟩

She Whose Voice Rides on the Wind
GRANDMOTHER TWYLAH NITSCH

*A*s Grandmother Twylah Nitsch explains it, in the Seneca Indian tradition relatives and friends often visit infants when they are about six months old. Everyone puts a stone on the blanket where the baby is, and some random stones are placed there, too. The baby then takes hold of a stone, and that is the baby's first decision.

As a youngster, Twylah was called strongly to the stones, and for a long time she had a favorite, called Geeh-yuk. It was three sided, had many markings, and was black and gray-white. When she finally lost her stone, she gained something else: the ability to help others look upon stones and understand the messages they carry as the oldest parts of the Earth. By examining a rock's color, texture, shape, number of sides, and markings, she can derive a phenomenal amount of information about the person, such as where the person has been, where the person is now on his or her Earth-walk, and where the person's potentials might take him or her.

Stone reading is just one of many gifts she has developed throughout her life. Though everyone calls her Twylah, hundreds of students also know her as Two Wolves, or Yehwehnode, She Whose Voice Rides on the Wind. The daughter of a Seneca mother and an Oneida-Scotch father, Twylah raised four children in her home on the Cattaraugus Indian reservation in western New York, near Lake Erie.

Twylah learned the philosophy of the stones, trees, and natural world

101

ASK
YOURSELF 1. AM I HAPPY IN WHAT I'M DOING?
2. IS WHAT I'M DOING GOING TO ADD TO THE CONFUSION IN THE WORLD
3. WHAT AM I DOING TO BRING ABOUT PEACE AND CONTENTMENT?
4. AND HOW WILL I BE REMEMBERED WHEN I'M GONE?

firsthand from her mother, her Wolf Clan grandmother, and her grandfather, Moses Shongo, a Seneca medicine man who looked to her to carry
on his tradition of teaching. On both her grandfather's and her mother's
sides of the family, Twylah is a descendant of the great Seneca chief Red
Jacket, whose spirit, she says, helps and guides her in this lifetime. Wisdom
and prophecy have been passed on in her family, she says, as far back as
they can remember. *Twylah is a descendant of the great SENECA CHIEF RED JACKET*

"My grandfather's teachings are very simple," Twylah recalls. "Each person, for instance, should ask himself or herself four questions that can serve
as guides: Am I happy in what I'm doing? Is what I'm doing going to add
to the confusion in the world? What am I doing to bring about peace and
contentment? And how will I be remembered when I'm gone?" Those are
important questions, Twylah says, for "all of us come to this Earthwalk as
'I am,' to learn how to become 'we are.' In doing this we are concerned seven
generations into the future."

While the basis of her traditional philosophies is simple, Twylah makes
use of many elaborate systems of divination to teach and share her wisdom.
She is deeply loved by hundreds of people for her common sense, her
warm grandmotherly presence, and the light she bears. To share her teachings more widely, she founded the Seneca Indian Historical Society and the
Wolf Clan Teaching Lodge. Over many years, she has initiated about 350
people—of all races and religions—into the Wolf Clan Teaching Lodge.
Members reside as far afield as China and India.

Twylah's teaching lodge is patterned after the lodge of the traditional
Wolf Clan, one of eight Seneca clans. The Bear Clan teaches medicine, the
Turtle Clan the moral code, the Beaver Clan cooperation, the Hawk Clan
conservation, the Deer Clan physical fitness, the Heron Clan farming and
nourishment, and the Snipe Clan (named for a small bird) discipline. The
Wolf Clan teaches Earth law.

The Fifth World

At the age of ten, Twylah first heard the prophecy of the Earth cleansing. If people lost their spiritual values, the prophecy warned, the Earth
would be cleansed. The prophecies made a deep impression on her. "There
have been a series of worlds," she explains. "The first time the Sun cleansed
the Earth, next the Moon did; then water. The fourth time, this time, the

Earth will be cleansed by all three of these forces. Those prophecies also foretold that a band of people would come to this continent from the East. They wouldn't know who they were or what their future held. They would seek answers by digging into the secrets of the Earth, water, and Moon—lacking any understanding about these powers. When they begin digging into the secrets of the Sun, the prophecies say, it will create the next cleansing."

"Most people know only about the Third World, Atlantis, which was cleansed by the great flood. But altogether there are seven worlds in the history of the Earth. From the First World we inherited the gift of beauty. From the Second World we inherited family structure, thus learning about the balance between physical and spiritual energies. From the Third World we inherited clarity of purpose through self-discipline. In the Fourth World we developed diversity of wisdom. The Fourth World, though, also spawned the syndrome of separation and control, such as wars and religions. We have now entered the time of the Fifth World, which began at Harmonic Convergence [August 16-17, 1987].

"North and South America were the site of the First World. While we are now in the Fifth World, there are obviously many hangovers still around from the Fourth World. In the Fourth World the greatest division came when humankind became impatient and decided to create a god and place him as a male deity someplace out in the clouds. That has been the greatest separation between humankind and the Great Mystery. But this had to happen in the history of the Earth. There were lessons that we needed to learn through this experience. The Fourth World was all about separation and control. Some of the wars separated the people so that they could not be strong; it separated them.

"When we honor the Great Mystery, we are at peace. But there's a certain blindness that people enjoy hiding behind. Their eyes are closed to certain experiences. Then they can say, 'Well, I didn't know.' This perpetual blindness seems to be like a disease. People say, "The world's a mess, but as long as it's not depriving me of food and shelter, I really don't need to do anything about it.' Yet we do need to make deep personal decisions about this. Some people choose not to see, to be blind, not to be responsible.

"The people of today are beginning to open their ears, their eyes, their mouths, and most of all their hearts. And they're coming together and listening to each other. That's because we've come to the end of the Fourth World. This Fifth World that we are entering means that each person must use their gifts of birth to accomplish their missions in life, and this is the contribution that each one is obliged to offer. Everyone has a place on the great Medicine Wheel of Truth. When we all do what we came in to do as a mission, everyone will be happy. There is no room for someone to be controlling someone else.

"In the Fifth World, illumination will be the central theme. Spiritual awareness will be common. Illumination radiates from the center. The focus is on truth; all the knowledge in the world is useless without faith. We humans have to be willing to take a chance. What is wisdom? It's an inner knowing of truth, without a shadow of a doubt. But it can't stand alone—it's tied to the other qualities on the Medicine Wheel. This life is not a game, but is based on the wisdom of the trees, the grass, the stones, and all of life. Wisdom is also having a dream. If you have no dream, you can't tap into wisdom. If a person has an idea that flashes into their mind, that's the beginning of a dream. But they must bring life into the idea and develop the dream, or it will pass on.

"Nothing works without the focus on truth, wisdom, and faith. If we don't have faith in ourselves, nothing's going to work. You can have all the wisdom in the world, but if you don't have faith and aren't willing to step out and do something about it, nothing is going to happen.

"Illumination is coming in the Fifth World. Any time there is a drastic change, it takes the environment and the people within the environment about twenty-five years to have this transition occur—to have the trend really felt and appreciated by the people. So if trees are burned down, for example, and then new ones are seeded, it's going to take about twenty-five years, if they're untouched, before some of them will look like trees again. So it will take some time before we see the full influence of the illumination of the Fifth World. It's happening, and you can see it, but you have to look.

"It's only those people who are stuck in jobs that prevent them from getting out and hearing what's going on in the world who are not seeing.

They still are the majority of people, and they're trapped. They're the last to move. Look at the people of this world who are starving and have no way to go, and yet look at all the people who are loaded with money and could care less. They could care less about the people who could use a little help now and then.

"We, as humankind, have to be willing to take a chance. Some are forced into taking a chance whether they like it or not. They go to work one day and they have a job, and the next day they don't have a job, so they are forced to do something else. It was a drastic experience when the steel plants closed down in Buffalo years ago. The people were up in arms wondering, 'What are we going to do?' Some of them who hadn't saved anything, they had bought houses, furniture, and everything, and they lost it. Others who had saved some money got their kids through school and a few other things. But there's others who had lived just from hand to mouth, and they had made enough money—the same amount of money the others had made—but they just figured it would go on forever.

Who knows who are the smart ones there? The ones who had prepared for an event such as that or the ones who had not prepared for it? I'd say the ones who had not prepared for it, because they had to do something. The others would sit back and think, 'Well, I'm safe; I've got my house,' where I can live maybe for a couple of years,' or 'I'll try to get a job, and even if I had such and so . . . The ones who were out with nothing, they're the ones who had to do something. Forced action I call it, when you have to do something—when you are forced into doing something no one wants to do. Everyone is afraid of change, thinking, 'I don't want to do this; I don't want to leave my job; I don't want to do that because this feels secure to me.' But we need to change. We need to take a chance and change."

"One of the principal things we need to do as we move into this new time is to become aware of personal fears. That would be the biggest thing. People give energy to fear and it blocks their growing. When a person becomes frightened of something, then they have that scary feeling in their solar plexus. Then they know that's a fear. Becoming aware of it—for instance, how many times it has happened, and can a person remember when it first happened, and to really look at it in that way—that can help heal and release that fear."

Ancient Tools for a New Time

In this time of tremendous change, Twylah believes one traditional tool that can help us tremendously as we move into a new era of world history is the concept of council. "A council is the gathering of heads, hearts, and minds. Our people are not aware of this today. People today do not know how to listen, really. People today are mostly interested in having other people listen to what they have to say. But in order for anyone to learn anything, we have to learn how to listen first—listen to the wisdom of the person who is talking. Everyone has something important to say, in some way or other. This is an important part of our lives. In the councils years ago, they would have a talking stick and a questioning stick. People today are only aware of the talking stick, but to learn we have to ask questions.

"The two sticks would be placed in the middle of the circle. The council is a circle, and everyone sits equally around that circle. Everyone in the council who comes in and sits in that circle sits in their sacred space, and they're equal; no one is any better than anyone else. This is the main thing. So the people would be sitting in a circle. A council represents a circle, and a circle is the shape of harmony; that's just something that should be remembered. The council is the shape of harmony; a circle is a shape of harmony. Years ago, while sitting in council, people recognized they all had to have an equal input if they wished. If they did not want to take the council stick and say something, that was their own decision. No one looked down on anyone who had not spoken. Oftentimes someone else would say something and they would nod their heads in agreement.

"The two sticks are placed in the center. One person will go in; it's usually the person who has called the council. At that point, the people know that there is a subject that's going to be discussed. Nine chances out of ten, that subject will go around and around, and it means that people have to come together to listen as one head and one heart and one mind.

"Anyone who comes into the council must feel that they are healthy. That's the first thing: that they have a healthy mind and a healthy body, that they are willing to listen to what has been said, and that they must be rational. They must listen to reason, and they must be reasonable themselves. They must come into that council with an open mind. The person who called the council together would go and pick up the stick. Now, this would mean that anyone could do it—anyone who felt that they were willing to open that council could pick up this stick. Now, prior to that, years ago there would be certain ceremonies that would be conducted to help the people feel that they were one body, one mind, one spirit—that they would be listening to one law. The person then would pick up the stick and would welcome everyone there, and would say what the issue was. Different people would discuss something that had come up, and the council would explore varied ways of solving the problem. The idea to solve a problem is to listen to everyone's point of view and then, as everyone heard various points of view, they would talk about concessions.

"Concessions would be if you wanted something done your way and someone else wanted it done their way. You would have to give up some of the things that you wanted, and they would have to give up some of the things that they wanted. Then you could come together in a reasonable way. If you insisted that it was going to be your way, you would be expected to get up and walk out because you would be unreasonable. The moment a person becomes unreasonable, they cannot think straight. Their mind becomes crooked. This means that the two people would come in with ideas that they wanted such and such a thing to happen, but they would also come in with the idea that they would have to give a little in order to have this happen, because they couldn't have it their way 100 percent. So this means they would have to be reasonable.

"Each person in that council would have an opportunity to ask questions, and when they wanted to ask a question they would go and get the questioning stick. Whoever had the talking stick, they would give time to listen to that question. They'd stop what they were saying, and they would listen to that question, and they would respond. If they couldn't answer the question properly, they would ask, 'Does anyone else have something to say about this?' Now this could create going off from the original question, so there would only be maybe one, or possibly two, questions. Usually just one question was asked at that precise time, so that the process would have an ongoing purpose instead of someone trying to pull them off the original issue."

Through the use of council, a group faced with a problem could tap their collective wisdom and gradually develop consensus on how to resolve the issue. In our times, when we face countless problems, Twylah says we would do well to look beyond our accustomed forms of leadership and problem solving, and to consider making use of the council format.

The Clarity Quest

There is yet another tool that Twylah feels may be useful as we move into this new time, a tool that supports individuals facing major life problems, or confusion, or life transitions. Called the Clarity Quest, this technique is less arduous and time consuming than the traditional three or four-day Vision Quest of fasting and praying in the wilderness. Twylah recommends a Clarity Quest for anyone going though a major unsettling life change.

"First," she advises, "clarify the question you are wrestling with, or your intention for making this quest. Then retreat for twenty-four hours into a darkened room, bringing a candle that should be lit only when you need to make a note. Be at peace in the dark. Allow no interruptions. Drink distilled water only, to help cleanse your blood. Some light food is permissible, but not too much. Sit in each of the directions of the Medicine Wheel—East, South, West, and North—at sometime during the twenty-four hours, and contemplate the lessons associated with each direction. Pray and give thanks. At the end of twenty-four hours, you will have clarity on the question or issue you have brought on the quest with you."

Her Kitchen Classroom

Twylah has a strong, high voice, eyes that are sharp yet warm, and an ironic sense of humor. But perhaps her most notable trait is clarity of mind. She keeps the many complex threads of her teachings woven into an intricate yet ultimately beautiful whole. This feat of inner organization is part of her nature, she says, and is made all the easier because it is directed toward a sacred purpose. "When our energy isn't directed in a sacred manner," she chides, "it is scattered."

Twylah's house is filled with beautiful art—dozens of paintings and sculptures, each a tool that she may use for teaching. However, the most-used artifact in her house is her kitchen table. Nearly every day she spends time sitting at the kitchen table, where visitors come from all over the world to talk and ask for her guidance. "There's a lot of people who come in here, and I cannot get them to do some of the things because they want to sit and listen to what I have to say. But then on the other side of it, I have to teach.

The flowers will reproduce themselves longer than I will be here. If what has been given me to share with others, if it needs to get out, I have to spend the time to do it. I could stop tomorrow. And I could say I don't want any company anymore, and let it go at that. I don't think I really could though. I could do it physically, but emotionally and mentally it would destroy me. I wouldn't last, and I wouldn't need to last because I would have said, well, this is it.

"We learn from each other. When anyone comes in here, people say to me, 'Twy, you're teaching all the time, you're telling people what to do.' And I say, 'No, I'm learning all the time, because every time we go through a chart or the Medicine Wheel someone adds a bit of their own wisdom to it, and this is what life is all about; it's the sharing.' This is the meaning of working with the Great Mystery, because we cannot do anything without the Great Mystery. The Great Mystery is the source of life. Even to take our hands and touch the fingers together—it takes the Great Mystery to do that, because the Great Mystery is the thing that keeps us going on.

"The teachings I share are based on truth. When we come into the Earthwalk, we come in with truth encoded in us. But we can lose sight of that. The only ones who do not know who they are, are the two-leggeds. So sometimes we have to open up and receive messages from the Spirit to remember. It is evident that the messengers of the Great Spirit wear many faces. They can be manifestations of nature, creatures, or earthly forces."

As a lifelong student of these messengers and their messages, Twylah has written several books, including *The Language of the Stones*, *The Language of the Trees*, and *Entering into the Silence: The Seneca Way*. The books all help readers learn from nature and the wisdom in their own hearts.

"Messages are all around us," Twylah explains. "For example, when anyone finds a feather, it's a message of peace. No matter where you walk, if you happen to walk along and you see a feather, pick it up, hold it, and bring it to your heart. It's a special message of peace to you. If you're walking along and you're thinking of something that might be puzzling, and you're moving it through your mind and you pick a feather, hold it and look at it. It can often bring in a thought of wisdom in connection with what you're thinking about.

"Let me tell you a true thing about a feather. In California I was walking down to the store. I was walking down the street, and as I stepped off the curb, there were four feathers from a pigeon. I said, 'Woo,' and I picked them up. 'Oh, you're beautiful'—and I'm talking aloud. Then I happen to look, and there are four people sitting there on this porch. I went to the store, and on my way back I thought, well, they must wonder why was I so excited about picking up a feather. So they were sitting there on the porch, and I thought, well, I'll talk to them—you know, I'm a bit of a nutty person anyway. I said to them, 'Obviously you wondered why I picked up those four feathers and was so excited about it,' and they said, 'Yes, as a matter of fact.' And I said, 'Well, I happen to be a Seneca Indian, and we honor all kinds of bird feathers, and when we walk and we pick up a feather, we look at these feathers as messengers of peace. I thought you might be interested.' And they said. 'Well, thank you,' and then I walked on. Other times I would see the people sitting on the porch when I would take my baby granddaughter for a walk in the buggy, and I would see these people and they'd smile. I thought, well, seeing me each time must remind them of that lady who picked up the feathers and thought it was so great."

"Those People"—"The People"

As she sits at her kitchen table and talks with people about their lives and about the events unfolding in the world, Twylah frequently refers to "the people" and "those people," a distinction that she learned from her family. "When I was a little girl," she explains, "my grandmother would say, or I'd say, 'Well, who's coming today?' Because we'd always have many people coming around. She'd say, 'Well, the big heads, the big 'I ams,' and we'd always kind of laugh about it.

"'Those people' are the ones who disregard the wisdom lessons of life. They could care less. The only time they become interested is when they don't have enough food and they don't have enough lodging and they don't have enough people to wait on them. 'Those people' need to recognize the importance of walking in harmony with this Earth. 'Those people' are those involved with the symbols of separation and control, such as wars, religions, the boundaries of countries and governments, and social hierarchy. These things separate and slow the growth of mankind because people do not have an example of truth from which to establish a firm foundation. 'Those people' see growth as using the gifts of the Earth, thinking they are inexhaustible. Progress is geared to speed. The moment one project is completed, man's impatience launches the next one; it's called exponential growth. This process of growth puts a strain on all the Earth's resources without any sensitivity to its need for restoration. Through this activity, 'those people' have wantonly fractured the backbone of the future—not only their own, but for every entity connected with the Earth as well.

"'The people' are the ones who are honorable. They honor all the animals, they honor each person, they honor sacred space. They honor trees, they honor everything that pertains to nature. Many of them would be farmers, people who work with the soil. People who like to walk in the woods, people who are gardeners, and generally people who touch the earth are 'the people.' They recognize that when we focus on the history of the Earth, we have a firm foundation from which to grow. Every place we look is an example that sets the pace for growth based upon the natural restoration of resources. Honoring the Earth builds a moral consciousness based upon love and respect, the spiritual and physical marriage that produces harmony."

In the context of 'the people' and 'those people,' Twylah warns, "The Ancient Ancestors of the beings who inhabit the Earth have made signs to awaken the dormant crystals that lie in the vaults of every manifestation of this planet. The Ancient Ancestors are stirring the matrix for a rebirth. Humankind has a choice: awaken, or be swallowed into oblivion. It has happened before, when the crystals were misused."

When the Sun Touches Us

Many indigenous groups in the Americas recognize the Sun as the principal source of not only the Earth's physical energy but also of the Earth's spiritual energy. Grandmother Twylah also believes this, and emphasizes an important distinction. Native people, she says, do not worship the Sun as God, but rather as one manifestation of the Creator or the Great Mystery, a manifestation that serves as the principal source of physical and spiritual energy for the Earth and the creations who share life upon the Earth.

Many native elders, including Twylah, recall ancient prophecies warning that great trouble—the next cleansing of the Earth—will come when human beings begin to experiment with the secrets of the Sun—nuclear fusion—for profit-making purposes. "We need to understand that the Sun is love. The Sun symbolizes love, and if we look at the Sun as the symbol

THE SUN IS LOVE

of love, then when we walk out in the Sun we say it's a beautiful day because the Sun is shining and it's warm. It's touching our bodies, and when we feel the warmth of the Sun it's the same kind of feeling that we have when we fall in love with someone. It's the same feeling; it's that gentle warmth. But when we misuse love, then we get burned.

"When the Sun touches us, it creates a loving situation. So long as we give honor, and praise the gifts of the Sun and think of all the things that the Sun does to perpetuate life, we're OK. Without the Sun we could not see. Without the Sun we could not feel. And the only way we can feel and see is through the gift of the greatest source, which is the Great Mystery. We cannot function without that and all the gifts here on the Earth. Within us is encoded that feeling of love that is the feeling of truth. Love and truth walk side by side. People who look and don't see are missing the boat, or people who only look at what they want to see are missing a lot of gifts that sight brings in.

"This idea that someday people would foolishly play with the power of the Sun, that has been a universal prophecy. It is not just any one seer, it has been a universal prophecy. I would go as far as to say that in every philosophy it says the time would come when people would recognize the importance of the Sun. And not giving the importance to the Sun would create blindness. In the Fourth World there's no doubt about it, people ignored the Sun. But what will come in the Fifth World will be illumination. So the fires are coming back. The spirit is awakening. We'll see again that the fire, the Sun, is love.

⟨⟨⟨ SEVEN ⟩⟩⟩

Somewhere Under the Rainbow
MEDICINE STORY

Master storyteller Manitonquat, widely known as Medicine Story, is the *powwah*, or spiritual leader, and the *minatou*, or keeper of the lore, for the Assonet band of the Wampanoag Nation. With depth of feeling and dramatic flair, he recounts the ancient myths and legends of North America, or Turtle Island. He has traveled the world to tell these tales. Each story offers listeners insights about how to be at peace, how to meet the challenges of life, or how to have a balanced relationship with nature. This is the medicine of Medicine Story: his stories help to heal the hearts and minds of those who listen.

If he were to tell the story of Medicine Story, he says, it would probably fill many volumes. "I've lived a number of different lives. Looking back it seems like they were totally separate lives. When I was growing up, I felt that kind of separation because my mother and father were separated, divorced from my infancy, and I spent my summers with my father's family and my winters with my mother—totally different environments.

"My father's family, the Indian side, was from what's now called southeastern Massachusetts, the ancestral lands of the Wampanoag people, the People of the Morning Light. Probably the biggest influence on me there was my grandfather, because my father didn't have much interest in me after the divorce. He was friendly enough when I saw him, though it wasn't like having a father at all. But my grandfather, he spent all his time with me, and he told me all his stories and showed me all the places he knew because it was his great passion to learn all about the olden times of our people. He knew all the campsites, and where they moved from place to place.

"I got his name. My name is his name, which is Francis Story Talbot, so I'm the second. The Story part just happens to be a coincidence, as I understand. He certainly was a storyteller, but I understand he wasn't named that way; that is, he was named for some friend of his parents whose name was Story.

"My grandfather was born down in Dighton, Massachusetts, and I go down to the Dighton powwow every year now and do ceremonies at the Dighton Council Rock, and sort of pay my respects to my grandfather and his background, there. His people came from the Pokonoket community and the old Watuppa reservation near Fall River, which the city of Fall River took away from our people around the turn of the century. Now we have a replacement that we call Watuppa, although it has nothing to do with Watuppa. It's in the Freetown State Forest, which we are struggling to take back from the dirt bikers and to make a sacred area. We've been doing ceremonies there for a dozen years, but it's still a battle to try and secure the place for ourselves completely. We have started to build a longhouse, and we plan to make a roundhouse and dig a well and build some other things down there, too.

"Now, the origin stories my grandfather told me about our people said we came out of the sea onto an island. Eventually the tops of these islands were to be destroyed, so the people left the islands in boats and came to a mainland where they went into the mountains and lived—until after a while they were overrun by invaders. So they migrated some more, and they began to head north; they went across flats, and floods, and ice, and this migration went on. Who's to say what period of time we're talking about? It could be thousands of years. But evidently every now and then some of the people moving would say, 'Well, this place is good enough; we will stay here.' And others would say, 'No, my vision tells me I must go toward the rising Sun.' And so people dropped off along the way—on the East Coast, probably up around Nova Scotia, and maybe Hudson Bay and Labrador. I'm not sure, but I think Algonquin people lived there, too. Some said 'OK, here we are at the ocean. We can't go any further. We'll stay here.' Others said, 'No, it's too cold. We'll move south.' And so you have the

Algonquin. When you look at the map of the language families in North America, you'll see they stretch out all across Canada. There's Cheyenne, and Blackfeet, and Cree, and Eastern Algonquin, down through the Mic-Macs, Penobscots, Narragansets, Pequots, and Mohicans, and down into Virginia and circled back up into Ohio, and the Shawnee and then other people going out to the Chippewa, because their legends talk about coming from the East.

"When I heard these stories from my grandfather, I took all of it the same way I took Robin Hood and all the other great stories. They were stories. It wasn't real life. Real life was you had to go to school and you had to go to college. You had to get a job and like that, and I didn't see any correlation. I can remember being in college at twenty-one years old, and my grandfather saying to me, 'I can't understand why you're still in school at twenty-one years old, because I was working for my family when I was ten.'"

"And I said, 'Well, you know times have changed since your day, and you can't get anywhere without a college education.' So he said, 'Well, what do I know?' And that was that. I've often thought about that conversation, and I say he really knew better than me. As I see it now, the only things that I learned that were really important I've learned from him and from other elders.

"There are those who think that everything happens by direction, and that there's a purpose to it. Well, there must be some reason why I had to go and get all that education, and why I'm in kind of a unique position of being a university-educated traditionalist. There's not many of us around, traditionalists with university backgrounds. There are a few, and I guess our job is as communicators both ways. If people can understand the old people and couch what they have to say in terms that can be understood by both modern native people and nonnative people, then I guess that's good."

Black Comedy, Nervous Laughter

After completing his education at The Gunnery, a private school in Connecticut, and at Cornell University in Ithaca, New York, Medicine Story moved to New York City to work in the theater.

"Yah, I did all that. I wrote, directed, and acted, eventually concentrating on directing and producing, just so I could get things mounted. That was the hardest thing to do, to find people who could do that—mount a production. I created my own company, and it ran under various names: the Community Players of New York, and the Cinderella Theater, and finally we settled into our own theater and then became known as the Off Bowery Theater on East Tenth Street. It was in an old art gallery, which had been a studio for one of those big painters like de Kooning. This was back in 1961, and it was sort of a fulfillment for me of what I was trying to do. It also came to an end there.

"I built this little theater, I used to sit in there at night after everybody would go home, and I would use my imagination to people the stage with characters and ideas and whatever, and write about it, and that was very exciting for me. But I also came to the place where I realized that I didn't understand why the world was so terrible, why people were doing the things that they were doing that were so awful.

"I mean, I lived in New York City. People were dying all around me. You lived in the middle of crime and drugs and violence, racial tension, pollution, you name it. That's the pits in New York City. I had four friends of mine in the theater kill themselves within the space of a year. Three of them worked in my theater. And you know it kind of brought me up short. You'd turn on the radio and pick up the newspaper and find that people are doing it to each other all over the world. People are starving. But why is this? I had no answers, and I finally said, 'I've had it with this business of writing plays and making cheap jokes about all this. I haven't got anything constructive to offer, and I don't see that anybody else in the theater has anything to offer at all.'

"It was all kind of like nervous laughter. Black comedy was the big thing; I was into black comedy a whole lot. I did a wonderful play called *The Ashtray*, which was about the electric chair. It was a comedy; the scenario was a television first—a live show from the execution. In the play, they were playing it up in a big commercial television way. It was funny, and I kept all the realistic, excruciating elements in the thing.

"It was OK. I was able to laugh at it all, but finally I wrote one play that was for one actor who was playing himself. He played an actor coming out to try to fill in some extra time between one-act plays. The manager would send him out to entertain because he was very entertaining backstage, and he was talking about his life, and he was trying to relate to the audience.

As the play went on, he'd get more and more upset that the audience was so removed and so condescending. He would get into a real conflict out there. Pretty soon they would begin to dim the lights on him from back-stage, and in the middle of his raging act the lights went out altogether. In the dark, at the peak of his rage, he screams out at everybody, 'Dammit can't you see, I'm trying to tell you that I love you.' And then the lights would come back on and he'd be crying, and he'd get up and he'd say, 'I got real tears. I'm pretty good at this.' Then he'd go off, lightly removing him-self, trying to make contact. But it didn't work, so he backed off and went into his actor's stance again. Years later I look back at that play, which was called *Artist Unknown*, and I realize that that was really from my uncon-scious, a statement I was making about my inability to really connect with the world, with people, with the audience, and to just say something meaningful, and to really be there. 'I love you' was the connection that wasn't being made, and I had to leave the theater in order to find what was reality and to find if there was any answer to the questions about what was so wrong. I sensed that there must be.

"That was about 1967. I had read a lot. I knew people like Paul Good-man and Alan Watts. I had a broad background in the religious and utopian thinking of the times, so I had a sense that there was something there for human beings, but nobody had really put it together completely or satis-fyingly enough to me to make sense of it. So in 1967 I went west with my brother, Jim. There were seven of us altogether. I had a girlfriend in tow who was from California, and so I had talked her into going back with me. And Jim was with his rock band, so we all went out together. We all got a big flat together in San Francisco, and I just was into everything that was going on out there—all the different exotic religions and mystic practices and humanistic psychology, and drugs and Tim Leary and the Grateful Dead and Jefferson Airplane, and the whole thing was just an explosion out there. I went from high to low, and finally had to get out of the city and into the country, 'cause I had to put my head together."

A New People, A New World

"In 1972, I went to my first Rainbow Gathering and my life turned all around again. Early in that year I received word of a great gathering that was planned to be held in the summer in the Colorado Rocky Mountains.

Since it was to be people of all races, religions, nationalities, classes, and lifestyles, it was called a Gathering of the Rainbow Tribes. There was to be a walk, a pilgrimage to Table Mountain, a place sacred to the Arapaho. The people planned to fast and stay in silence all day on that mountain while praying for world peace and understanding.

"Now there are old prophecies that at the end of this world many people of many different nations and tribes would come together to seek a new world and a new way. This would be according to the vision the Creator placed in their hearts. Then, you know, seeing how sincerely they sought this, how deeply they desired it, the Great Spirit would hear the cries of their hearts and take pity on them. At that time, the prophecies said, the new world would be born in the midst of the old. This new world would be very small at first, like a newborn baby. But it would be full of life and learning and growth, full of trust and love, like a newborn. Because of this, the new world wouldn't hate the dying old world, but instead learn how to survive and become strong within it. It was said that the sign the Creator would send of this new beginning would be a white buffalo.

"Over twenty thousand people came to that first gathering, and everyone was treated with respect. It was wonderful. One night it rained. The next day, when we came out in the meadow, we saw that a huge patch of white snow on the side of the mountain that faced us had been eaten away and carved into the perfect shape of a buffalo. People began to cheer and sing, and many of them wept joyfully.

"Then, starting at midnight on the third of July, everybody began a walk over the eight miles to Table Mountain. All night long that line moved in silence, carrying candles and torches. At dawn, thousands of people stood still upon the mountain, people who had come from all over the world to be together and share that moment, to watch the Sun rise on a new day, a new people, a new world.

"People stayed together all day on that mountain. We fasted and stayed in silence until, sometime after noon, someone started singing an Arapaho chant. All of us took up that chant to honor the traditional caretakers of that land. When we left that gathering, everyone had the feeling that something very important had happened, and was happening all over the world. No one could say exactly what it was, or knew what to do about it. So everyone went home and went on with their business. But the next summer a lot of the people decided the only way they could learn what to do with this new energy was to gather again and keep on gathering until the spirit directed something different. That's how it's been. Ever since, the Rainbow World Family Gathering of the Tribes has been held during the first week of July.

"The rainbow is based on the recognition that we are all spiritual people. So part of the idea is a spiritual gathering with no dividing lines. There's no laws, no regulations, no hassles. It's a try at anarchy. Does it work? Yeah, it works. When problems come up we sit down and talk about them. We figure it out as we go along."

The vision of the rainbow was dreamed after the cultural watershed of Woodstock, when a commune named the Hog Farm and a clown named Wavy Gravy helped feed 400,000 people. That spiritual service was immensely inspiring to the founders of the Rainbow Gathering.

As they saw it, the rainbow is a sign of the unity of all people in the universal family. And as the fliers for the annual gathering proclaim, "The people who gather are a tribe not of blood but of spirit, for all are born into it. We are bound together by our desire to live in peace, to be in the cathedral of nature, and to heal ourselves through union with the earthly mother and the heavenly father. The Rainbow Gathering is an opportunity to celebrate human diversity, to venerate the Earth, to deepen connections, and to party—to share a community that is beyond the rules of violence, prejudice, and caste." Each summer the gathering moves to a new state and sets up camp in one of the national forests. At the gatherings there is no exchange of money. The Rainbow Tribe relies on cooperation, respect, goodwill, and equal rights. And for one intense, joyful week every summer, it works.

Medicine Story attended the first fifteen Rainbow Gatherings consecutively and is one of its grandfathers. He has also attended Rainbow Gatherings in Europe and at the Arctic Circle. As he has matured, the gatherings and the vision they represent have been deeply important to him.

"One reason my life turned around was this vision of twenty thousand people getting together on top of a mountain praying in silence for a new world to be ushered in. The whole thing was so powerful. I knew something was happening. I didn't know what, or how, but I knew I had to be a part of it. Also, I met a number of young Indians who, although they weren't very traditional, came from people who were traditional and had their traditions together. They invited me to their reservation, to the Sun Dance and the Sweatlodge and things like that. And so I opened up into a whole world of traditional old ways that I knew nothing about. So those two things came together at the same time, this rainbow communal world vision, and the old ways, finding that there were still the old ways, and going to seek them out. I kept balancing those two things.

"Pretty soon I left the commune where I was living in the mountains and went together with a bunch of people on a bus that we bought and called the Rainbow Rider. We traveled all around, building barns and picking apples and things like that, and spreading the joyous rainbow message. But at the same time I had a little truck and I would go bopping off to Sun Dances and peyote ceremonies, and just getting in with different people, different teachers wherever I found them, and learning the sweatlodge ways. I was beginning to understand the philosophy behind all of that, which to me made the picture complete, made me understand what had really gone wrong.

"It was jelling for me all the time as I listened to these old people talk, and I listened to the rainbow people in council. Finally, in '73, I can remember this time when we were talking to this black man from Liberia. He had come from a place that had been tribal and had been taken over and completely modernized and industrialized. Firestone Rubber owned the country and all that. He was looking back to the old tribal ways, and talking about how it used to be. And we felt like we were brothers there, and we understood the same things. Yes, this is what was really lost in the world, and what people didn't understand, and yet was probably the most important part of life. It became very clear to me at that point that those tribal ways are the ways that enhance love and cooperation among people, and that modern society is based on fear and competition and struggle."

Recalling the Original Instructions

"I began to learn more and more about this. Eventually, in 1975, I went to work with *Akwesasne Notes* in upper New York state as a writer and the poetry editor. The editor wanted me to come, so I went there, and I sort of rounded out my education at *Akwesasne Notes* in two ways. One was to get the input of news of indigenous people all around the world who had the same relationship to the Earth and each other and the circle and all that. And I realized that there was this universal thing that all human beings must have had at one time, before civilization began to get built up on fear. At the same time, I began to learn in more detail from the Mohawk people about their concept of the Original Instructions.

"When I listened to the chiefs of the Longhouse and to the common, ordinary people, whose language was formed by these sensibilities, I began to put all that together with what my grandfather had told me via stories. Then I went back to my own people, and we began to make spiritual gatherings together. I got together with Slow Turtle and his daughter Ramona, and Gkisedtanamoogk, and others who had been out traveling— and we explored our own tradition and added to that from what we had been learning. And from all of this I began to deepen my appreciation of the Original Instructions.

"Native people refer to the Original Instructions often in speech and prayer, but rarely attempt to say exactly what they are. They are not like the Ten Commandments carved in stone by a stern authority figure. They are not ideas. They are reality. They are natural law, the Way Things Are—the operational manual for a working creation—and they cannot totally be understood in words. They must be experienced. The Original Instructions are not imposed by human minds on the world. They are of the living spirit. Other creatures follow them instinctively, and they are communicated to humankind through the heart, through feelings of beauty and love.

"Black Elk spoke of it very well when he said that everything we do is done in a circle, because the power of the world always works in circles and everything tries to be round. In the old days, when we were strong and happy people, he said all our power came from the sacred hoop of the nation. That circle, that basic circle, fits into the larger circle of the universe. And the universe is circles within circles, and everything is one circle, and all the circles are connected to each other. Each family is a circle, and those family circles connect together and make a community, and the community makes its circle where it lives on the Earth. It cares for that part, but cares for it as a circle—which is to say in a cooperative way and an egalitarian way, where everybody is cared for and everybody is respected. The way of the circle is the way of respect. The way of the circle is that everybody is equal, every being is equal, everything is sacred and respected and given consideration. That's why the Longhouse prayer you'll hear me speak is, to me, one of the most powerful and meaningful, because it acknowledges everything, and it contains the whole attitude of our ways. It's basically greetings and thanksgivings to all the things that give us life.

"I start everything—the people of the Longhouse start everything—with that particular prayer. It acknowledges everybody, everyone in the circle. It brings the circle together as a circle so we can put our minds together and give greetings and thanksgivings, beginning with the Earth and all the creatures of the Earth: the human beings, the animal creatures, the plant creatures, the insects, and all the species of things are one family of the Earth. Sometimes the person speaking this prayer will go into great detail, thanking the maple tree for giving its sap, and the strawberries for their fruit, and so on and so forth, but carrying their instructions on outward throughout the whole universe, acknowledging all our relations.

"So the first part of that prayer is acknowledging those relationships, and remembering that we are all related to everything we see as sacred and important. The other part is thanking. By thanking you are giving appreciation. Whenever you appreciate, it makes you higher; it tunes you to a higher vibration. And it makes whatever you are appreciating feel better. If I appreciate you, you'll feel better. If I appreciate the birch tree, the birch tree will feel better. This is a very profound attitude, I think, about how people can live in a good way and be happy. So I think part of our Original Instructions are to live in that circle, to remember our relationships, to respect all beings. Part of our Original Instructions are to be thankful and to keep a positive attitude toward the community and toward life.

"The Original Instructions urge us to find our place in the cosmos, to know our true nature and our goal in existence. There must be a response—not an intellectual answer—but a felt understanding of the nature of this existence, of its purpose and of our part in that purpose. That is the reason for the spiritual quests, the religions, the rituals, the searches, pilgrimages, meditations, and mystic disciplines of humankind. Something in our consciousness is just not satisfied with only eating, sleeping, creating, and reproducing. Something in us wants to know what it's all about and how we fit into it."

I Had a Vision

"In 1973 I had a vision, and so then I was already well on the way. I knew enough then to be propelled outward on a spiritual journey. What happened was that I had been invited to lead a sweatlodge for a group of people at the Rainbow Gathering in California. We sat in a healing circle, and we called it the Tribal Healing Council, and I've kept that format ever since then. A number of people were doing it in those early times.

"They wanted me to come to a healing arts fair and lead a sweatlodge. I was the only native person they knew who did sweatlodges, but I had never led one before. I didn't consider myself to be at the level that I should do that, so I didn't accept right away. I said I should confer with some elders, so I took a little journey, and I did a sweat with some relatives who I had done sweats with before, and I told them the whole situation. They told me that I should follow my heart, that I should go into the sweatlodge and ask for a vision and then see what the Creator gave me. But they did give me a little help, because they said, 'Would these people do a sweatlodge whether or not you lead it?' I thought about that for a while, and I said, 'Yah, probably. They'll want to have it, and they'll probably do it. They know how to pray, and all that sort of thing.' And then the elders said, 'Well, people don't know what they're doing. They can hurt themselves. So maybe it would be a good idea if somebody showed them the right way.'"

"So I did the sweatlodge. I felt that was the important argument—that they would go ahead and do it anyway—and perhaps I was supposed to be sort of a bridge between these cultures and help them along just to make sure they didn't hurt themselves. Basically, that's what the elders were concerned about—that, and that they didn't mistakenly teach something that would be wrong. So I decided that what I needed to do, to do it right, was to fast. I began fasting four days before the gathering, and when I got there I was pretty light. And lo and behold, there were so many people who wanted to do the sweatlodge that I had literally to be in the sweatlodge from about noon to about eight o'clock at night—maybe more than that, 'cause it was really dark when I got out. Anyway, it was a continuous revolving door at the sweatlodge, and here I was, when it was all done and it was dark, and I had already been fasting and was light, and I had been relieved of body fluids by the heat of the lodge. I was about to blow away like a wisp of smoke.

"Before I had gotten started at the sweatlodge some people had invited me to a teepee up in the woods for a peyote ceremony. Now, the way those work is you have to get there by sundown and stay in the circle until sunrise. So I said I didn't think I could make it by sundown, but they said they would hold my place and keep my spirit there. And so I said OK.

"So my only thought as I staggered out of the sweatlodge was to find this teepee. Here I was, going through the woods in the pitch black dark. I couldn't see anything at all. I was really weak and going from tree to tree hanging on, and suddenly the whole place was just light, and it appeared to be a forest fire. I understood that this was a visionary thing, because there was no heat and I had no panic. I knew there wasn't a real fire that I had to run from or scream about or whatever, but it was like something being shown to me. And all these animals started coming out, running around. It was almost like it was a performance in a way, but they were very real. They were all chattering away in the different animal languages, none of them understanding each other, but all in a panic and running in different directions and looking at each other and not knowing what to do and stumbling over each other.

"Then suddenly, in the midst of all this, there appeared this large bull elk, massive, and the elk was very dignified. He just stood there. All these other animals that had been running around started to slow down and look at him and say, 'Well, wait a minute, what is this elk doing? He must know something we don't know. We're all just panicking and he's not.' And so they all came over to him and just sat down. They waited patiently, looking at him, and when they were all seated and quiet he began to walk very slowly. They all got up and began to follow him, and they began to walk on the plains; they walked on the slopes; they walked up into the sky. And they all followed him up, and as they went up into the sky they formed the rainbow, and the slope became the rainbow.

"When I finally did find that medicine teepee I told of this story, this vision, and they all said, you know, 'What do you think about it? It seems pretty important.' And I said, 'Well, it seems to me that the elk represents the native people of North America; it's a very indigenous North American creature. And I think, more than that, this elk represents the knowledge of the old ways. All the animals represent all the people of the different languages and cultures and so forth who've lost their direction, and who are panicking and who don't know where to go. Then they suddenly turned to see this elk, to see that this great tradition is there, which is a way of safety. And they saw that by learning to follow that way they could save themselves.' So I thought, I guess if that's what is being said to me in this vision, then I am supposed to be an interpreter of those ways to the general culture of the world, to the different cultures of the world. There are so many that need to know the old Earth wisdom from our elders. It was at that point that my name changed. I had been Story all my life, but it was suggested that I should be called Medicine Story—which in our old language, the Wampanoag language, is Manitonquat."

Let's Figure Out the Next Step

Since 1981, Medicine Story has made his home in Greenville, New Hampshire, as a part of the Mettanokit Community—an intentional, egalitarian community, in which the members choose to live together and to give all community members equal access to resources according to need. The community has been through many changes over the years, but continues with an average ten to fifteen members who caretake the land, pursue individual careers, share chores, and pool their resources.

Medicine Story's wife, Ellika Linden, is also skilled in the theater and as a puppeteer. Together they have developed the International Children's Peace Theater, which has offered performances in many different venues. In addition to his international work as a storyteller and dramatist, Medicine Story volunteers time in prisons. He is also deeply involved in Reevaluation Counseling, a technique that helps people to face and heal the deep wounds that lie in the human psyche. Such personal healing, Story feels, is essential for human beings, but he believes people must take action in the outer world as well.

"I heard something really important this year. I heard several important things from scientists, or people who are in touch with scientists who know things. One thing I heard that is obviously true if you think about it—but we don't stop to think about it—is that at this moment in time, for the first time in the five-million-year history of this planet, we have the capacity to change the relationship between the Earth and the Sun. I thought, 'Oh, oh, that's scary, that's really scary.' The ozone layer, particularly, and this blanket of pollution that's creating this Greenhouse Effect—these are two basic aspects of our relationship to the Sun that are being altered by human beings. How do we have the arrogance and the daring to do such a thing? You think of the power of the Sun, and you think of all that it took to create just the right conditions for life. We look at all the other planets, and we see what the conditions are there, and we have what is just right here—no warmer, no colder, just the right amount of atmosphere, water, hydrogen, nitrogen, all the stuff, you know? And we're messing with it.

"All the places where the lobbying is going on, and all the major industrial countries, they say, 'Oh, we can patch that up enough, you know, so let's go ahead and do business. Let's not let that get in the way of making a buck.' And they don't really realize the seriousness of it.

"The way it is for me is, if I had to heal the world right now, I'd say, 'Stop, just stop. Don't do anything right now. Don't do anything. Because we're still destroying it. Now let's figure out the next step to be healing rather than to be destroying.' What's needed is a consciousness of conservation, of simplicity—an awareness that we don't need to be producing at the level we've been producing in order for us to live. We have the highest standard of living. We have more than the highest standard of living. I mean, we look crazy to the Europeans, but then everybody in the world is trying to emulate us.

"I think what's missing in the environmental movement—which is coming, is coming in more and more—is this sense of the spiritual connection, the sense of sacredness. Now people are talking about Gaia—about the Earth as a living being—and that all things are connected, talking in a very spiritual way. That is finally beginning to come in the general environmentalist's concept, rather than just the usual mechanistic thinking about this and that. You know, fix it and make it right. That's good. That's so necessary, because what I feel in people is a very deep malaise. There's a deep wound in people—that they have been so cut off from the source of their being, their mother, their Earth Mother."

Medicine Story has addressed this theme in depth in a manuscript entitled *Return to Creation*. The title comes from ancient carvings in Dighton Rock on the Wampanoags' ancestral lands in Massachusetts. According to the tradition of the Wampanoag people, the carvings were set into the stone a long, long time ago by the Wampanoag prophet known as Weetucks. In essence, the carvings say that some day a whisper of fear will cross the land bringing disease, violence, and starvation all over the Earth. Many will die in confusion and ignorance. But those who remember the sacred teachings, the Original Instructions, would be able to save their children and heal the Earth.

The carvings on Dighton Rock show one person listening to the Great Spirit and returning to Creation. The other person is continuing on a path that leads to his own destruction, shown by a bolt of lightning. Medicine Story has no doubt that now is the time to return to Creation. In his art, with his stories, and with his life, he says now it is time "to begin a whole new world, a world in harmony with all Creation, a world of people guided only by their heart's joy in love and beauty."

EIGHT

Prophet of the Earth Changes
SUN BEAR

*B*urly and bighearted, the man called Sun Bear has traveled the world to warn of upheavals upon the Earth. He encourages people to prepare for even greater changes, not just by storing food and water, but also by remembering their spiritual connection with the Earth. He has shared his warnings with an even voice and a strong undercurrent of hope. Still, he has become perhaps the most widely criticized Indian alive, not so much because he warns of disaster, but more because he has revealed to people around the world some of the ceremonies that Native Americans have used for thousands of years to live in balance on the Earth.

These teachings have drawn to Sun Bear the enmity not only of white people who feel threatened by the teachings he shares, but also of some native people who feel he should not be sharing the teachings at all. Some native people believe strongly that native teachings are for natives only, and that Sun Bear has violated a trust by taking those teachings to the world.

Criticism is not foreign to Sun Bear. In his life he has stood alone and been vilified many times for following his convictions. "I can think about a lot of times when I've had to do things that seemed to go against the grain. One of the things was, I made a decision against going to Korea. I went to prison for seven and a half months because I felt it just wasn't the right thing to do. The U.S. government told me I should fight for my country, but why should I fight the Koreans? They didn't take my land from me and the

Indian people, the U.S. government did. They didn't like that, of course, so they sent me to prison at Lompoc."

"Oftentimes my stand has not been in harmony with everybody else at the time. When I first started teaching nonnatives, there were no other natives who were teaching this philosophy. I was the first person to come out and do it the way I'm doing it. And I got a lot of flak, especially from some native people who were oriented more to militancy. They thought that my going and sharing things with nonnatives was not right. So I got hassled. But I've continued on in this path because I believe it's what has to be.

"My life path is teaching people how to find and follow their own path of power, and how to be responsible in all of their actions to all aspects of life upon this Earth, not just for this generation, but for all generations to come." As Sun Bear has followed his life path around the world, his influence has been become widespread. "The medicine that I believe in and offer through the Bear Tribe is not a medicine of the Sioux of yesterday or the Chippewa of yesterday. It is a medicine of today, as well as a medicine of tradition. This is the kind of medicine that will bring balance between the races on the Earth Mother. I don't speak about medicine in the name of all native people; I won't do that, nor will I speak for a single tribe. I can only speak of the teachings that my vision has given me.

"My vision and my work are for today, for the people who are here now, and that's why I don't stick to any particular old-way ritual but incorporate whatever my medicine calls for, from everywhere. It's not really a traditional view that I hold, and yet it is. I don't believe that technology is a bad thing; if I want to communicate with a lot of people, I'll pick up a telephone, use a computer, or go on a radio or television program. Technology in itself is not a bad thing; it's the greed and misdirection of its users. We're not advocating going back to the Stone Age, but rather going forward into the New Age.

"I don't think of the world as little separate boxes or pockets. I think of the Earth as being a whole planet that belongs to all of us. And I think each human being has the same right to grow, the same right to knowledge, everything. Until we are willing to work in such a way that we create a world of humans living, working, and sharing together, and taking responsibility for the Earth that way, we're going to be locked into these little pockets of prejudice and hatred that will continue to destroy people.

"All the prophecies of the native people speak of a time when the human beings will face a choice between going on the same way with greed and technology, or going toward spirit. I feel, and many others feel, that now is that time when we face that choice. We need to go toward spirit now. These prophecies were given to warn all people on the planet, not just the natives, but all the people on the planet. That way they can make the necessary changes in their lives. I'm very strongly trying to encourage native people to become self-sufficient—to learn how to dry meat again, and how to store foods, and restore their balance with the Earth, so they aren't dependent upon the Bureau of Indian Affairs, or the government, or anything else. That's the only way we can go. We have to shift our dependencies back to the Earth and back to each other as human beings."

Piercing the Veil

Sun Bear was born Vincent Laduke on August 31, 1929, on the White Earth Reservation in northern Minnesota. He is a member of the Chippewa Nation and has ten brothers and sisters. A large part of what he shares in his teachings has to do with the prophecies of the native peoples of America, which identify this time in history as a time of cleansing upon the Earth Mother. Many prophecies from many traditions indicate that this is a time when the Earth will shrug off the poisonous aspects of greed-inspired technology and a way of life that tells people they are separate from the rest of Creation.

"My people, the Chippewa-Ojibwa people, have what we call the Migration Scrolls, and these scrolls tell about the journey in the Four Worlds of the Chippewa. Each world has ended and then been joined to the next by a period of cleansing. We've already been through three of these worlds, and the last of them is coming now with the present cleansing that the Earth is going through. The Migration Scrolls show that the bear is a sacred animal of this continent. The bear represents the Great Spirit, both in the scrolls themselves and in some of the ceremonies that we perform. The bear spirit works for the Great Spirit and all Creation. According to the scrolls, the bear opens, or pierces, the veil to each new world with its tongue. It wasn't until I was doing what I'm doing now that I fully realized what that meant. I feel that I'm doing what the scrolls say: With my tongue and what I say, I'm helping to pierce the veil to the next world that will come after the cleansing. I do this by teaching people, and warning them of the Earth changes coming and how they can survive those things.

"The prophecies of the Hopi people foresaw both world wars, one to be fought against the sun sign [Japan] and against the swastika [Germany]. They foresaw the invention of the automobile, the airplane, even the atom bomb. Ancient prophecies also spoke of the time when the sons of the white men would grow their hair long, wear beads, and live in communal societies. When that time came, according to the native prophets, the cleansing would be at hand. It happened in the sixties with flower power, the anti-Vietnam protestors, the Berkeley Free Speech Movement, and so on.

"Native prophecies say that those mixed-blood and white people who grew their hair long and wore beads would come to us, as native healers, and ask for guidance—that they would be incarnations of the Indians slaughtered during the conquest of the continent. The prophecies say that they would return as rainbow people in bodies of different colors—red, white, yellow, black—and that they would return and unite to help restore balance to the Earth.

"The story of these Rainbow Warriors is told by many peoples in many different ways. The Hopi tell it and others tell it. We feel that we are in that time now when the Rainbow Warriors are coming about. The human race is no longer at a point where anybody can necessarily hold up their hand and say they are pure this or that. Even among the Indian tribes, you know, they might be all Indian, but they are Indian from two or three different tribal groups or something like that. So it's a time when we are all having to acknowledge that we are all human beings upon the same planet, and that's what the Rainbow Warriors is all about.

"If you wake up and realize that we are Rainbow Warriors now, that we are a rainbow people upon the Earth, then the next step is becoming a spiritual warrior—someone who is willing to put their energy into something that helps to heal the Earth and restore the balance, and who is interested in doing that consistently, not just showing up for a weekend demonstration or something, but people who are willing to use their life energy to create a world of balance and harmony for our children after us."

Medicine Wheels of Stone

"The death of the forests, the poisoning of the waters, the shaking of the Earth—that was all foreseen by the native prophets," Sun Bear says. "And this is what's happening. This is happening, and many humans are not ready to make the necessary changes for the survival of the planet, so the Earth Mother herself is doing it—making the necessary changes—on her own. I've been speaking and teaching about Earth changes for many years, and now they are coming on in greater intensity all the time. I have a book out now called *Black Dawn/Bright Day* that deals with Earth Changes—the things that we see happening to the Earth: the volcanoes and big winds and earthquakes and all that.

"I feel very sad that humans are not willing to take responsibility and make the necessary changes. My thing is reaching out on the planet and trying to find those humans who are ready to make conscious changes in their lives, and to move in a sacred manner. That's what the Spirit says I have to do: awaken those people and give them a different perspective so they can survive the changes. Those people who are not willing to make changes, they'll just perish and become part of the fertilizer for the Earth Mother."

Sun Bear says he believed, even back in the early years, that if any person came to him and asked to learn medicine ways, he should work with him or her—not necessarily because that person might be a reincarnated Indian, but simply because the person wanted to learn to walk in balance on Mother Earth. Sun Bear's call to teaching took a giant leap forward in the late 1970s when he had a vision that changed his life. In the vision, he saw a bare hilltop with a circle of rocks on it, with spokes that led to the center. He saw what looked like animals coming toward the wheel from all directions, but as they came closer he recognized that they were people wearing headdresses and animal costumes. The people were from all the clans, all the directions, and all the colors, and in their hearts they carried peace. They came together to make prayers and ceremony for the Earth and all the creations who share life upon her.

From his vision, Sun Bear understood that the time was drawing near when, for the sake of the Earth Mother and our evolution as human beings, we had to return to a better and truer understanding of the Earth. He saw that we would have to put aside our petty fears and learn to live again as true brothers and sisters. We would need to find others who shared our heart's direction, whatever their racial background, and join with them in groups to remember our purpose as instruments of the Great Spirit's will.

He understood from his vision that now was the time to help bring the Medicine Wheels back upon this land as a way of sharing this understanding with many people. A Medicine Wheel is a large circle of stones that is symbolic of the universe. Common to many tribes, the Medicine Wheel is frequently used to explain the cosmology of the American Indian and to show that all things are related in the circle of life. The wheel is also a place for dancing, singing, and ceremony.

Sun Bear says, "The Medicine Wheel is based upon a person's relationship with the Earth and with all of the Earth's realms: the animals, the plants, the minerals, and the humans. I feel it was revealed to me in this time as a means to help with the healing of the Earth Mother."

Since the time of his vision, with the help of a group of supporters known as the Bear Tribe Medicine Society, Sun Bear has organized several Medicine Wheel Gatherings each year in the United States and abroad. As the brochure for the gatherings explains, "Medicine Wheels of stone once spread across this land, constructed by the original native inhabitants. These wheels were the ceremonial centers for the native people, a place where the sacred teachers would share their teachings and conduct ceremonies. These wheels were found all across the Earth, from the great standing circles at Stonehenge in England to the mandala circle of India." Since the 1970s, Sun Bear's intent has been to revive the tradition and teachings of the Medicine Wheel.

The first Medicine Wheel Gathering was in 1980, at the base of Mount Rainier in Washington State. Over six hundred people came. Since then there have been dozens of Medicine Wheel gatherings all across the United States and Europe. Many thousands of people have come to the gatherings to meet with Native American teachers, as well as with traditional teachers of Earth wisdom from Africa, Tibet, South America, and elsewhere.

In a Sacred Manner

"If we are going to stabilize the world through this time of Earth changes," Sun Bear says, "then there are going to have to be some funda-

mental changes in the way people think about the Earth. It's very important that they stop thinking about the Earth as something they can just take
from—and that they can bulldoze off a hillside and take all the timber just
to create a shopping center, or something else. They have to start learning
to take and do things with respect—respect for the natural resources and
energy.

"One of the programs I'm working with now is called the World Earth
Fund. I'm trying to raise funds from different places to plant trees and help
restore the balance upon the Earth, and to help humans become conscious
of taking responsibility for themselves. People have to adopt a totally new
consciousness; that's what has to happen. People have to become totally
committed to this, so that the person who is smoking a cigarette doesn't
throw the butt down on the ground, and children are learning the same
thing, so that respect for the Earth comes into their hearts and minds totally.
We have to do things with respect. There can be no more taking and living in the old way. You can't just go out and shoot some animal for sport.
You have to get to where you know that that creature has the same right
to life as you do. If you have to take it for food, that's a different thing, but
you have to learn to do it in a respectful way. Respect everything.

"Beyond that, human consciousness has to evolve and expand. This is
a part of what I'm doing. I'm reaching out to a lot of the ancient teachings
and bringing them together, and making comparisons, and sharing with
people so that they can understand. Maybe the gods and goddesses that the
ancient Egyptians were addressing are the same spirits that the native peoples of America or elsewhere were addressing. We have different names for
the spirit keepers of the Earth. For example, Isis was goddess of the Nile and
the waters, whereas we have spirits that we call the Thunderbeings. These
spirits have been around for thousands of years, and they are probably the
same, but with different names. They have responsibility for the waters.
Their work is to keep the Earth in harmony and balance, and we are supposed to work with them. Now, people are going to have to understand it,
so that in their life path everything is in harmony. They must relate to each
other and the world in a sacred manner, and no longer be involved in the
conscious and unconscious destruction of the Earth."

The Nature of Wisdom

Sun Bear is the author or coauthor of six books, including *At Home in the Wilderness*, *The Bear Tribe's Self-Reliance Book*, *The Medicine Wheel: Earth Astrology*, *Buffalo Hearts*, *Path of Power*, and *Black Dawn/Bright Day*. He is also the publisher of *Wildfire* magazine, formerly known as *Many Smokes*. Through his writing and his world travel, he has encountered many knowledgeable and wise people.

"Knowledge is a beautiful thing, but the using of knowledge in a good way is what makes for wisdom. Learning how to use knowledge in a sacred manner, that's wisdom, to me. And to me, that's what a true elder is. A true native elder, or an elder of any people, is one who uses their knowledge in a sacred manner. That means that they advise their young people on proper respect for the Earth and all Creation. They understand how to deal with the other people around them in a loving and harmonious manner, rather than fanning the old fires of prejudice and hatred that some of these people do. These sicknesses, they have to disappear completely. We don't have any time for them. We don't have time to be cutting each other down and creating havoc between humans, whether it's tribal groups, or nations, or whatever it is. And we don't want to have elders who are ordering our young people to go off to war and get slaughtered on battlefields. We don't need that anymore. That sickness has to end.

"To me, the wisdom the elders have to manifest is in teaching people how to live in harmony and balance with each other and the Earth. Instead of telling young people to be out spreading hatred for others, they should be telling their young people to help cut wood for the old people, to cut wood for the women who don't have husbands, and to take responsibility for their people in a sacred manner. That's what we were taught in the old days.

"When I grew up in northern Minnesota, we'd go out and spear fish in the spring of the year. When we'd get a few extra ones, we'd take and give them to our neighbor, a woman who had four or five children and didn't have anyone to go fish for her. So we'd go and do the fishing, and then bring the fish to her. Teaching people these concepts of harmony and balance, this is what the elders should do. This is what wisdom is.

"Wisdom to me is understanding the right use of knowledge. And it can be at any level or in any field. Use your knowledge in a sacred manner so that what you are doing for a living, that's your buffalo hunt, that's the way you support yourself and provide for your family. Look at that and ask yourself, 'What am I doing here? Is this a job that is beneficial to something or someone? Is it a right livelihood?' That's good wisdom. Learn how to apply your knowledge in such a way that your life is helping all living Creation. Like when we go out on a Vision Quest to fast and pray in the forest, we are praying to the Creator, asking 'How can I help? What can I do? How can I best serve the Earth Mother and my people? How can I best serve all generations to come?' Those are the things that we ask when we go out on Vision Quest. We are asking for how we can help all the generations to come, and that's a very important thing. That's the way my life path has to be. That's the way I look at my life all the time. I say, 'Well, how does this help my fellow human beings? How will it be ten years from now, or one hundred years from now? What will my actions and words have done?'"

"If I can live my life in such a way that it's helping over that time span—for the generations to come—then I feel that that's wisdom."

Major Things Will Happen

Much of what Sun Bear teaches has to do with survival and self-reliance on the land: practical skills such as farming, herbology, foraging, hunting, building, beekeeping, butchering, preserving, canning, composting, bartering, and so forth. However, all of these skills are taught from a point of view that has spirituality as its foundation.

"We are setting up a project now where we are dealing with dried foods, like rice and beans and stuff like that—putting them into nitrogen packs and others ways of preserving them over a long period of time so the food will remain good to eat. That way people who see what is happening on the Earth, and what is going to be happening, can provide for themselves and their families. They can prepare themselves for survival. My first step is just teaching people to have a right-mind approach to life and living. After they have exhibited that, then I'd like to see them stick around during the time that the Earth changes are taking place, because then they have beneficial gifts to offer. So I show them ways of survival.

"We are told that during this time of Earth changes, between now and the year 2000, there will be a period of three years when hardly any food will be produced upon the planet. During that time people will have to have food stored, or they will starve. I see that starvation happening now in Sudan, Chad, Angola, and Ethiopia. Those are the first four. I see seventy million people dying in Africa and elsewhere. It will be increasing in intensity. There are very major things that are going to be happening.

"You can see what's happening on the East Coast right now. One small example is a thing they had on television the other day about Lyme disease, which is becoming a major disease. They don't have any cure for it yet, and it can get real serious, what with people going blind and getting arthritis and so forth. And you've got Mad Cow disease in England, and an epidemic of rabies in the wild animals in Pennsylvania and New York now. So why? Why is this happening? It's part of the Earth changes. What is happening is that we have created imbalances with nature.

"Around where the Bear Tribe is headquartered in Spokane [Washington], the farmers do very little spraying, so now there are a lot of birds around. As a result of that, the little nuthatches and chickadees are around; they haven't been sprayed to death. They go around to the trees and check the trees for ticks and eat them. So we don't have ticks around there; we have a natural balance. The birds eat them. In parts of the Northeast, everybody has sprayed their lawns and put out electronic bug zappers and disturbed the balance of nature. The bird population is plummeting. And so now they can't even spray the woods for the ticks that spread Lyme disease. What's happening is that all the destruction the people have put out upon the Earth is catching up with them.

"The Earth to us is an intelligent living being. It has a natural intelligence in itself, and it is able to talk to us, to communicate with us, to guide us in what to do—if we pray and open up to it and come into harmony with it. When we go into an area, we stop and pray there, and the spirit there will tell us what we're supposed to do, how we are supposed to treat the Earth there. And that's how we keep the balance. We go and ask permission of the Earth, and the Spirit will tell us where to plant our garden, where to build our houses, how to live there, and what ceremonies to offer to the Earth. This is what we are supposed to be doing as keepers and protectors of the Earth—to ask permission.

"In the old days, my people all knew that they had a responsibility to the Earth, and to all of the other beings upon her. They recognized the circle of life, and they were aware of all the gifts that all of their relations gave them. They knew that by praying—by centering their thought in a respectful way—they gave some of their energy back to the plants, the waters, and the animals. This keeps the energy circle from being depleted. Prayer is a good way of giving energy to all our relations; chanting, and drumming, and rattling are other ways. These all change what scientists today call your brain waves. They allow you to become more relaxed and at one with the things around you. And when you put praying, chanting, dancing, and drumming together in a ceremony, you have one of the most powerful ways of giving energy back to the Earth and all of her children. You can't just take all the time. It's important to remember that: ceremony gives energy back to the Earth and so helps to keep the life energy circulating upon the planet in a healthy way.

"The people who preach against this, and who think that talking with the spirits of the Earth is in some way wrong, need to take a look at their book a little closer. In the Bible it tells about how Jesus spoke to the waves and told the sea to be still. Jesus talked to the Earth all the time. He told his people, though they didn't hear him, that 'you see me doing these things; you can do even greater things.' But they don't do it because they don't have the faith to do it. So they better read up and check their own book."

A Green Grass World Arising

"I get to travel all around the world, leading groups and making ceremony and so forth," Sun Bear says. "I see a great many people waking up and asking questions, and wanting to know things, and wanting to come into harmony and balance. At the same time I see many things that are tragically happening, the destruction to the Earth. Many people are not willing to make the changes—to consciously make the changes that are necessary. So there's a lot of destruction continuing. People are not being as careful as they should. At the same time that the cleansing is happening, and much of the old system is going down, and the people who are clinging to it are being destroyed, there is a new world of love and harmony and balance coming about. It's springing up like fresh green grass out of the Earth. This is what's happening at this time.

"There are a lot of manifestations of this fresh-green-grass world. People are reaching out for new knowledge, and acknowledging that they need to take responsibility for restoring the balance upon the Earth. We see that while the cleansing of the planet is happening, many of us will be teaching and showing people how to do some good for the Earth, whether it's learning how to plant gardens organically, or learning how to recycle garbage upon the planet so there will be better harmony, or using renewable energy like solar. All that's part of what we are doing—teaching people to walk in balance."

NINE

Odyssey of a Warrior Woman
OH SHINNAH

*I*n the Land of Many Snows, a woman-child was born during the Moon of Frozen Waters in the Cycle of Strange Storms. The year was 1934, and the child was given a name that said much about who she would become: Oh Shinnah. In the language of her people, *Osha* means "Earth," and to *shinnah* is to make the sound, the heartbeat, the song of the Earth.

Now that she has become a grandmother, Oh Shinnah heals, but will not let herself be called a healer. She has mastered many mysteries of the shaman, but will not let herself be called a medicine woman. She is blunt about it. Make no mistake—she is a warrior woman, and she has accepted a charge in life to speak and sing on behalf of the Earth, and to confront fixed reality.

"My training started before I was born," she explains. "My spirit was consciously invoked by my mother, father, and great-grandmother. They did ceremony in the mountains of Colorado to call my spirit in. I was born into a crystal spectrum. When my great-grandmother helped deliver me, she designed a nine-pointed star in crystals around the place where I was delivered. My cord was cut with a crystal knife sharper than surgical steel. My first memories are of a quartz crystal hanging off the cradle board.

"My father and my great-grandmother were best friends, and they taught me many things that were peculiar, and in peculiar ways. She used to take me out on the streets of Durango, Colorado, and blindfold me, take the blindfold off for about eighteen seconds so I could look around, and then put it back on. I'd have to tell her not only everything that was around me, but also how I felt about the people I saw and how they were walking. In this way I learned to detect, even from body language, what's going on with a person. I learned a lot of things while I was growing up.

"Make no mistake—I am a warrior woman. I had to go through all of the spiritual, physical, and mental training that the men go through to become warriors. I did the Run for the Sun when I was eleven. That's an eight- to ten-mile run done on the winter solstice, a puberty rite for boys and girls who are pledging to be warriors. You run in the dark of the early morning because you have to arrive at sunrise where the Ceremony of the Mountain Spirits is taking place. You have to arrive with water in your mouth. You have to run the whole way with water in your mouth and not swallow it, then spit it into the hole when you reach the ceremonial site. I repeated the run when I was forty just to prove I could still do it.

"The prophecies of many native peoples speak of the days of purification; we live them now, and in them we have the opportunity to do something real with our lives. It requires surrender and sacrifice to become a warrior; one must develop a strength so present that one will act, instead of react, always for the good of the whole, regardless of emotional impact. Our lives are short, but each life can make a difference."

Flowers in the Great Spirit's Garden

Oh Shinnah's teachers have been elders of both North and South America. From her father's people she inherits traditions of the Tineh, known as the Apache. From her mother's people she inherits traditions of the Mohawks and the Scotch. From her great-grandmother she inherits traditions that she believes may be older than time.

"My only real contact with the Iroquois Six Nations was through my great-grandmother. On some levels I can't really say my great-grandmother either, because she wasn't born on the reservation; she was a full-blood Mohawk born in New York City. I'm a fourth generation Theosophist. My grandmother, Sparrow, was a Theosophist, and a Balinese temple dancer. When she was very young she met Madame Blavatsky, who took her to Egypt. She was the first Native American woman that we know of to spend a night in the Great Pyramid.

"My great-grandmother taught me a lot, but Mad Bear Anderson, who was Tuscarora, is the one who really taught me. He was in the Merchant Marines with my father, and he was like a protector. I was confronted one time at the end of the Longest Walk by two people in the Indian community who are not very friendly toward me. They got the Mohawk people there together and called me in. Mad Bear yelled out the door—you see he was never aggressive toward people. The way he'd usually work around aggression toward me was making me sing for the people, and that changed everything. He'd tell me, "You be strong. I know your father—we were in the Merchant Marines together," so he's been one of my stronger teachers. I'm really sorry he's not still here in the physical."

The Longest Walk in the mid-1970s was a demonstration in which Indian people walked from California to Washington to demonstrate the many injustices perpetrated against them by the government. The United States has broken every one of the nearly three hundred treaties it has signed with native peoples over the course of the last two hundred years. In general, the Longest Walk helped awaken and bring solidarity to the native community. When Oh Shinnah was confronted at the end of the walk, it was by some Indians who challenged her status because she is not a full-blood.

"I never tell anybody I'm full-blooded, nor that I'm a traditionalist either, because I'm not. My way's more eclectic. If somebody were to ask me what my tribe is, I'd say Eclectic. Most of the traditions that I learned came from the way of the Tineh, the people called Apache.

"There are some Indians like this—often the tribal chairmen who have received authority in the governmental system the white conquerors have imposed on the red nations—we call them 'apples.' They're red on the outside and white on the inside. They've been whitewashed. Everything has to be white—the White House, the White Knight, and Mr. Clean—and that's really ridiculous, isn't it? Anyway, they called me into this meeting, and before they got three words out of their mouths, they wanted me to prove to them that I had Mohawk blood. They wanted paper, and I looked at them and said, 'You've all been whitewashed haven't you? You have to have a piece of paper from the white man for me to prove that I'm an Indian.' I said, 'My life proves who I am, and I have nothing to say to you.'"

"I said, 'I would think you would be proud to have me as a Mohawk person.' Those who confronted me are exactly what my father told me about, because I used to be angry about my light skin. My father told me that it would reveal to me the two-hearted person who couldn't see the heart of another individual but could only see the surface of their skin. It's been a real refining process for me."

Part of the concern of those who confronted Oh Shinnah was that she was sharing native ceremonies with nonnative people, something they felt should not happen. Oh Shinnah says the wisdom and ceremonies she shares come from many traditions around the world. She says she teaches very little of the native tradition, and then only what her mentors have given her authority to teach. "I must say I have mixed feelings about non-Indians leading Indian ceremonies. There is a prophecy that states a time would come when Indians would reincarnate on this planet as part of the dominant society, which is white society. In this prophecy, these people would wear feathers and beads, and talk with the flowers. Indians spirits would incarnate in the dominant society to change the attitude of that dominant society. So learning native ways is very natural to them.

"People are being drawn to native ways because Mother Earth is experiencing trauma and calling to them. Native people are the keepers of Mother Earth. Our Original Instruction from Great Spirit was to take care of her. If a person has a sincere heart and wants to walk the path of the sacred, it should be accessible to them. The prophecies say we should do this. It is wrong for us not to share our spirituality with those who have lost theirs. But people should be very cautious with traditions they don't understand. People who participate in a ceremony and are not clear about what they are doing can create inharmonious results.

"As far as I'm concerned, it doesn't have anything to do with the color of your skin—it's the way you live your life. The only thing we have to give is the way we live our lives. If you live on this land, and you have ancestors sleeping in this land, I believe that makes you native to this land. It has nothing to do with the color of your skin. I was raised not to look at people racially. What I was taught is that we're flowers in the Great Spirit's garden. We share a common root, and the root is Mother Earth. The garden is beautiful because it has different colors in it, and those colors represent different traditions and cultural backgrounds.

"A lot of the factionalism in the Indian community has to do with loss.

The people, so many of the people—especially some of the younger ones who haven't been raised traditionally—feel that everything's gone and now the white people want our religion, too. This is the one thing we should freely give, because it doesn't belong to us—it belongs to the Great Spirit. If we can appropriately reveal anything of spiritual value to anybody, we should do it. The spiritual belongs to everyone."

Communication with Source

Oh Shinnah has had much varied training and many experiences in life. She holds bachelor's degrees in both voice and music from the University of Denver, and a master's degree in experimental psychology from the University of Chicago. She is an accomplished composer and singer who, early in her career, performed at the top folk-music clubs around the country. She also helped develop improvisational theater techniques, working with Second City in Chicago and the Committee Theater on the West Coast.

Oh Shinnah has studied healing and Native American traditions with Grandfather Roberts and Keetoowah of the Cherokee Nation, Buck Emmett of the Navajo-Apache nations, Jose Peldiecahn Mendez of the Mayan Nation, and Goman Rinpoche and Neychung Rinpoche of Tibet. A close friend and colleague is Dr. Dolores Krieger, author of the much-acclaimed book *Therapeutic Touch*. Oh Shinnah has also been instructed through what she calls "direct contact with Source."

"Let me tell you how my vision came about. I've been pronounced dead in this life three times. You see, I'm a recovering Catholic, and at about age twenty-eight I became very, very suicidal. I was in the hospital from a serious attempt at suicide, and pronounced dead. My soul journeyed to the other side, where great-grandmother was sitting waiting for me. She was shaking her finger in my face saying, 'Naughty, naughty, naughty, no, no, no.' She sent me back. I fought through this gray fog, back to my body in the hospital.

"Seven days later they told me I had Hodgkin's disease. Well, by then I had opted for life, so I thought, 'This is interesting; if I can't kill myself one way, I've designed a whole other way to do it.' The doctor told me my death was about two years away, but my soul mobilized for life. And I never had any chemotherapy or radiation, though my condition was monitored. I worked on it myself, and had one Blessing Way chant, which is a sand-painting healing ceremony. For nine years this struggle for life continued. Then I had a one-year retreat to discover and heal my pain and loss. We're only here a short time, and somewhere along the line I made up my mind that if I was going to be here I was going to play the master game. No more playing little games. I was going to educate myself and use all sorts of Earth energies and elementals, everything at hand, to make the world better instead of worse.

"At age thirty-three my heart led me to seek vision. If it wasn't real, if there was no Spirit, if there wasn't this compassionate loving force coming from Great Spirit or the Great Mystery, or if I wasn't held in the arms of Great Mother Goddess, I didn't want to be here anymore. A medicine man put me up on top of a mesa. I fasted for twenty-eight days with just three sips of water a day, absolutely no food. I did sweats every day until about the twenty-sixth day when, dehydrated and weak, I could hardly think or move.

"It was on an Apache reservation, because my Vision Quest leader was Tineh. Every day I was shaking my fist at heaven and saying, 'I want the real thing, direct communication with Source. I don't want the spirits to come and talk to me, or to read signs in the stars and the clouds. I don't want the animals to come and tell me things. Give me direct communication with Source, if it's real. If it isn't, I don't want to be here anymore.'"

"No longer being able to stand, I lay down in the dirt and just let go. I said, 'OK, take me.' I had an out-of-body experience that they told me lasted about eighteen hours. After so many days, unknown to me, this medicine man was sneaking up there, just to check to see if I was still alive. When he saw me go out, he stayed and said I was gone probably about eighteen hours. He said if I had been on the ground twenty-four hours he was going to bury me."

"Ultimately, there was direct communication with Source. It wasn't being in the Light, it was being the Light. It wasn't seeing infinity, it was being infinity. That's when I really realized that infinite nature is in all living things. There was direction and counsel to give my life over to this work, even to neglecting my own personal life. It claimed me. The direction was to become a spokesperson and to follow truly the path of the Great Mother Goddess, bringing in compassion and sharing it with all others. The feminine energy is what's going to change the world, not the masculine energy.

Actually, it's the feminine combined with masculine energy; really, it's the coming together of the two of them that will make a difference.

"This is my understanding of how it works. In the Beginning there was the Void; and the Void was filled with the All-There-Is, therefore, non-Void. Perhaps in the Void the Unseen Mystery experienced loneliness, breathed a sigh, and thus was born the God and the Goddess, yin and yang, father and mother, masculine and feminine, the man and woman in all of us. The wings of the bird carry positive and negative charges, male and female. Likewise, it takes two wings to fly to the spaces of the Great Mystery.

"For five thousand years, we have been strongly influenced by the red, masculine-charged ray that emanates from the planet called Mars. In my tradition, in the Star Way taught to me, this planet is called Dog Soldier Star. The Dog Soldier is not a true warrior; the Dog Soldier will fight just for the fun of it. Mars' reputation is his love of war; he'll go out and create wars just for the fun of it.

"The red ray has also meant a suppression of the feminine for five thousand years. It began further back than that, but the real repression of the feminine started when the Hittites came out of the steppes of Russia and influenced Hebraic peoples with their concept of God as male, two-legged, and white—a vengeful and unforgiving deity. Because they didn't understand the Moon and a woman's menses, they separated the women from the men and called the women unclean. Women became subjugated to men, and there was a suppression of the Great Mother Goddess. Her image disappeared all over this world. The Goddess is an essential part of the equation of life; you can't have the masculine dominate or you have imbalance. The Goddess is the Weaver of Life, nurturing, compassionate, always loving, the life-giving essence of existence. Through her we may find peace and reason once again, with strength to continue our path of life on this beautiful planet.

"For the last five thousand years we've had a male-dominated, male-oriented society bent on war and conquest. Somewhere on this planet, for five thousand years there's been war. We've had aggressiveness, a use-and-throwaway society. At the turn of the century we began to be influenced by the violet ray, which emanates through the planet you call Venus, which we call the gateway to the above and the beyond. Its name is Surrender, and it's the gateway through which you must go to reach the above and beyond. Venus emanates a violet ray, a feminine ray. It is represented by the eight-pointed star, each point symbolizing one of the graces you must obtain to follow the way of the Goddess: patience, humor, forgiveness, humility, willingness, courage, responsibility, and unconditional, compassionate love.

"At the turn of the last century the violet ray began to come in, pulling against the red ray. We had the First World War, the Second World War, Korea, Vietnam, Cambodia, Iraq, Iran, Nicaragua, El Salvador, all these red-ray expressions. We had the industrialization of the world, and the peak of capitalism, which created a user society: 'I'm gonna get richer than you, and I'm not going to share.' That's one side of the spectrum. We also had the birth of women suffragettes, women's liberation; the birth of nursing, caretaking; women deciding that they'd rather be married to men than houses; the homosexual and lesbian communities coming out of the closet and declaring themselves people instead of hiders. It doesn't make any difference how you lay your body down, either, as long as you don't give away your masculinity or your femininity. So this is where we are—in the scariest part of it, when these two pull away from each other.

"Ultimately, the masculine and the feminine must be balanced. But for that to happen, the feminine violet ray must continue to strengthen. Even though we would be influenced by other rays, the violet ray is a permanent ray. Once it's really here it will never go away."

Sisters of the Violet Flame

When Oh Shinnah was twenty-seven, she became affiliated with an ancient order of women who are dedicated to serving the feminine principles associated with the Goddess, The Sisters of the Violet Flame. "This order predates ancient Egypt," she explains. "The sisterhood was the feminine counterpart to the original Essenes. Now, The Sisters of the Violet Flame have nothing to do with Elizabeth Clare Prophet, even though she has a group with a similar name. We want no association with her. Our tradition goes way back beyond recorded history; this sisterhood has been in existence for many, many centuries.

"How did I become affiliated with it? It was a conspiracy between my great-grandmother and a French woman named Simone, who was also a sister and a follower of Gandhi. I had this dream, a dream in which I was told to go to O'Hare Field in Chicago. I was to go to Braniff Airlines and stand by a rubber plant and wait for somebody to meet me. At that time I wasn't using my Indian name—I was using another name as a folksinger. Sure enough, this very tall woman wearing a cape embroidered with all these symbols—moons and stars, all sorts of things—walks up to me and calls me 'Oh Shinnah.' She looked into my eyes and said, 'Will you go with me?' Well, I said yes. I would have followed her anywhere. We went outside where there was a car waiting with three other women in it, and we drove out of Chicago into the forests. When we arrived there was a group of women and this huge fire. Simone told me she had been instructed to initiate me into The Sisters of the Violet Flame, that I was to become head of the order, and that I was going to help reestablish the order.

"The initiation is putting your body through a wall of flame three times. If you fall into the fire nobody can move to help you. I've changed this rule because of a dramatic and traumatic incident. I won't even go into that now, only to say this rule no longer applies. My first jump was real easy. My arrogance took me through, but it also burned out in that fire. She made me state what it was I wanted to leave behind—things like the inconsistencies, things that troubled me, my losses and guilts, and so forth. Then she told me to take through the fire only the things that I wanted. Anything that hadn't been declared would be burned out of me on one level or another, and that happened. It's happened to everyone that I've initiated as well. The first jump was easy, except that my feet didn't quite make it over to the other side. I realized that the pit was gauged just beyond my ability to jump, so the second jump was a little scarier. My feet didn't even make it to the other side—it's a deep pit, you know—and I slid down and got an incredible burn.

"The third leap was initiation. I knew that I couldn't go through that fire. I knew if I went through that fire I would die. All of a sudden this energy moved through me. What Simone told me was true: the initiation is no longer to be a priestess of the Mother Goddess, but rather to be an embodiment of Great Mother Goddess, which is a whole other ball game. The third leap, it was like my body was suspended in the fire. It turned this violet blue color, and I felt like I could stay there forever. I've been radically different since then.

"The work of the Sisterhood is to honor and channel and bring in this violet ray of energy. We have an obligation to commit to memory as much esoteric information as we possibly can. I was given a list of books that had to be read and passed on to future generations. All the world's esoteric information is out there now, but it may not always be available. That's why we are initiated in the oral tradition. If it's committed to memory, not word for word but as much as possible, it will never be lost. Books will burn, but your memory won't.

"We have an obligation to be caretakers and teachers, to share this information. One of our biggest responsibilities is to the unborn. I was instructed by Simone to bring my heritage into play, that the feathers I use would be different from the feathers she uses, and the way I build the sacred fire would be different from the way she builds the sacred fire. To date I've initiated, I think, twenty-seven women. So all this touches on what The Sisters of the Violet Flame are all about."

The Emerald Tablets

Oh Shinnah's odyssey as a warrior for the Earth Mother has led her on many other high adventures. "In the early 1970s—I think it was 1971—I went to Mexico as a seeker after I had my vision. The vision told me that if I could find one person who could listen to this vision all the way, from beginning to end, without interruption, that was the one I should follow. Well, in the end I learned there isn't anybody to follow, because if you follow in the footsteps of the guru you become a shadow. There are teachers who can teach us things we need to know and to integrate into our lives to make us better people, but a guru is not one that you follow. A guru is a dispeller of evil.

"In Mexico, at Palenque, there's a rainforest right behind the temples— just incredible, so beautiful. Walking there alone, I found this river. I went off the trail, wading to a log in the middle of the waters. Totally unaware of any danger, I sat there. Then this herd of frogs went by, none of them bigger than my little fingernail. I would scoop them up, holding five or six of them in my hand. It was like a birthing place, just wonderful. I sat there for many hours, just thinking. It started getting dark, as the Sun is very filtered through the greenness of the trees. I could tell that if I didn't want to get trapped in the forest in the dark, I better leave, so I went back to the trail, walking the path. As I walked, my eyes were diverted. There on a large leaf was this butterfly that must have been as big as a large plate, with luminous turquoise rims around it, and luminous turquoise veins in its wings, which were translucent. You could see through its wings. Right below it, on the forest floor, were these parrot feathers, which I picked up and bound with a bit of leather strap hanging from my belt, with a key on it. Then I tied them in my hair.

"Coming toward the end of the trail, I saw a Mayan man watching me. I took a step toward him and a little brown snake went between my legs. I took another step and a second little brown snake went between my legs. I took a third step and a third brown snake went between my legs. This man was observing all this. When I got to the end of the trail, he asked me, in Spanish, what I had seen. So I explained to him about the frogs, the butterfly, and about this hole I had looked into where these white—I mean albino—granddaddy longlegs, thousands of them, were pouring out. Also, I had parrot feathers in my hair, and then the three snakes at the end, which he had seen. He said, 'I want you to come and talk to the old man.' I said OK. We ran down to the compound, to the small store where the old man was in the back room. He checked me out like a horse they might want to buy. Finally the old man said, 'Do you want to go to our village?' I replied, 'Where's your village?' and the old man answered me with a laugh, 'Two weeks' walk into the forest.' I said, 'Sure, let me go tell my husband and daughter,' and they said, 'No, they can't come.' Well, that was the end of that marriage. We stayed together a while longer, my husband and I, but when I elected to go, the marriage was as good as over. He recognized then that there was no holding me back from spiritual realization.

"So I went, and when we got there I realized no one in the village spoke English, and hardly any of them spoke Spanish. It was the strangest experience. The old man, the elder who was my teacher, and the man who spoke Spanish, the three of us would go into this cave, and I would think of a question, and he would, in Mayan, answer the question before I spoke it, and then the interpreter would tell me his answer in Spanish and broken English.

"It was explained to me that in their prophecies it was foretold that there would come a woman who was a grandmother (I was already a grandmother at this time), who would carry back into the world a meditation associated with the Emerald Tablets of Thoth the Atlantean. It would be her responsibility to share this meditation with the rest of the world. The reason they knew it was me was because of the frogs, the spiders, the butterfly, the parrot feathers in my hair, and the guardians—they call these small, brown snakes guardians. I found out later that if one of those snakes bites you then you are dead in eighteen seconds.

"The Emerald Tablets are from Thoth the Atlantean, also known as Hermes Thrice Born, or Hermes Trismegistus. During the Atlantean era, Thoth was the son of a human being and one of the seven Lords of Light. When he realized that Atlantis was falling because of the abuse of crystals, Thoth went to Egypt and began to teach the people there how to live in a sacred manner. He took with him one copy of the Emerald Tablets, and then made three more copies and sent them in the Four Directions. The only one that we know about ended up with the Mayan peoples in the Yucatán. However, in 1934 a man named Doreal, a member of the White Brotherhood, brought the tablets back to the United States, though I believe they are now in Egypt, where they are kept safely in a museum.

"The tablets, the sacred teachings of Thoth, were eventually translated into several languages by this Brotherhood of the White Temple. Some copies of the translations are available, but they are difficult to get. They are powerful. When you read them you find there's a rhythm to them. So it's not even the words, it's the rhythm that communicates to you. As you read them, your energy changes. You won't understand a lot of the content in them until you're ready, and then suddenly it makes sense to you when before it didn't.

"If you study and comprehend them you can learn the keys of life, of space and time, and they help take fear out of a lot of your life. Its very individual, very explorative of who you are as a person and what you need in any given moment. I teach this meditation to help people gain access to the teachings of the tablets, a moving meditation that is quick and more in harmony with Western people, and it gives you direct communication with the Lords of Light. I think the energetic form creates a tunnel to the Sphinx, which is the Halls of Amenthe. It's incredible.

"By connecting with the Emerald Tablets, you can accelerate your development. They take fear out of life. They put life back into life, instead of death in life, as we have so much now. In a way, the tablets are like the

Akasha, the Akashic Records. You can connect in five minutes, or ten minutes. I taught it to Goman Rinpoche, and he looked at me after he did it, then shook his head and said, 'Where were you fifty years ago when I needed this? I've been sitting in meditation all of my life, very long hours, and all I got was a big fat bottom.'

"Years later I started teaching individuals. Then I had a dream where one of the Lords of Light came to me and told me that I had to start teaching groups, because this meditation was needed in the world. It requires that people fast for four days before learning these things, with the exception of those with medical problems, or people who are pregnant or nursing. This meditation is very powerful, so it is helpful for initiates to be clean, clear, and centered."

Oh Shinnah is still teaching the Emerald Tablet meditation as she travels the world. After she has taught a group of people, she follows the guidance of her elders and bonds the people who are learning into clan systems. She says Grandfather David Monongye named the clans Saquasohuh—which means Blue Star. "According to Grandpa David," she explains, "when the Blue Star appears in the sky it heralds the really heavy part of the Earth's purification. When it comes again the purification is over. The Blue Star came for the first time in 1963 for the seven days leading up to JFK's death. We don't know for sure when it will come again, but I think it's going to be about 2010 or 2011.

"The Blue Star is the star of creation. It's Great Spirit's star. It's neither male nor female. It's a nine-pointed star. In 1963 the scientists who observed it thought it was a supernova, but later found it to be a star never seen before. We have veils in front of our eyes, and when we reach certain levels of consciousness, the veils drop, and for a brief time we see as we have never seen before."

The Center for Grandfather Coyote

Though she is now an elder herself, since her youth Oh Shinnah has had long-standing relationships with many distinguished elders. She has been adopted, for example, into the families of Rolling Thunder, the late Hopi Grandfather David Monongye, and Matthew King, the treaty chief of the Lakota People. Since childhood she has recognized and appreciated the wisdom of older people.

"Grandchildren can often learn more from their grandparents than they can from their parents. As you get older you begin to see the world in a different way. When you are raising your own children you are trapped in the immediate now. But when you have grandchildren you begin to see the world more inclusively. You begin to see the possibilities of change in good ways. You see that when you give your grandchildren the way of spiritual teachings and practices, it takes hold in them in a way it won't take hold in your own children. There's a certain wisdom that comes with you because you've had the experiences that are necessary to become archetypal, to go to the subjective level. When you are twenty you can't make the same kind of decisions around the same happening that you can when you are fifty.

"I tell people, 'If you don't have a grandmother or a grandfather around you, then go and adopt one, because you cannot understand the cycles of life unless you have old people around you.' The wisdom that comes with being an older person is wonderful. You just can't get it or have it when you are twenty.

"People on this planet need older people in their lives. Women, being mothers, know things different from what men know being fathers. In our tradition, the father names the child because he gives the child identity. The mother gives the child life through the processes of her body. It takes two to make a baby, but it takes a woman to complete what the seed has sown. Because of this, women have a closer association with nature—it's automatic for us. I think we have a closer association with spiritual ethics because we are the givers of life. Men are beginning to change now, and to look for the grandmother and grandfather within themselves, too, but it's essential for the people to listen to the old folks. There are things that we can only learn from the old folks. There is no other way."

Because so many Native American elders are suffering in neglect and abject poverty, Oh Shinnah has co-created, with her friend Dolores Krieger, Ph.D., R.N., an organization called The Center for Grandfather Coyote. "Native elders are a national treasure," she says, "and they are dying. They starve. They freeze by the sides of the road. They lack proper medical care. With them end ancient traditions. It's important that they be honored for who they are and what they know."

The Center for Grandfather Coyote runs two programs to assist elders on reservations: Support an Elder and Adopt an Elder. "With the Support an Elder program," Oh Shinnah explains, "people send in donations—whatever they can afford—and we put it in a general fund. When we get a call about an elder who's going to be put out of their house because they can't pay the rent, because they chose to stay warm instead of cold, or to eat, we send money. We pay the bills; we don't send them the money personally, we pay the bills. We pay the electric or the telephone bill or an emergency medical bill. We also send food, clothing, and blankets.

"Adopt an Elder is even more interesting because we canvass several reservation areas and find really needy and worthy elders. Then we find people who want to go into a relationship with them, and we put them together. You correspond with and directly send support to one person, who in turn lets you know what they need. It might take a large family or an organization or a network of friends to meet these needs, but it works beautifully.

"The basic idea of caring for elders is real simple. You ask them what they need and what they want. That's all it is. And then listen to them. Also make sure that they're not inundated by people. When I traveled with Rolling Thunder, nobody could talk to him unless they talked to me first. The only way they could get to him was through me, and the only way to get through me was to be there for a real reason. I did the same thing for Grandfather David Monongye. I wouldn't even let Marlon Brando talk to him."

Grandfather David

"I met Grandfather David through my father when I was three years old, and my father took me there quite frequently. When I was ten and eleven years old I used to get on my horse in Silverton, Colorado, and ride all the way down to Hopiland by myself with my wolf dog, and never run into a fence. You can't do that anymore. Grandfather David was grandfather to a lot of people, but he adopted me, too, when I was about thirty-four. He had always been my grandpa since I was three, but at that time he formally adopted me.

"He was probably one of the most enlightened people I've ever met in my life. There was something about him—I mean he was very human, that was one of the things that was so beautiful about him. He was one of the keepers of Hopi prophecy. He had absolutely no prejudice or anger anywhere in him. He was a peacemaker. Many people say he lived to be

116, but no one knows for sure—some elders think he was older when he crossed.

"I'll tell you a quick story about Grandpa David you'll understand. The light without is attracted to the light within, which expands the light within so that you eventually are attracting to yourself beings of a higher vibration as your vibration increases. I saw that light, that outer light, only around three people, and two of them were at the United Nations Conference on Ecology in Sweden. There was a conference going on for Third World people at the same time. There were maybe five or six thousand people in this one auditorium. They were all just standing next to these two men. One of them was a Brazilian Indian, who had to be smuggled out and couldn't go home. There was also a man from Nicaragua, whose government told him if he left and came back they'd kill him, and if he didn't come back they'd kill his family. These two men were screaming at each other about 'my problem's worse than your problem; we have a greater need than you have.' The energy was just horrible.

"Grandpa David was the last speaker. He took off his headband, reached into his pouch, and got out his cornmeal to pray. He just stood there in silence. I saw his energy expand and move around this room. I wasn't the only one who saw it. As it moved, a wave of silence—a wave of profound and utter silence—encompassed this whole room. It was beautiful. When there was total silence he made his offering, put his headband back on, and looked at the people and said, 'I want you to know that we are all brothers and sisters.' This is where I heard about we're flowers of the Great Spirit's garden and we share a common root. Those are Grandfather David's words. But, you know, he had a sense of humor, too. He used to teach me when I was little; he used to tell me, 'Don't be so serious.' He'd teach people that if you didn't maintain your sense of humor, all this horrible stuff that is going on in the world could really destroy you. Oh, he was exceptional. He had an affect on everybody he came near. He really expressed unconditional love."

The Heart of the Earth Mother

"The message I carry on behalf of the Earth is really quite basic and simple: If you're not a part of the solution, you're a part of the problem. There is no middle road. I don't think we can destroy the Earth, but I think the

Earth can destroy us. It's really stupid for us to continue a path of trying to consciously destroy our life-support system: the lungs of the Mother, which is the Brazilian forest, and the Heart of the Mother, which is the Four Corners area in the Southwest. It's stupid.

"We call the Four Corners area the Heart of the Mother Earth. It's bounded by four breathing mountains, and protected by Rock Crystal Boy and Rock Crystal Girl. I'm going to give you the English names for the mountains because the Apache names take two weeks to say. They are Mount Blanca in Colorado, Mount Taylor in New Mexico, Mount Hesperus near the Utah-Colorado border, and the San Francisco Peaks in Arizona. We call this land the Heart of the Mother.

"We can't have romantic notions anymore about what's going on. I worked with some scientists from Boulder at the observatory there. They told me the space pictures they took when we went to the Moon show that the Earth is not really round; it's shaped more like a plum, kind of flat on one end. So the electromagnetic poles of the North and South help hold the Earth in balance, but there are also East and West poles, and they are essential as well. The East and West poles, though, are not in a horizontal line but a diagonal, because we're not round. The West pole would be the Four Corners area, and the East pole would be the Lower Himalayas of Tibet.

"Now, I think that's fascinating, you see, because I helped bring about a meeting between the Hopi who are the keepers of their prophecies and the Tibetans who are the keepers of the Tibetan prophecies. Goman Rinpoche and Neychung Rinpoche, who were two of the keepers of Tibetan prophecy, met with Grandfather David and other elders who were keepers of Hopi prophecy in the late seventies. During the meeting the interpreter kept interpreting the word *dharma* as 'the way,' which closed the doors to real conversation between the Indians and the Tibetans because native peoples here already have a way. Finally Grandpa David—these little lights went on in his head, and he jumped up and said something to Goman in Hopi, and then Goman jumped up and said something to him in Tibetan. Grandpa turned around and said something to the interpreter, and the interpreter told all of us that he had been corrected, and that dharma was 'universal truth.' Then the doors opened.

"It was discovered that Tibet was the focus for masculine ceremonies that help to hold the Earth in balance. The Indian peoples in the Southwest, Hopi especially, are the keepers of the feminine principle and have ceremonies to help hold the Earth in balance. I believe the ceremonies relate to the electromagnetic poles. Remember, when you work with ceremony, any ceremony, you are basically working with energy. The ceremonies of the East and West poles have to do with the masculine and feminine balance of the Earth.

"In the late fifties the situation changed in Tibet, and it changed everything as far as ceremony. That's when the Chinese invaded and the Tibetans who held the masculine ceremonial form had to flee or were imprisoned. One of the reasons why the Dalai Lama told me he was still there in the Lower Himalayas in Nepal was because the ceremonies they were still trying to do were helping to hold the balance of the Earth. You see, the axis of the Earth is changing, and if any of the major poles are disturbed during the axis change, the electromagnetic field of the Earth is grossly disturbed. We relate to this as a time of purification. It is a time of purification. In the Bible it is called tribulation. But those gross disturbances could cause the Earth to go into slippage, which would lead to wobble, and wobble could lead to spin. If we go into spin, and the planet starts spinning wildly, then all life on this Earth will cease to exist within twenty-four hours. Then we start all over again.

"This is a living being here, this Earth. She has consciousness like you. And what do you do when you get sick? You throw up, don't you? OK. Well, let's talk about Mount St. Helens and all the volcanoes that are going off, all the earthquakes and the floods and wind storms, all the climate changes. It's not just what's going on with the ozone, it has to do with this Earth saying, 'I'm stronger than you are and you better straighten your mess out, because if you keep hurting me you're going to get hurt because you'll go into spin.' We're already in wobble. And wobble has a lot to do with the wind currents and the way the wind is blowing so strong, the tornadoes in areas that have never experienced them before, winters with no snow in Alaska, but snow in Florida and California—the list goes on.

"It's all changing. My sense is that the wobble could proceed and accelerate, but I also have great hope. If I thought the wobble was inevitably going to become spin, I would just go find a cave somewhere and move in. I've given my life over to this work of healing the Earth and I don't even have a place to live—haven't for years. I think my children are the most wonderful children in the world because they let me go. It wasn't me letting them go—they let me go, because they recognized early on that I had a voice that was going to be heard.

"So now the Tibetans are off center from their pole, and in the Four Corners area there are many corporate threats to the healthy balance of that pole. The greed for the coal and uranium is what's doing it. What's happening is they use, I'm not exactly positive on my figures, but about eighty to ninety million gallons of water per minute to process the coal. This is underground unrechargeable mineral water. What's happening is the water table is dropping. Some scientists from Boulder, Colorado, say there are places under the crust of the Earth in the Heart of the Mother where it's shaped like an hourglass, and that's where the water is holding the continental shelf—the north and southwestern continental shelf—in place. As the water table drops, these thin areas begin to dry out and to create sink holes. If we continue the way we are, this can and will have grave consequences, not just for the feminine pole but for the whole Earth. Remember, in Tibet the keepers of the masculine principle have been forced off center. So what's going on with male consciousness?"

A Spiritual & Political Revolution

"There are a lot of people who haven't explored the possibility that they are destroying their own lives. They don't believe that the Earth is a living organism. They live in the greed of the now, you see—they're not even thinking of future generations; they're not even thinking of their grandchildren. They're thinking of how much money they can make right now. And this government supports this lack of consciousness. Anybody that spends ten million dollars on an inauguration party in the shadow of the worst ghetto of this country, where little black children die of malnutrition today—I mean, really, that's inexcusable, absolutely inexcusable. I don't see how this country can continue to support this lack of concern for land and life. I believe in 'of the people, by the people, and for the people,' but with the way it's set up now we have 'of the rich, by the rich, and for the rich.' That's what it is.

"There has to be a revolution in this country. I think it has to be a spiritually political revolution. I'm not talking about picking up guns and shooting people—I'm talking about a spiritual and political revolution. If we're going to continue with this system, we have to put people in office who are not going to allow big business to continue the rape of this planet, because that's where it's coming from. It's like the styrofoam, and it's like the medical trash that was dumped off the shores of New Jersey. They're giving them ten years to solve the problem. We don't have ten years. We are in an accelerated destructive phase right now. I'm encouraged because I believe the children of the future will change it. I don't think we're going to change it. But I know I've been involved in starting that change. You know, when I had my vision I made up my mind that I didn't care if anybody ever remembered my life, but they'd sure know that I had been here. And they will."

⟨⟨⟨ TEN ⟩⟩⟩

Where the Medicine Wheel Meets Medical Science

J.T. GARRETT

*A*fter exploring the issues of health and healing from several vantage points, J.T. Garrett has found some gentle ways of uniting science and the Indian tradition. Currently the deputy director of the North Carolina Commission of Indian Affairs, at other times in his career J.T. has been the deputy associate director of the Indian Health Service, the administrator of the Cherokee Indian Hospital, and a director of safety and industrial hygiene in private industry. Public health has been his main concern, and to this he brings not only his academic and professional experience, but also his training in Native American medicine. J.T.'s mentor was a respected elder medicine man, the late Doc Amoneeta Sequoyah.

J.T. was raised on the Qualla Boundary, which is in the western part of North Carolina. It is the domicile of the Eastern Band of the Cherokee Indians and the only Cherokee reservation on the East Coast. The Oklahoma Cherokee are called the Cherokee Nation; they were removed from Virginia, West Virginia, Tennessee, North Carolina, and Georgia during the 1830s in a tragic government action that has come to be known as The Trail of Tears.

About three hundred Cherokee Indians were able to escape capture and remain in the Appalachian Mountains of their traditional homeland. Some sixty years later, in 1899, they were chartered as a tribe and granted the right to live on their own land, the Qualla Boundary. "It's a reservation,"

J.T. explains, "but we call it a boundary—the Qualla Boundary. And that has a whole different connotation than reservation. You cross the boundary from one place to another. The Boundary is a line that is drawn between the white world surrounding Qualla and the isolation of the Indian world. I was raised most of my younger years on the Boundary, and it was different."

Building Bridges

"When my father was in the Navy, we had a chance to move to different places in Virginia and Florida. So I had a chance to see the bridging of one society to another. For me, it was not difficult. But for some it was very difficult to move from the reservation into a different society and environment.

"The members of my family were earth people, farmers and spiritual leaders. My grandfather, Oscar Walkingstick Rogers, shared many, many stories with me, and somehow instilled the notion that one day I would, somehow, learn Indian Medicine. I was interested in the ministry from the age of twelve on, and I fully intended to go that way. Eventually, though, I had internal conflicts with the dogma of religion."

As a teen, J.T. lived in Florida, spending many hours by the ocean, watching and listening to the rhythm of the waves. One night as he sat on the beach, he saw a big ball of light out over the water that came steadily toward him. Eventually, the light engulfed him, in a joining that took several hours. It was a profound experience that moved him deeply.

For a time, J.T. moved back to the reservation with his family, where he was reintroduced to Indian Medicine. But he leaned away from the medicine path; it seemed too unusual. However, the medicine way continued to exert a force like a magnet. In college he studied biology, botany, chemistry, and then business administration. During the spring of his senior year, he was taking a test when all of sudden he passed out.

"As the story was told to me, not only did I pass out, but I also lost all bodily control. I was actually dead for a period of time. According to the nurse, there was no heartbeat. A couple of the guys, including one good friend of mine, carried me out to the infirmary. They even went so far as to call the coroner's office, because they really weren't sure what was happening. During that period of time, I had no idea what happened. I had no idea, but I have a feeling that it was a revisitation of some kind—for me to realize that I had a special direction to go in.

"One thing I do remember from that experience. It was the first time I visited with what I call the White Spirit Eagle, which is similar to the White Buffalo. I saw a huge eagle. Its wingspan covered the land, and I had the opportunity to look through the eyes of this huge bird. I could see there was a lot of decay on Mother Earth, and there was too much being destroyed. People were in conflict. Then suddenly I knew that part of my role was to shift over into the direction of public and environmental health, and to help people bridge the gap into a natural, spiritual understanding by using the teachings of Indian medicine.

"I made a list of things that were literally like messages for me, and I wrote them down as fast as I could. The nurse was trying to take my pulse, and I was sitting there writing things down. She said, 'Sit down and be still,' and I said, 'No, I've gotta write it down.'"

"Anyway, from that experience all of a sudden I knew that I was to visit several Indian Medicine people and find my link with the circle. All of that led me toward public health. It just seemed like one thing led to another. Eventually, I went out in the work world and suddenly found that I had good intuitive as well as professional work skills. I went into industry and became a safety professional, then moved into insurance and Worker's Compensation in private industry. I worked in the business world over ten years, being promoted to the position of corporate coordinator of safety and industrial hygiene for the Bendix Corporation.

"Following that, I had this real strong urge to return home to North Carolina. This one day, out of the clear blue sky, I just came in and said to my family, 'We're going back to North Carolina.' And we did. In a matter of weeks we were back home on the Cherokee Boundary. I got a call from Mary Sequoyah, who was the daughter of Doc Amoneeta Sequoyah, an elder Cherokee Indian medicine man. He wanted me to visit him. The first time I went in to see him, he turned his back and wouldn't talk to me. I was pretty anxious, and I said, 'Look, I'm here. I don't know why I'm here, but I don't have much time, and I've got things to do. I've got to catch a plane, and I've got appointments to keep.' And he didn't say anything for another hour before he finally took me up on a mountain behind his home. I knew this would be a profound experience for me. As a matter of fact, I was a little afraid.

"What I remember the most about him was his dark eyes, the penetrating eyes that just cut right through you. Finally he turned to me and said, 'You know what your problem is? You've learned too much to listen. Now you have to listen, and relearn.' That was his first statement to me, and it was pretty profound. At the time, he was right. I wasn't listening much. I was on top of the world with a good job, making money, an important position. But all of a sudden, when he said that, I developed a whole new taste for humility. From that point on we became, over a period of several years, very close. He became my grandfather, and he started teaching me Indian Medicine. He said to me, 'I'm passing the medicine on to you.' I remember thinking, 'But I'm not ready.' Still, it happened. Now if I had to describe it, I'd say my medicine is for bridging, the bridging of two cultures and two approaches to medicine. That's what I try to do. I now realize that the eagle in my vision represented the two people—Indian and non-Indian. Like the eagle feather, there are light and dark colors, like day and night, man and woman, and so forth. And it takes both to fly. They have to be connected."

Giving the Choice Back

"Doc Amoneeta told me a number of times that I would come back to the Boundary. I said, 'No way, not me, I'll never come back. I'm not going to go through that again. It's too difficult a life for my family.' And he said, 'No, no, you'll come back. And when you come back, you'll be this big person with a hospital and all.' But I couldn't imagine myself doing anything like that. Lo and behold, they built a new hospital, which was, in fact, the way I came back. I came back as administrator of the Cherokee Indian Hospital on the Boundary, using my experience from industry. We became certified during the first year of operation. It's exactly as Amoneeta Sequoyah described it.

"I had the pleasure of setting up an Indian Medicine Circle at the hospital, to see what we could do to improve community health, and to include our proud heritage and culture in the health care. The Indian Medicine Circle allowed people in the community to come to the hospital and sit within the circle—in other words, to make the hospital a community-based service. Those with special healing abilities could share their medicine within the context of the modern hospital. We had a community circle and other circles to welcome people of the community and spiritual talents into the hospital, so we could bring our traditional culture back. That way the hospital was not a separate island of Western technology in the middle of the Boundary, which is itself already isolated.

"Anybody in the hospital who wanted to go to a medicine man, or have a medicine man visit them, could do so, as long as the mode of treatment didn't interfere with the treatment modality used by the clinicians in the hospital. And if it did, then the patient could sign a waiver, or release themselves from the care of the hospital physicians. That way they could make a clear choice about which medicine pathway they wanted to follow. That was the whole idea. There was no judgment made about the way they were going. It gave the choice back to them, so that they could become a part of their own care.

"The other thing I did was to set up a special room dedicated to Doc Amoneeta Sequoyah. I called it the Indian Medicine Room. We kept in that room a sacred rattle, some herbs, and things that were special to remind us of our Indian Medicine heritage. Doc Sequoyah and others would use that special room for counseling, particularly for alcohol and drug-abuse counseling. That room took on its own personality, and many things were accomplished there to promote our Indian culture and heritage. Four years later it seemed like it was my time to go on.

"That's when I moved to a position in the national Indian Health Service's headquarters in Rockville, Maryland, and moved up to deputy associate director for the office of health programs. I spent six years there before I came back to North Carolina to serve as the deputy director of the North Carolina Commission on Indian Affairs."

Indian Medicine

"The Indian Health Service is based primarily on the biomedical model, designed to provide acute care. Indian Medicine people would refer to that as physical medicine. In other words, it's just that; it's treatment of the physical body. Unfortunately, Indian Medicine hasn't taken its proper place in the annals of medicine. Even *Dorland's Medical Dictionary* refers to Indian Medicine as a form of quackery used by native people. In fact, it's a form of medicine that has far greater depth than a medicine that's just used for some treatment or cure. Don't get me wrong, I truly appreciate our modern medical system, but human health care must go beyond that.

"Each person under the Indian Medicine model has their own medicine, which is sometimes referred to as a 'medicine bundle.' These are the things that become a part of a person, which help a person realize that they have choices they can make in their own life. They have protectors, or guides, that are working with them. They have their own strength and power, and they have Universal Spirit that they can tap into. All that is a part of the person's medicine bundle.

"The things that are in a person's medicine bag, or the bundle itself, are of particular value, such as a special herb. As an example, my herb is yellowroot, since my weak spot is my throat—getting a sore throat. If your stomach was the weakest point, then you'd carry an herb to settle the stomach.

"I am responsible for my own care, and I make choices to heal myself, or keep myself healthy. You know the old saying, 'Physician, heal thyself.' That's another way of saying, 'Be sure you've got a medicine bag for yourself.' You can't help others if you can't help yourself. At the same time, there are some things that one can't help oneself with, and that's when you visit a medicine person.

"Indian Medicine is interesting primarily because it provides a way of life that encourages a focus on wellness. Indian Medicine is basically a wellness methodology that emphasizes improving one's lifestyle and making better choices for encouraging good health, or 'good medicine,' which is the traditional Indian way."

It's a Way That You Go

"From working in the Indian Health Service for many years, and from studying the ways of Indian Medicine, what I've managed to do is encourage and enhance the focus of health promotion and disease prevention, as opposed to just clinical care. I've also tried to enhance the understanding of why a spiritual and mental-health way has to be part of the healing for such problems as alcohol and drug abuse.

"Indian Medicine is actually physical, mental, spiritual, and natural. Think about it. Who separated the concepts of physical and mental? It wasn't some physician; it was a philosopher. The whole concept of the bio-medical model, though, grew from this separation of the mental, physical, and spiritual. In Indian Medicine there is no separation, and no such thing as a treatment. It's a way that one must go, a way of living one's life, a path to follow. It's a choice that one makes.

"The 'Rule of Opposites,' as I call it, is also a part of Indian Medicine. The eagle feather teaches us about the Rule of Opposites, about everything being divided into two ways. The more one is caught up in the physical, or the West, then the more one has to go in the opposite direction, the East, or the spiritual, to get balance. And it works the other way, too—you can't just focus on the spiritual to the exclusion of the physical. You need harmony in all Four Directions.

"Some people tend to romanticize Indian Medicine, and others tend to shun it as if it were more fallacy than fact. But with Indian Medicine, there's a memory that we are tapping into that goes way back. In the forests and fields around us are thousands of plants that researchers have discovered can combat a wide range of ills. Western medicine owes a great debt to Native Americans. Indian Medicine has already been through the trial-and-error phase many hundreds of years ago. It's valuable to learn these traditions from the elders. They are the keepers of the secrets. While some aspects of Indian Medicine are culturally unique and need to be kept sacred or secret for traditional preservation, there are many teachings that have application to all of us today."

A Sacred Art & Science

"Indian Medicine is the traditional sacred art and science related to the preservation of health and well-being. Therefore, Indian Medicine coincides very closely with the public-health model of preventing disease and improving the health and well-being of a population.

"The term 'medicine ways' implies a way of life based on a unique Indian cultural heritage. Indian Medicine taught an individual responsibility for health choices. The proper choices were taught in ceremonies, herbal formulas, personal discipline, and meditation or prayer chants. The family was included for balance and harmony. Any modern health approach would do well to focus on harmony and balance, rather than just on diseases and cures.

"Indian Medicine can be summarized as an individual health management system that uses everything in the person's environment to maintain harmony, which includes our modern clinical medicine. The personal discipline on the physical, mental, spiritual, and natural planes is directed toward a high level of personal involvement, quality of life, and well-being. Indian Medicine is culturally oriented, but the ways or teachings deserve relearning. The focus should be on giving health responsibility back to the individual for promoting health choices and personal health maintenance. Indian Medicine ways can certainly provide an alternate approach to the modern concept of health promotion and disease prevention.

"Earlier Indian Medicine helped people find a path, or helped them get back on the path of balance and harmony. This balance included internal harmony with the family and one's own environment. That's because the focus of Indian Medicine is on faith in sacred beliefs, individual involvement, family and clan involvement, knowledge and use of natural helpers such as herbs, meditation, ceremonial practices, balance and harmony, and an individual seeking their own way to health."

The Four Directions

"Many of the teachings of Indian Medicine have value to us today. The concept, for example, of the Four Directions emphasizes the way that individual choices in lifestyle lead to a path of preservation, conservation, and wellness. The Four Directions convey the importance of respect for oneself and the environment. I use the traditional Cherokee approach and go counterclockwise.

"The North is the Path of Quiet, representing the mental aspect of health. The mental aspect has to do with raising one's inner consciousness to the level of receptivity, so one can learn by listening to the mind and spirit. Even seeing and reading are considered a form of listening. Learning is a matter of choosing and accepting at will.

"The West is the Path of Introspection, representing the physical. Traditionally, stamina was important for spiritual attainment. Running, walking, dancing, and certain aerobic activities are necessary in the lifestyle concepts taught in Indian Medicine. Relaxation includes meditation and the sweat bath as activities for physical, mental, and spiritual awareness. There are also represented here ways for release, or 'give-away,' to achieve a high level of consciousness.

"The South is the Path of Peace, representing the way of youth and innocence. Youths learn self-sufficiency and conservation of everything and everyone within the framework of the circle of family and environment. They learn how to live in harmony with the ecosystem. The legends and stories of this direction teach respect and understanding, and also having fun. The South should be fun.

"The East, the Path of the Sun, represents the spiritual aspect. The first value emphasized here is respect for the dignity of everything, whether we understand it or not. Indians are taught that everything has its own spirit, including every animal, bird, tree, plant, and even every rock. This teaches respect for ourselves and our environment.

"These Four Directions provide a road map for anyone seeking balance and harmony. As Doc Amoneeta once said to me, 'The medicine traditions will bring us back to the reality of health. You don't look at what's wrong with a person, but what a person has done wrong.' The Indian approach provides a 'medicine bundle' of practical values that can be applied to everyday stress control and lifestyle choices. Prevent the preventable illnesses and diseases. Provide activities that encourage good choices, especially with children, including physical fitness, nutritional eating habits, and the avoidance of alcohol, drugs, and tobacco. Create the habit of health-wise awareness. This includes practical ways to avoid illnesses and diseases, and ways to treat common illnesses.

"Establish health fitness as a way of life. Exercise, and take relaxing walks in the park or on the seashore. Establish values and ethics that include the physical, mental, spiritual, and natural aspects for establishing one's own 'good medicine.' Bring the circles together in the family, community, churches, and businesses, and focus on improving universal health and wellness. That's what can make a difference, and that's Indian Medicine."

Remedy & Ritual

"You know, as I think back on it, I didn't become a physician because I didn't want to practice that kind of medicine. I didn't become a psychologist because they also have a set of rules, a code of conduct, which is not necessarily in harmony with Indian Medicine. Anytime you are doing something to someone, such as giving them a treatment, you are controlling them. That's the opposite of Indian Medicine, which acts as a helper to give you information or something else so you can help yourself.

"When I would orient new physicians in the Indian Health Service, I would say that the medicine approach of the Native Americans includes certain things such as harmony or equilibrium of all these forces: social, psychological, community, family, clan, and so forth. The healer and the patient share a system of beliefs about the nature of health and the nature of disease. They share this! It's not the doctor saying, 'Well, you have something called ABCD.' Sharing is what's going on. It's a different approach. And even though the patient might be sick, the patient and his family participate in the healing process.

"The other thing I would try to convey to the young physicians is that you don't just give a remedy of sorts, you also give a ritual. In other words, you don't just treat a person, you also do a little health education, too. Now, many physicians won't take time for that. They don't have time for healing. They're too busy treating or trying to cure. Too often the human element is taken out, which is actually a part of the healing.

"Illness is the result of some kind of imbalance that has to be corrected. The Indian healer traditionally enlists the participation of others in song, dance, and rituals. Can you imagine a physician saying, 'Let's bring in the singers and dancers and prayer chanters; let's go through a sweat-bath ceremony for personal healing'? The physician today simply does not have time to get involved with the healing of the patient; they are only going to get involved with treatment of the symptoms. This is not intended to say that our current medical care is bad. We need it. But even many physicians would really like to get more involved with healing.

"The other thing is that the traditional healer would surround himself with other helpers, and that's very important. Anytime that I'm working with a person, I include others in the process to create a healing circle, and that's very powerful."

Disease As Opportunity

"When you think about it, disease is an opportunity. As my father lay dying of cancer, I didn't think to ask him, 'Dad, what did you learn or what am I to learn from your experience?' He was trying to say, 'Stop smoking,

America' because my generation was overwhelmed with the romanticization of cigarettes. He tried to say that we need affordable health care so that people would go for checkups before it's too late. I was too involved with his dying to listen and learn from his disease. It goes back to what Doc Amoneeta said to me, that I had learned so much that I had forgotten to listen. But from my father's experience I ultimately listened and learned something that I have internalized and personalized. I have regular checkups, I don't smoke, and I learn from nutritional and health education messages.

"In the nineties people are going to be looking more for things that they can internalize and personalize, more so than in the eighties. I've heard psychologists say over and over, 'Don't internalize this, or personalize that,' but you have to identify some experience that you can learn from and then internalize it. That experience then becomes a matter of change—it modifies your energy. You can learn to internalize the messages of a disease experience and use it as an opportunity to change illness energy to wellness energy.

"Every day of our lives we ought to get up and, as we open our eyes, give thanks—be thankful that we are here. If we all started off the day as the ancient ones did, by greeting the rising Sun—in essence giving thanks—we could see tremendous changes in attitude and behavior, changes that would make a big difference in our lives.

"We are the ecosystem, and it's a part of us, internally and externally. The ecosystem is water, air, and earth, and we are water, air, and earth or minerals. Our frustration with the environment and all environmental issues is coming to reality now because we are beginning to realize that we are a part of our environment. We haven't been just killing Mother Earth, we have been killing ourselves. Now we need to heal Mother Earth and heal ourselves."

The New Cultural Medicine

J.T. regularly meets with native elders, not only from the Qualla Boundary but from around the country. They tell him that there has been a change in the last ten years. "During the seventies," he says, "their concerns were the harm that humans were doing to the Earth, and all the crime and social distress. I heard a lot of frustration in that. But as we entered the nineties, suddenly there was a new theme of concern for the Earth and getting back to the helper or protector role. There's an awakening around that. Even such large organizations as the Environmental Protection Agency are shifting from a purely scientific role to one of educating the public about what can be done to participate in protecting the environment. It's a different approach, and the elders are relating that, too.

"The other thing the elders see is a renewed growth in natural spirituality. It reminds me of the experience I had with the large white eagle in my vision, where its wings were spread over the people. What's coming about is not the gloom and doom you hear so much about, but a cleansing that is actually occurring now, and has been occurring over recent years. People getting together and sharing, by holding hands—even that's a cleansing process, and all this is coming about in a positive way. This new natural spirituality is going beyond the scope of the dogma of religion. It's a realization that we need to return to core spirituality, which encompasses everybody.

"I learned all the ancient beliefs, ways, and stories, and a system that almost seemed to outdate itself. Then, as Amoneeta Sequoyah passed on, I suddenly realized that there is this emergence now of what I call the new cultural medicine. This is a time for all systems of healing to come together in the traditional way of the Medicine Circle. There will emerge a new understanding of illness, disease, and healing that will enable patients or clients, families and healers, to share and make better choices. It will include healing through individual choices and self-care, as well as clinical or medical care.

"With the elders, I envision cultural healers, social services, and community providers merging their ways to improve social and family conditions, including approaches to drug and alcohol abuse, AIDS, and other maladies. What we need is a return to the Universal Circle used by Native Americans for talking, healing, and praying—bringing all people of all traditions back to the harmony and balance of family, clan, and tribe.

"An important part of this new cultural medicine will be remembering that the basic idea of worshiping the Sun was actually a way of getting in touch with the nerves—our own nerves, our own natural network. In other words, just as the Sun generates energy, we also generate energy—energy that isn't moving in just one direction. It's a similar thing with telephone lines. I've heard telephone workers say there's as much energy outside the wire as there is carried through the wire. Likewise, energy from the Sun is more than just ultraviolet rays; there is also energy for healing and for growth processes. We actually become a part of the network of healing energy through everything, including the forces of the Sun. Even the plants that we use as helpers, or medicine, get their energy from the Sun. There is that force, and there is a universal force that we are able to tap into for healing. We are in fact a part of the networking force that is the Universal Circle.

"The Sun is our beginning, and the new cultural medicine comes back to the Sun. People who understand the new cultural medicine recognize that we are part of this total energy. It's not just Indians, or the Sun Dance, or the Cherokee Green Corn Ceremony, but the emergence of people all over who are recognizing their 'Indianness,' recognizing that they are part of the total energy and the spirit of the past that will bridge to the future.

"In the nineties we are going to see a shift in dominance from the white culture to a culture of color. There will be a new consciousness that is in fact part of all of us, that we share with life on Mother Earth and nature itself. Therefore, all it takes is this thought, this willingness to come together, to create a difference. We can't create or destroy energy, but we can modify it. And that's how I see our role in the nineties: to modify the energy and bring us back to a level of harmony and balance. For me, that realization gets us past the level of gloom and doom and destruction to a renewed Earth. We really do have a role and a responsibility right now, and we can fulfill it.

"These are not things I am hoping for, but things I have seen already beginning to emerge. I have the deepest respect for our elders and the messages they bring to us. I know there are ways and teachings from our Indian traditions that will help us save Mother Earth, and also help us save ourselves from ourselves."

⟨⟨⟨⟨ ELEVEN ⟩⟩⟩⟩

The Sacred Roles of Women & Men
AMYLEE

*A*myLee, the Shieldmaker, She Who Catches Rainbows, is hardly an elder. She is a woman just entering mid-life, with bright eyes and tremendous vitality. But she is also a wisdom keeper. Born of Iroquois parents, AmyLee has, by circumstance, become the last woman in an ancient lineage of woodland Indian women who have practiced medicine ways.

At Hawk Hollow Nature Preserve, her medicine place in Tippecanoe, Ohio, she presides as a licensed rehabilitator of birds of prey. She also serves as a guide for two-leggeds (human beings) and shares the ancient healing ways.

AmyLee founded and directed the American Indian Rights Association at Kent State University, and has developed and conducted a series of American Indian values courses. She is also the director of a Native American resource center, and has appeared with Native American leaders and dignitaries such as Mad Bear, Rolling Thunder, Grandfather Sky Eagle, and Vernon Bellecourt.

A talented artist and a skilled fashioner of crafts, AmyLee has long, lush, reddish-brown hair that, when spread out, is evocative of her totem, the magnificent red-tailed hawk.

"My life doesn't compare to any elders," she says. "I've only lived a few years, and I would not even presume to sit in a circle with elders and talk about my life. I would listen to theirs. But as a point of reference, for someone to know where I come from, I'm the last in a long line of women who have been called to a medicine-way path, women of Iroquois lineage.

"Interestingly, the mothers in the lineage had only one daughter. Sometimes they would have only one child who was a daughter, sometimes they would have several sons but only one daughter. That way the medicine lineage has been handed down, mother to daughter. Now, this may be unique to our path or not—I don't know that much about other paths—but in our medicine ways the passing on of ritual and other wisdom from the elders skips every seventh generation. The woman of that seventh generation, she gets to go out and do other things. We vicariously watch her do that; she gets to do things that we don't get to do.

"I don't know how far back this lineage goes, but very far. I do know that my mother is one of the seventh-generation women, that the lineage skipped her generation. I am the first person in a new count of seven, but I am also the last generation of the whole lineage. It was foretold to me that I wouldn't have children, but I certainly feel I have free will about this. Also, I feel I do my best to align that free will with the greater will of the Creator, the Creation. And I don't see in Creation's plan that I should spend my energy putting it into one child. Instead, I have all these baskets of seeds that I have been gifted with from my grandmothers to hand out to other people, and that's my purpose and work."

A Good Way of Being

From early childhood, AmyLee was gradually exposed to the teachings and medicine of her elders. "It was pretty much passive. It wasn't, well, we're going to sit down and teach you this today. It was experiential—sometimes just observing ritual that I wasn't qualified to participate in, and other times even being the center of that ritual as I became a woman. I started my Moon times at age nine—I was into womanhood really early—so I got to participate in adult rituals at a very early age.

"I learned that medicine is simply a good way of being, a way of bringing things back into balance—that's what medicine is to us. And it's honoring those things when you're out of balance; it's honoring them to help bring you back into balance. I'd like to talk about some examples of that, but first let me offer some insight into the character of some of the elders in my life, for instance my great-great-grandmother's medicine ways.

"Great-Great-Grandma had three medicine bundles she kept by her door. One had medicine for her to give as a midwife, to help babies come into the world. Another had medicine to help those who were leaving the world; she wasn't pushing them out of the world, but she was helping their transition be graceful and peaceful. And the third bag had medicine for those who were still going to be in this world but had some major complaint about it—something hurt, or they were bleeding or out of balance. She lived alone. Most of the women in our family do live alone. Men leave because medicine women really don't have the ability to take care of men, but a medicine man usually needs a woman to take care of him.

"Great-Grandma, she had similar medicine. My own grandmother, though, her gift was with her hands, phenomenal hands. People from all cultures would come to her because by then we were off the reserve. Our family left the reservation when both alcohol and missionaries came. They didn't know which would be worse, but they didn't want any part of either one.

"My grandmother was a servant to people of all cultures and all colors, and was not a medicine woman just for our own people. People would come; I don't even know how they heard about it 'cause I was just a little kid, but my job was to help them up on the porch, to sit and wait, and to run and call them in. One by one they'd go in, and I saw her do everything with those hands, like zapping a wart, a big ugly growth—it wasn't really a wart, it was probably a cancer of some sort—off of a man's face. She just zapped it with her laserlike hands. In fact, my mother had a bad burn as a child, and Grandma zapped it and healed it. It was a major scar right down her face, but she only has the scar come out when she gets tired. It's very visible when she gets tired, but otherwise no one would ever see it.

"So anyway, this man's big growth got zapped, and my job as the apprentice at that time was to pick up that yucky thing that fell off and move it to a sacred space. I don't know anything about the American Medical Association and how they deal with medicine, but just think of how they'd do it. You know, they'd lance it and they'd do a biopsy and they'd freeze dry it or destroy it. And that would be it. The man would feel healed, and he'd pay a high bill and would go on his merry way not having really learned much from that experience, and the growth would wind up in the garbage heap. Then the source of that imbalance would have to find a new home in his body to teach him the lesson he didn't get to learn.

"With Grandma's way, my job was the yucky part—to carry that thing around and put it in a sacred space. She and he would sit together then, and they would work through ritual and discuss what that meant, what a teacher that growth was to him. He would leave there knowing that he could be grateful to that ugly growth, which was a major teacher to him. It taught him humility; it taught him to not judge people by appearances— you can imagine the things it taught him. And so it was my honor—it didn't seem it at the time—but it was my honor to help Grandma bury that thing out in the back, out in the field to release it and give it back to the Earth so it could go do other things, so it could become other things. That's just one of the kinds of things that Grandma's hands would do."

Her Own Healing

When AmyLee was between the ages of about twenty-one and twenty-three she entered a period of withdrawal and would not leave her house. Some people would call this condition agoraphobia. "I'm not real certain what pushed me into agoraphobia, and Indian medicine doesn't always have to dissect things and overanalyze them. I was content to live through it and to heal it as I was living through it. Quite possibly some would say I was pushed into it through different traumas, or the fact that my grandma had passed into spirit and I was staying in her home. Perhaps that was part of it. I really honestly don't know, and I would be very irritated for others to project onto me what they think pushed me into that time of solitude, because maybe it's the same thing as that growth on that man's face. Maybe it was my teaching, my teacher at that time.

"It lasted for a block of time. I can't even think of how long it was, but I did not go outside the house. I would go outside at night; night was fine 'cause no one would see me; I'd be invisible. At this time I lived in somewhat of a town and I didn't drive, so I'd order my groceries. I could call people on the phone but I couldn't answer the phone. I had an answering machine so I could hear their voices, and when I was ready and after I'd rehearsed, I could call them. I could tell them what I had to say, or I would leave notes, or I would write letters. I write great letters. And so I ran my life by mail and by telephone.

"I didn't think of myself as being on a medicine path at the time. I didn't know where I was. I just knew I was inside, and that's where I felt safe. But medicine is what pulled me through and restored the balance. That was a time of great, heightened creativity, when different art was emerging for me. The art felt hideous at times. It was then, at the darkest moment, that I looked at the art, and it was ugly and isolated and lonely. I don't know why, but I hadn't looked in the mirror for a long time. But then I looked in the mirror and I had started to look like that, too. Such a moment is usually the first flash before you get the light turned on.

"I didn't know which came first, and it didn't really matter—I just knew I wanted to heal both of those images real quick. I didn't want anyone to ever see that art and think it would come through me, nor did I want to look into that mirror and have anyone else see what I had seen. The art was powerful and potent, too, because it wasn't simply doodlings and scribblings. They had medicine in them, and that's why I didn't know what to do with them. And so the way I started to heal was by making Medicine Wheels and putting pictures of what I wanted inside of them. That turned it around. So I don't know which came first, the picture or the ugliness that I saw. Maybe the ugliness wasn't there except in my perception. I don't know; it doesn't matter. But I restored balance to myself by creating beauty again through art, and then somehow or other it came back to me.

"I had tried to get out. It wasn't a total isolation before. I had tried. I would rehearse in my mind, 'Yes, I can do it, I can go enroll in class,' because I hadn't finished college. I visualized walking across the street and going down to the college. And I would even get dressed and get down to the end of the street. But just a gust of wind or something small would send panic through me, and I would run right back and lock the doors and not be seen for a month or so. So there were tense times. I registered for classes by mail, every quarter, but I never made it. I dropped the classes by mail, too.

"I studied at Kent State in Ohio, and I went to the State University of New York, too, but Kent State primarily. My major was peaceful change. The incident with the National Guard at Kent State changed my life; it changed a lot of our lives, Kent State did. It was almost a defiant act on my part to go to Kent State in the summer, the day that it reopened after having been closed because of the killings. I remember thinking—the warrior in me thought—'Yes, it's OK. I'm willing to put my life on the line.' You know, you're overdramatic about it at that age, but it was a valiant move to step out on that campus."

Like the Last Dinosaur

As the last woman in a long line of Iroquois medicine women, AmyLee is carefully and deliberately opening the medicine bundles of her family tradition to give the contents away. "I simply accept invitations to share, to share whatever ways and wisdom I've been loaned. My main task and responsibility, being the caboose, the end of the lineage, is to take all the baskets that I've been given and inherited—some very physical and tangible, some not, filled with all the gifts of the grandmothers, the seeds—then carefully, selectively to reach my hand in there and plant those seeds in different places. Some are never going to germinate, some are just going to be there in the ground, and yet some will grow in different hearts and they'll grow in a different way. They'll become hybrid. What I share with nonnatives in particular, those seeds will be nurtured by their ways, by their energies, their genes, their culture. And so they'll grow a different plant, and yet that's part of the changing times, too, to grow different plants to feed a different people now.

"I truly believe—and this is the saddest thing, bittersweet if you go a step beyond what's immediately visible—I truly do believe that Native American Indians are not only an endangered species but one that is on the brink of extinction. I know the Peregrine Falcon made a U-turn and came back, and yet I wonder about that and the analogy to us. The Peregrine Falcons, the ones that are now descendants that are making the comeback, they came from parents who were in captivity. There's something changed about them. And I wonder if maybe they were ready to go on to another dimension and we stopped that. Just like I wonder if maybe we've pushed whole groups on to another place by our carelessness, too. We know one species of plant or animal checks out of this planet every hour, becomes extinct, mainly because of our influence, our impact.

"We're going to find ourselves alone some morning. We're going to wake up and there won't be birds and there won't be air to breathe and there won't be anything left. So you see, I probably look at this world a lot differently being the last in a lineage, because I'm not going to give birth to a child that I'm going to be worried about when I'm gone, and although I'll be concerned about all of the world's children, it's a different feeling. I look around and walk around this world like a dinosaur sometimes, like the last Brontosaurus must have felt, stomping around and munching some leaves and looking at some of the other species moving on to other dimensions. 'There goes Tyrannosaurus Rex'—that's how I feel.

"One thing that is central to any sharing I offer is honoring the appropriateness of medicine in specific places. Native American Indian medicine, religion, spirituality, is based on the Earth. It astounds me, sometimes appalls me, that more people today haven't reflected on that. They travel all around picking up shards of our religion, and the tattered fragments of our ways, and sometimes whole bundles of our ways, and then sometimes they transplant them to where they are.

"But I'm not certain that was ever part of the Original Instruction and intention for these medicine ways—that they be able to be transplanted. I look at the harsh, hot, fiery, jagged, painful Plains Indian Medicine, and that is so appropriate for the harsh, hot, jagged environment they have in the Plains. They need that kind of medicine there. And yet I look at the lush, deep woodland medicine of my people, and if we were to transplant my medicine to the Southwest, say Arizona, it probably wouldn't even be noticed. It would evaporate. That doesn't mean that our medicine ways as woodland Indians are less effective or less powerful, or are weak; it's rather that it's the strongest and most appropriate medicine for the woodlands. If you try to transplant the hot and jagged Plains Indian Medicine into our woodlands, then you start fires and create trauma by trying to force that harsh way into the lushness. To try to transplant medicine from one place on the continent, or planet, is not always the appropriate thing to do.

"So, ever present in my mind and heart when I share is a question: Is this way going to work here? Will it transplant here? Not only does it have to jump from one culture to another, it has to jump from one region to another. And I'm not sure that's a fair expectation of medicine."

We're Here by Invitation

AmyLee has many insightful observations to share about conception, birth, and abortion. "Some of the medicine seeds I've planted include reminding women that not only our responsibilities but our joys of life are because we are women on a female planet. Some women think, 'What's that mean, female planet?' But they've been calling her Mother Earth all their lives. I usually share that with women in a context of the seasons and the rituals that women caretake. I also remind them that, in our teaching, every man who's here is here by invitation of a woman, because a woman can't conceive unless on some level she gives permission to that soul who's knocking at the door to come on in.

"So, you're here by invitation. You should feel good. You should feel welcome here. This happens for all of us. I show this to women who haven't put that together yet, who've been really angry at men. Remember that you are here by invitation. And so that's the starting place. The other issue that's of great concern to me is the irresponsibility that I've seen, and part of it's just a backlash from the so-called sexual revolution.

"We've forgotten the sacraments and the sacredness of certain things, and certainly sex and procreation would be among them. We seem to have forgotten the sacred part of those things conveniently so our egos could play around and enjoy some things. But it's got to come back into balance. The symptoms we're seeing that are highly out of balance are horrific: the statistics on abortion, all of the new diseases, all of the sexually transmitted diseases, and the increasing rapes. They really are sexual. I know that in a way they're not crimes of sex, they're crimes of violence, but they're sexual, too.

"All this imbalance has got to change, and I think women are going to be very instrumental in bringing change, bringing it back into balance. We have to be, because we're the ones who are the Earth, and the men are here by invitation. We have to set the scene for that as we have set the scene for so many other things. We can't complain about the way men are; we raised them. So I remind women of that responsibility, help them see it and accept it. It goes even beyond that, too, to reminding them that if you believe a soul is invited in through you, which we do believe, then once it's in that mother, that vehicle to its physical existence, the soul calls all the shots for however long it's within the womb. The incoming soul might make that woman go eat pickles and ice cream, or encourage her to go to Lamaze class, or seek out a midwife, or even have an abortion.

"Usually women are in shock when they hear that, because they're thinking about all the pretty things: 'Oh my baby wants to love me, wants me to knit booties or to make little moccasins.' And then, 'Well, my sister had an abortion. How dare she?' But could it be that the baby's soul asked her to do that? Women in the group will just start sobbing when they think the soul might have had something to do with it, because they're carrying all this guilt around that the abortion was their decision alone.

"But on the other hand, just because it was the soul's decision to come in and be aborted, this doesn't alleviate the burden of responsibility. There's so many different levels. Let's just take one at a time. Two ought to cover most lessons of this. So the soul chooses the parents, the genetic structure, and it calls all the shots, and the woman's ego is pretty much on hold. She may not know that. She may think she is just acting responsible by eating tofu and going for that walk every day. But when she makes the agreement in whatever dimension that is with the incoming soul, she willingly makes the agreement: Yes, I'll be the vehicle to give you physical existence. I'll loan you my blood, my tissue; you can even share my heart until you have a heart of your own. And all these things will be yours.' The problem comes when the baby is born and the women sometimes forget to claim their power back again. They still let that little life outside of their womb call all the shots. And it gets very uncomfortable for everybody and gives that other soul unfair control—sets them up for some hard lessons.

"I needed to clarify that because otherwise it sounds like I'm gung-ho on abortion clinics, and I'm not. But on the other hand, it does help women who are still carrying that guilt around with them, because it's never too late to have that funeral service, that releasing and grieving ceremony. I encourage women to do that, whether or not they ever got to wrap the fetus in a bundle and bury it in their own custom. Even if it's years later, you can still talk to that soul, and many of the women already have. They don't need me to tell them that. They've even had two-way conversations with the soul of the fetus they carried, and have seen the soul come into physical existence through somebody else; they free themselves at a later time. So some women are aware of these things, but so many other women seem to be seeking permission and confirmation. That's what they're hungriest for. There isn't really anything else I can offer them except encouragement and confirmation of stuff that they've already been feeling and thinking and dreaming.

"I'm certainly not an advocate of abortion. Some people will say, 'Well, why would a soul choose to come in and just be aborted in the first trimester or the second trimester? Why would a soul choose that? Why would a soul choose to come into an alcoholic family or an abusive family or a minority? Why would a soul choose anything? Why would a soul choose you? Why would we choose to learn the lessons we need to learn? There's always more than one reason for everything, and once we can remember that it makes life a lot easier. But one reason, perhaps, that all these souls are coming in and being aborted, is that maybe this is their give-away to us as women to remind us to stop playing this foolish game on ourselves. Women go to abortion clinics and pretend that it isn't a life they're giving up. They pretend they're just sloughing off the lining of their uterus, that it just isn't real, that life doesn't happen until the first breath, like some people have said, or it was not really a baby—it wasn't really a soul after all. They're playing those games on themselves.

"Maybe these souls are coming in and bringing this horrible awareness to us, a necessary awareness of the horrible ways these things are done—how those bodies, the little bodies, are just cast off with no honor, no burial, no sacraments offered to that soul. So maybe that's one reason why a soul would choose to be aborted, to be a teacher to us, to remind us that's not the way to be.

"Truly, the way is not birth control. It's conception control. That's the original intention and instruction. Just talk to that soul, and either you open the door to it or you don't open the door. It makes so much more sense. I'm not even sure you could use the word control. You could call it intelligent conception, or willful conception, or even consensual conception—I like that one. It would be by consent, not just to that woman and that incoming soul, but also to that man, who's playing an important part, too."

Distorted Sacraments

As she travels around the country teaching, AmyLee offers lessons on many themes, including the creation of new life. "The honorable way for a man and a woman to join and create new life, a baby, would of course be for them both to invite that soul to come though. Sometimes though, one or the other does that without the other's knowledge. The woman dreams the baby, invites the baby, and the man's just having a good time. On the conscious level people often feel they are just getting together to have a good time. But certainly on another level the woman has to give permission.

"For consensual conception, there is a lovely and gentle ritual for either inviting a soul in or for making sure that no souls come in. The ritual involves mental dialogue with all souls that are in the area, and also connection with each other so you can sensitively read the other person enough to know if there is a weak moment. You can both agree, 'Oh, we're not going to have any kids, not ever, or at least not in this decade. We both agree, and we're meditating on it, and we're talking to you right now, soul; we don't want to do it.' And yet in the moment of that rush, that burst of sexual energy, one of them might think, Oh, we could create a baby,' or 'He'd have your eyes or your hair,' and then the doors open. So it would have to take people really working together to know each other well enough to be sensitive to those moments when the door would open, and to cover the door quickly.

"I think this is one vehicle to get us to remember that we are the creators when there is sexual union. I think that's one reason a lot of us seek that, and crave it, too. We all know that there are many drives to bring men and women together. But at one time sexual union was a sacrament. Lots of sacraments have been so distorted. Look at the tobacco sacrament; now people are poisoning themselves with it. Look at wine as a sacrament; it's become a poison to my people. So sacraments have been misused, but they retain their power, and to get our attention they're going to wreak havoc in us until we restore their honor; honor them and acknowledge what they are.

"So the tobacco is going to keep giving us cancer and polluting our air; it will give us cancer even if we don't smoke, if we're sitting in the same restaurant. It's going to keep doing that until we remember it's a sacrament and use it in prayers. Iroquois men saying a prayer do not take the tobacco smoke in their bodies. They put their prayer into the smoke and then they puff it outside their bodies. Also, we need to restore the rightful place of sacrament to the wine—to alcohol, too—so it will cease to make us drunken idiots, fools, drunken drivers, alcoholics, and the other things that come from that. Same thing with sex. We've used it and misused it in the same way, for self-gratification of things other than our highest purpose, our connection with the Creator.

"When there is that moment of intensity in the sexual exchange, you feel a closeness to Creation, to the Creator. And so it would seem natural to savor that moment, and to prepare for that time, and to treat it as a holy time. That doesn't mean you have any less sexual drive. Probably more so, because all levels of you are intimately involved in that exchange: not just a body, not just an ego, not just a mind, not just an emotion, but all, the whole package."

Sacred Moon Time

"One of the sharings I offer concerns sacred Moon time. It helps women so much, because they're still the daughters of the generation that called it 'the curse,' or didn't call it anything at all. They didn't talk about it. Just buy a girl a box of sanitary napkins and she begins to think her Moon cycle isn't sanitary. All kinds of hurtful ideas. One of my favorite rituals to do when I first get women together to talk in the Moon Lodge, or in a gathering about Moon time, is we close our two eyes, and we open our third eye. Then we all go back to a sacred place in our childhood, a special place where we're comfortable, and we gather something from that place to weave a basket. In our mind's eye we bring that something back — it might be moss or clay or grapevines or willow or sweet grass or whatever. We'll bring something in the mind to weave an invisible (to many) basket before us.

"Then we start to fill that basket. I take them back to their first impression, the first time they ever found out about menstruation. Was it the word, was it a health class, was it seeing blood on another's panties? What was their first impression? We go so far back, then, with vibration and sound, to those thoughts and memories and different experiences, and use them to fill this basket. We move through their own era, from their first remembrances of hearing about the Moon cycle to recollections of their own personal experiences. We go over everything, from PMS and Cathy Rigby playing tennis in a white outfit when she's on her Moon time, to not being allowed into the sweatlodges when they're on their Moon time. All the feelings that they have about these things. Then we just run through the vocabulary associated with Moon time: 'on the rag, tampons, fell off the roof, curse' — all these things. It's incredible.

"So the basket is overwhelmingly full and brimming to the top. That's their giveaway, so they can clear out all the old things they've been hanging onto about their experience of being a woman on this planet. Then they can really hear what I'm offering them about Moon time. They can pick things out of the basket if they want them back, but they also have the freedom to give them away, to empty some part of themselves. Then they can receive new information in a nice, open, receptive space instead of trying to figure out, 'Well, how can I insert that information AmyLee's giving me about the sacredness of Moon time? How does that fit in with the idea of the curse?' So they have the giveaway, and then they can also receive back. And it's a marvelous experience, too. It's never the same twice. Then the women proceed to share briefly about Moon time, about how the natural flow of women is twofold. One flow is energy from the Earth Mother. It moves up in a spiral through women and goes around to Grandma Moon, and then it flows back down through us. We are columns conducting the energy through Grandma and Mom, back and forth. It's a twofold flow.

"I remind women that during their Moon time there are apertures in that column, that spiral, and the energy from Mother Earth and from Grandma Moon starts coming out and spiraling in these apertures, which is why we move to a Moon Lodge at that time. Where there's an opening, where there's a door, an aperture, the intention is for Mother Earth's and Grandmother Moon's energy and that woman's energy to whoosh out of there—to be released. But where there's an open door, things try to enter as well. And so to protect ourselves, and so that the original intention of Moon time can be honored, we withdraw from the world and go to a Moon Lodge, where other women can care for us and we can be nurtured.

"The intention of Moon time is not 'cause there's no baby in there (excuse the double negative)—it's not just because it's empty in there so all that blood's wasted and just sloughs out. That's not the reason. In fact, it's the other way around. It's hard to describe to another culture, but a woman's primary responsibility is to be a conductor of the energy flowing between the Earth and the Moon. We give over our own will for a period of time, literally a period of time, each month. That's where that word, period, comes from.

"So we give over our free will at that time, and then those things are cleansed—not that we're dirty, it doesn't mean that we're dirty, but removed and freed from us for another cycle. So what happens when a woman invites a soul into her to become pregnant is that she gets time off from those other obligations between Earth and Moon. Then all those energies, including blood and tissue and other energies, can go to building a baby. She doesn't have those apertures opening."

The Making of Shields

Another of the inherited seeds that AmyLee is sharing in this lifetime is the tradition of the shields. She is, in fact, known as The Shieldmaker.

What is a shield? It's more, AmyLee says, than a beautiful disk made of wood and leather. She says the starting point in understanding shields is to acknowledge that "all life is created out of dancing Medicine Wheels—medicine meaning "good," wheel meaning "round thing." Scientists might call these Medicine Wheels atoms or electrons or something else. Some of these Medicine Wheels are very fluid, some are hard, some are gaseous—all the different elements. Some of these Medicine Wheels dance together to create shields. There are shields that some would call etheric shields; then there are physical shields. Our corneas are shields, our skin is a shield, our aura or energy field is a shield, our eyelids are shields, the ozone layer is a shield. So there are shields everywhere, and they serve different purposes. A shield doesn't mean necessarily to block out— sometimes it's to reflect back to those who would behold the shield. Sometimes shields are mirrors. Sometimes they are symbols of the person holding or wearing the shield, to let other people know the essence that the person wants them to know. There are probably other essences, too, that are on the backside of the shield. Just as when one wears a mask: it isn't what the mask looks like when you are looking at it, it's what the world looks like when you are looking through the mask. Well, a shield has more than one side as well. So it's in the eye of the beholder, but it's also in the heart of the shield-holder, the shield-wearer.

"I waited a long time before I began to share the medicine of the shields with women across the continent, because I thought, 'It won't work there. It's only for the woodlands.' But I carefully put out my toe in the big water several years ago, and began to share with a group of women I had known for a while."

Then in 1989, at summer solstice, AmyLee created an invitation to any

women who were interested in joining her in a year-long dance of ceremony and ritual to earn the right to build their own shields. Although she
printed only two hundred invitations, over one thousand women from
around the United States and Canada responded.

The making of the shield takes over a year of intense study and preparation. "The women of this shield circle—over one thousand of them—
each express their own unique intentions, and they go the full gamut, from
wanting prosperity, to wanting a partner, to wanting and needing comple-
tion with family, to wanting a baby. So far, so good. We're really doing well
with women getting their intentions fulfilled—more quickly than I would
have guessed. The shield-making process is on a seasonal basis, and by a
lunar system. They receive from me, via the mail, the suggested rituals, the
intention for those rituals, options of ways to do them, and a story showing perhaps how the ritual came into being or how it was tended in my
lineage.

"After this year-long process of preparation, we meet regionally. We
gather together to earn the right to build the physical shield, starting with
the hoop. By daybreak, after drumming and dancing and singing all night
with the hoops, the women give birth to their shields. My job is as midwife
to the women, to help them give birth.

"Shields are living. For several Moon cycles, as the women give birth
to them, they are almost like newborns. They are demanding, and they
want attention, and they want certain things tied on them, and certain
things taken off of them, and they want to be hung in a certain place. Then
you sit there and look at them and think, 'Well, it's just leather and wood,
and what am I doing with this? And then all of a sudden it becomes so
incredibly potent that you can't deny its energy. After a time of the woman
taking care of the shield, the shield begins to take care of the woman. It
takes care of the woman in many ways—perhaps as a mirror she can look
into as a reflection of her own potency, power, prominence, and effective-
ness. It also tangibly symbolizes whatever her intention was, which will
help create it. By putting these things in symbolic form, by earning the right
through the slow dance of ritual that lasts a year long, by moving in that
honorable way, that precisely directed way, each of the symbols on the
shield becomes a powerful invitation, or invocation, for the fruition of
the intention.

"Shields do not last forever. Most shields have their own life span. When the person is healed, the shield is released to do other things. How rude to keep medicine objects contained and restrained in one static form after their work is done. We let them go on to other places to do other things, whether it be hanging it outside in a tree to let the wind and the rain claim it again, or disassembling parts of it and giving it away, or giving it to each of the elements—burying some, burning some, putting it in the water, and letting the winds carry the rest.

"I think of the turtle and Turtle Island [North America], and her many shields. I think how those shields, the tectonic plates, shift and move. This is what we are seeing with all the many shields and Earth changes. I dreamed of Grandma Turtle and all her shields moving around, and all these women moving their shields on her, and then all the other shields moving like one big chiropractic convention as the energy shifts and gets into alignment for this next round in the world's evolution, this next dance."

Women's Purpose, Men's Purpose

"A woman's intention for being here is to be a nurturer—to nurture herself first, so she can continue to nurture children, lovers, elders, the Earth, and everything beyond. Men's purpose for being here is to protect themselves, us, the past, the future, everything. They protect the past by accurately remembering it and by sharing it appropriately. And they protect the future by protecting the environment so there can be a future. Also, men's purpose is to protect the present, to protect women, to protect the Earth, to protect themselves. It's easy to see that we are far out of balance with that.

"Now women feel that we need to protect ourselves, that we have to do the men's job, that we need to protect ourselves from our protectors. We're busy doing that, busy carrying little cans of mace, taking courses to protect ourselves, wearing those T-shirts, marching down the streets to take back the night. All of these things are protecting ourselves from our protectors. Well, then, where does the nurturing go? Some of us stop nurturing ourselves first and just go into the protector mode, and we continue to nurture the children, or whatever we're doing on our job, or whatever. Some of us stop nurturing men altogether. Some stop nurturing children or are abusive to them, and some just stop nurturing and just get into a protective mode. Some don't know how to protect, but they can't have anything left within to nurture if they're just abused and empty women, if they are beaten and maimed women. They have had no one to protect them, and they were never taught how to nurture. Women haven't got it in them to nurture because they weren't protected. If we can get back to the place where men remember to protect and women remember to nurture, that's where balance will be.

"Beyond my own lineage, this is something that Iroquois children are guided or groomed with. The Iroquois don't raise children, they raise corn. You guide children. So I would say then that I was guided to think of these things: to expect any boy, any male, any man, to always protect me, and as a woman I would always nurture. So it's a shock to a woman when the protection isn't there. And that's what so many women are wrestling with now. And men have to deal with the backlash of that, whether they've been protecting us or not.

"Just as it's important for men to let go as gracefully as they can of prominence in this world, it's important that women get ready to accept the pendulum of responsibility and power. It's swinging our way. There's a role of prominence, and as I understand it, female energy is emerging and will be the prominent force for some time, just as male energy has been for some time. It's important that we get ready to do that in an honorable way. The last time women had the prominence we were not necessarily that honorable about it. Certainly in times of transition, when power pendulums are swinging from one side to the other, there can be chaos and exaggerated pain and more disparity than the norm. And so perhaps now, in this small way, I am preparing, guiding women to get ready to receive the role of prominence, the prominent energy of the planet for the next cycle.

"So many women say, 'I don't want to be prominent or superior or the head; I want equality. I want to be equal with men.' Well, we always have been; they always have been with us. It's just that we haven't earned the right to live that yet. Because in order to be equal, we must know that we can trust the left foot to lead and the right foot to follow, or the right foot to lead and the left foot to follow. We must know that we can trust men, and men must know that they can trust us. And we need to know that we can trust ourselves. So we haven't earned the right to walk side by side yet. It's going to be a while, too. The dance has just begun."

When There Are Trails on the Face

"Every day should be a thanksgiving, of course. When you wake up, give thanks for that day. But then there are personal holidays. Each woman would have two. One is the sacred Moon time when she is initiated as a woman, when the little girl becomes a woman and the aunties get together and welcome her. But it doesn't end there, because there's also a holiday when the woman becomes the grandmother or the clan mother, when she ceases the Moon times, when she is no longer visited by Grandma Moon but becomes Grandma Moon instead of Mother Earth. When she becomes grandmother, then there's a holiday or holy day of honoring her for becoming that wise woman.

"I think it's important, and I encourage women, whether or not they've ever had aunties, to get together and surprise each other with a feast and games and gifts and responsibilities and songs and dances. Whether they ever had that when they became a woman, I think it's important. They can't really move into that clan-mother stage of life, grandmotherhood, without going back far enough to honor that they even became a woman to begin with. They can't just honor that grandma if they haven't honored the child who became the woman. You have to go back to that somehow, whether it's in a journal, or writing it out, or in a fantasy, or in dream, or in a painting. There needs to be some way to go back there, or to have friends come by and bring gifts, little-kid gifts to honor the little girl when she was changing, merging, and emerging into womanhood. I encourage women to do that for themselves, and to get the support of other sisters. Then when it comes time for menopause, we can have our parties and celebrations.

"If I could just pull one thing from my culture right now, if I could just give one gift, it would be the experience of how the most cherished members of our families are the old women. The older she gets the more revered she is. She becomes the clan mother, and the clan mother picks the chief. The clan mother also impeaches that chief if she doesn't like what he's doing. That's the wisest woman and most revered woman.

"If I could just give that to all women and men—to remember that. When there's snow up here on the top of the head, to honor that. That white hair means she's been somewhere, and obviously learned something. When there are paths and trails on the face, those are the trails that show where she went, what she learned, what she's done with her life. They aren't wrinkles that need an injection of silicone or whatever. Women need to remember this themselves, and to remember that men reflect it back to us. Remember this and respect it. That's what I want to give all women."

TWELVE

Massapowau for the People of the Morning Light
SLOW TURTLE

As executive director of the Massachusetts Commission on Indian Affairs (MCIA), John Peters is often called upon to wear a suit and tie, to sit behind a desk, and to negotiate with the governor and legislature. While he has a marked antipathy toward governments, taxes, and bureaucracies, he also recognizes that this is an important part of his medicine path in service to the Indian people.

However, the position of government official is only one of the roles he fills. He is also the supreme medicine man for the Wampanoag Nation—the People of the First Light. His title is Massapowau. In the Wampanoag language, *massa* means "big," as in Massachusetts; and *powau* designates the person who brings the people together. In recognition of this role, over his tie he wears a green soapstone carving of a turtle on a thong with seven beads. The beads signify the seven future generations of children who will be born on this land and his responsibility to think of them when he makes a decision.

In his role as Massapowau, which frequently blends with his governmental responsibilities, he counsels Indian people and presides over ceremonies. Though he shoulders many roles and responsibilities and is in constant demand, like the turtle, he is noted for his patience and careful deliberation.

When John Peters was about fourteen, in the mid-1940s, the elders of the Mashpee Wampanoag Nation decided that it was about time for him to get his Indian name. They made a ceremony and called him Slow Turtle. "They gave me that name," he explains, "because I was very slow responding when talking about things, and I moved slow. They thought that was a wise thing to do. At that point it was a description of me and the way I moved, and I guess you could say things had to be methodical for me. A turtle, well, he has a certain procedure before he even moves. He sticks his head out and checks everything out, and then he makes his move, so he has some attributes about him that you have to really look at.

"I'm the guy who gives those names out now, because I'm in that position, and that's how we name people. We sum up their characteristics and how they portray them out there in the world. So it's easier for me to remember that person by this name than by some Christian name that has no meaning whatsoever for us anyhow. The name to us is very special because each one of us has our individual name, like our own individual spirit."

Slow Turtle grew up in Mashpee, Massachusetts, where he studied with a medicine man named William James. They worked on a road crew together during the Second World War, when Slow Turtle was about fourteen or fifteen. James taught him about nature, plant life, preparing herbs, and also about people and the stories of creation.

Several years after completing the ninth grade, Slow Turtle became a police officer, a profession he remained with for ten years. After leaving the police force, he spent a year in Hawaii as a private investigator. While there, he saw a parallel in the campaigns the native Hawaiians and the Wampanoags were waging to control their lands. Later, while working on the construction of an airport on the island of Nantucket off the coast of Massachusetts, he received a sign from Spirit to return to Mashpee and to his people. Eventually he began to do 'Indian work,' as he calls it, full time. He was appointed the executive director of the MCIA in 1979.

One of sixteen major New England tribes, the Mashpee Wampanoag Nation has some 1,300 members, although less than four hundred still live by the sea in Mashpee on Cape Cod. Even Slow Turtle and his family, because of the demands of his work, have moved from Mashpee into Chelsea, a city tucked close to Boston in the heart of modern Massachusetts. Still though, through powwows and other tribal gatherings, they connect with their people and with Native Americans from as far away as the Southwest, Canada, and even Peru. "To lose one's culture is a dangerous thing," Slow Turtle says. "The whole concept of the powwow is people coming together in a unity circle sharing with each other—sharing a spiritual feeling, recognition and respect for the Earth and each other."

"Most of my involvement is with the Indian people and their purpose in life. I think the intentions of my people are entirely different from what mainstream society promotes. We're not here for private gain, but to find a solution to preserve the Earth Mother for all generations to come."

Slow Turtle is married to a strong woman, Burne Stanley, who shares responsibilities with him at the Commission on Indian Affairs. Their youngest child, who arrived after eight children, twelve grandchildren, and one great-grandchild, was named Autaquway, an Algonquian word for "the end."

When the state government steadily cut back on the MCIA's already meager budget in 1989 and 1990, Slow Turtle and Burne, along with others, founded the Massachusetts Center for Native American Awareness, a not-for-profit charitable organization established to serve the cultural, social, and spiritual needs of the Native American people.

They've Removed the Spirit from Government

Slow Turtle has strong feelings about the way Native Americans are still caricatured with stereotypes. "I mean, hell, I was over in London, and I got off a boat over there, and I come into the terminal and there was a big cartoon sign up there, 'Come to America and see all the Indians dance.' There were cartoon Indians all doing a dance. I say America is no good. I mean, this is the attitude of the people in America. In this day and age, this Indian is still out there because the European people don't know any different, some of them, and they'll be coming here looking for this naked Indian with his loin cloth and a tomahawk, out there dancing. And, you know, that was an advertisement done by an American from America for an American company. It was the airlines that were going to bring these Europeans over to see these Indians out here dancing. That really hurt me to be away in London and see that. How far will they go with their rhetoric and their racist attitudes, their prejudice?

"I have an opportunity to speak to a lot of foreign students that come here to Boston and go to universities and colleges, and I look at them and I say, 'I want to explain to you about being an American.' And I say, 'The only way you can become an American is to get rid of your culture, because you can't bring your culture here and really use it. It's not allowed.' America has no culture, really. If you try and exercise some of your ancestor's ways, they'll shoot you down, because that's not the way of the system. We'll always end up in limbo in this country because they have no respect for my culture; there's no respect for any culture.

"You see, we had democracy here before the Europeans came, but we had spirituality in our democracy. We had respect for each other, respect for differences in other people's ways of life. They don't allow for that in this system. They have removed the spirit out of democracy, so it can never work right, because there's no respect.

"In the native way, each one of us has our own spirit, so each one of us is different. With your democracy, you're talking about us all going down the same road, you know, reading the same prayer. When you go to your churches you all read the same prayer, someone else's prayer. In our way, in our spiritual way, you have to speak your own prayer; you have to make your own prayer. You don't use my prayer because that would be disrespecting me. It has to be your own words, your thoughts and feelings that are put into your prayer, not mine. We don't read each other's scriptures and say, 'Well, you know, this is what is said.' We understand in our way that every day is a new day. And life continues on. It doesn't stop.

"I don't know whether it will ever change in this country because we're going right back to the old European style. Every day I'm reminded of that. They've gone right back to the king days and dictator days here in this country. You've got a power structure here; you've got the pyramid type of government. The native people of this land, our form of government was always in a circle. There was never a hierarchy. And so we all considered each other equals. No one was ever greater or lesser than the other person. It didn't matter what kind of job you've got. It doesn't matter that I'm a medicine man—I'm no greater than anyone else, and I understand that. I just have a position. So we don't have that hierarchy situation, and for that reason we don't have the competition and the jealousies, and all that goes with it. And we don't have the fears, you know, that the rest of society has out there, and the anxieties, and all of those kinds of things where you have a few people at the top who have it all, and the rest are always wanting something that they don't have.

"That's what's happened here. You've gone right back to the same old days of the king, where the royalty had everything. When the Europeans came here and looked around to see how we operated, a lot of people liked the system. In fact, the natives here taught the Europeans how to establish a township that no one person had control of, where everybody had a voice in the community. That's the way our people are. Everyone has a voice in the community, and what goes on there. Because of Europe, the new-comers didn't know anything about a township. They didn't own anything in Europe, and they didn't have control over anything, so when they got here they didn't know how to run a town.

"Passaconaway, a great chief, he sat them all down and said, 'If you want to come into this area, you have to abide by the regulation, and that's that there will be no one person who makes the decisions. All of you have to make the decisions about what goes on in the community.' And so I credit Passaconaway as one who started townships where everyone had a voice in their community. That was a new thing to the Europeans. They weren't accustomed to that."

People of the First Light

"It's very special to be one of the People of the First Light," Slow Turtle says, "because you are on the spiritual land, in the area where for thousands of years your people have been—land in the forest and near the ocean. And so you are really connected. You have a base, and you have a connection. You've got the elements, and you're proud of it. Your ancestors are there. They've acknowledged all the same things that you've acknowledged out there. So it's a carryover sort of thing that's continuous, because if it's there for me it will be there for my great-grandchildren. Those kinds of things leave a good feeling. But today there's a question in our minds whether those same things will be there for our great-grand-children. We've seen a different kind of animal come in that doesn't have the same connection that we have, and so there's a question: Do we have the time to turn it around and get him to look at reality and look at what's happening?.

"I think this is it. This is the last go around. I used to kind of condemn my people for not taking the time to try and teach the white man about what's real out there, knowing he lives in a fantasy world and knowing the things that he holds dearest to him have no connection to reality. I mean, they are just a dream. His wealth is nothing, and amounts to nothing. The green paper's got no value, and he doesn't understand that. When you remove love and try to replace it with monetary things, you've got nothing. The whole thing is to try to love himself again, and get him to understand that he has to love himself before he can love anything else.

"To turn the white man around and give him that kind of information is really difficult. But we took on the role. We do a great number of programs in prisons. We went after the best of your lot. We went into the prisons and we laid our program out to those in there and we told them that it's a spiritual program. We're not a religion, because religion is institutionalized and it's designed to control people, and that's not what we're about. And so we came in with a spiritual program and said, 'The first thing that we want you to understand is that spirit has no color or race to it. It doesn't matter whether your skin is white, black, red, Hispanic, whatever. No one out there is any better than you, and you are no better than any one else out there.' And they begin to look at that. That's something to think about."

Since about 1984, Slow Turtle has joined with two close friends, Medicine Story and Wildcat, to pay regular visits to prisons in Massachusetts, Connecticut, Vermont, New Hampshire, and Pennsylvania. The visits are called the Native American Prison Program, but they are open to people of all races and religions. The programs often involve what are called Truth Circles, where the inmates sit in a circle and pass a talking stick, speaking what is in their hearts to the circle of men who have gathered. This simple approach of sitting and speaking what is in the heart is highly effective, possibly because the tradition of truth is largely absent from mainstream culture. The men feel the respect of the equality and the moments of truth, and they open up.

Sometimes the prison program includes a sweatlodge ceremony for purification, and sometimes guests come in to talk about something like manufacturing, physical therapy, or counseling. "We try to show that everyone has a special gift given to them," Slow Turtle explains. "We try to open minds to the notion that there are many avenues in life to examine and explore. That way, when it's time to make a decision, they can tap into the other avenues of experience they have explored.

"Why do we go into the prisons? To hit them; to begin to get them to take a whole different outlook on life and what life's all about. And to develop a way to get them to promote love within themselves, to get them to understand and find out who they are. 'Cause the people out here don't know who they are. They have no idea of who they are. The average guy on the street, he has no idea of who he is. He doesn't know why he's here. He has no purpose for being here. I mean, he can't appreciate the Sun up, or the Moon, or anything, because he don't see dollars and cents on it. And he can't appreciate a tree or an animal talking to you or something, you know, because he's so far removed from that, and he's become a loner, you know, he's all by himself. He's become engrossed with himself, and generally with his own anger, and that has driven him into thinking that he's someone cute. They think they're smart and intelligent, you know, and that's what tickles me. They really think they're smart.

"When I sit in prisons in a circle of men, I find that they are human beings. They are people that have been disregarded and trashed, but I find a lot of love and beauty in there, a lot of respect. I've seen people turn around from mean, real haters, to real loving people who are able to start communicating with people that they hated. And they don't know why they hated them, but now they're communicating with them and that's really something. When I see them start to interact with their families again, I know that they're on the road. They're really working on coming together. And the thing that happens is that most of these people who take this program and leave the prison and get on the outside try to start the same kind of circles out there in their communities, because they now have found out it's a whole different thing. It's a different way of looking at something and dealing with it—with life. And it's easy for them."

Just Speak the Truth

"It is a native tradition to sit in a circle and talk—to share what is in your heart. Often it would happen, but it wouldn't be in the same sense as in a workshop or in prison, you see, because the people in the tribal sense already know the thing that you're just learning here. They know how to be with themselves and each other. They would be able to present their problem and say it, and everyone would look at it from all sides and deal with that particular thing. When we sit in a circle in a workshop or in prison, we don't have the time to deal with anybody's real problems. But the people feel good for being able to get the problems out. So the circle really does something for them. We sit down and talk about their problem, and we all throw our views on it. This is what really makes a difference, when everybody puts their view on it, because I see something different than you see it, and so I can only talk about it the way I see it, and you can only talk about the way you see it.

"And you don't need to be adding on nothing. We don't want you to be stretching the story a little bit. Just speak the truth as you see it. It's difficult at first to be able to speak truth because we've been trained to deceive the other person, as if it were a weakness if you admit that you're grieving or that you're upset. We tell our men that it's alright to cry, and that there ain't nothing wrong with crying. If you were going to cry, I know that you love me because you're crying about me. There's nothing to be ashamed of. It's a natural function. And so why should you be ashamed of it?

"I had one of the guys that was the most feared inmate in prison down there in Connecticut, and he would stand up there and, in given moments, he would tell you some of his stories about what he had done. And he would stand there and cry, and say that he didn't know that he could ever be on a high like he's been in that program, and be able to feel the things that he feels, and know that he loves his wife and be able to tell her that. He said, 'I could never tell my wife that before.' He said, 'The only time I ever told anyone that before was when I was trying to get into their drawers or something.' And he said, 'That ain't the way it is today.' He said he was so glad to go back to prison, to find this program in prison. He said that because he had been out two or three times and nothing, no program had done anything for him. And he knew he would be coming right back to prison. But he won't be back there now. He say's he's got something to live for now. He's found a whole different way of life."

To Us, Everyone Is an Individual

One of Slow Turtle's duties as Massapowau is to act as a therapist for those who need support. He says many young people come to him. "I don't train them. I present them with a story as a way for them to learn. The story might not mean much to the outside world, but it does to them because

I'm into their heads. I might see them looking at a white-skinned person in an angry way because they had been hurt by other white people. I can see that anger emerge, so I try to take their anger and do something positive with it.

"When I feel that I've been able to accomplish something, and help someone spiritually, that's my reward. I can do this job here and take care of my needs, you know, but not everybody is as fortunate as I am, in the same sense. But I can deal with a lot of people who need counseling, and I can be very effective because it doesn't cost them anything, so we don't have to go through a whole lot of charades, you know, about the pay.

"My philosophy has always been that if I can't help you in two times then I'm not doing my job. Then I can't help you. These people that are paid to counsel keep their clients coming two or three years; they become married to them, and the person's practically paying their mortgage. But I can't do it that way. You know, when you go to school and learn about counseling and psychiatry, and those kinds of things, you learn a pattern. We don't have any pattern. To us everybody's separate, everybody's individual, and they don't fall into one of four types, or one of ten types. And so it has to be kind of an on-hand thing. I mean, I've got to have you before me, so I can see you, and I learn from you because your body's going to tell me more than your mouth's going to tell me. And I can tell the transitions that you are going through and what's happening with you. So these are the kinds of things that make it kind of special. You don't have to worry about giving the guy a show because he's paying you or something. You know what I mean?

"To us, to become a medicine person, it's the people from your nation that make you that. You don't make yourself. You don't go around saying, 'I'm a medicine man,' because you learn about the pipe or something, or because you counsel a few people. This is what I hear all across this country, these self-made medicine people. A medicine person is one who is accepted by the people that he ministers to. They are the ones who can unmake you a medicine person, OK, and so there's nothing that's got you locked in there that says, 'Well, my grandfather was one, so I got to be one, or my father was one.' That isn't the case. It's a case where, when the people have respect for you, they give their permission. So I'm subject to being removed at any time."

Find Out Who You Are

"The thing that really strikes me as very funny and very sad at the same time is how people are led by a person that they feel is their superior. They're taking them down a path, on a ride, you know. And I don't understand that, why people are so naive.

"We've spent a lot of time trying to get in a position to educate people about the reality of what's happening around them, and I think it's beginning to work. I see many people this year who don't believe in Santa Claus anymore. And there'll be less people believing in the Easter Bunny this year than there were last year because they know, they finally figured out, that rabbits don't lay eggs. So I'm sure that we're progressing along. It's been a hard road. I think people are beginning to stagger under the onslaught of false information that's in the system and in the airways, and they're beginning to understand that their government isn't very truthful, because they can't drink the water any longer and they can't breathe the air. I mean, it's about time for them to wake up.

"If people are going to get back into balance, one of the things they have to do is seek the truth. They have to start really speaking the truth themselves, and that's a difficult thing to do. The way it is now in the world, we don't mind lying. But that stuff doesn't go in our Truth Circles. When we start, we tell you right up front, 'Don't start telling one of those stories because everybody's gonna know you're lying; they're going to read you and your body ain't gonna lie. Your mouth is going to lie, but not your body. If they think that you're not truthful, they're not going to allow you to waste their time, their lives.' And so it may take sometimes months before they can feel comfortable and be able to sit down and talk without lying. That's what America has to do, is to be truthful with itself, start dealing with the truth. You know, you see a spade, call it a spade; don't call it a heart.

"People really need to begin trying to find out who they are. In our story of Creation we talk about each one of us having our own path to travel, and our own gift to give and to share. You see, what we say is that the Creator gave us all special gifts; each one of us is special. And each one of us is a special gift to each other, because we've got something to share. Our traditional form of government is always in that circle where everyone contributes. And when you contribute that way, then you become part of the whole. Being able to share that gift you have, whatever it might be—it might be that you can hook a fish or hunt better than the other guy—you are able to share that, and so it helps other people, helps everyone. You know, when you go to an Indian social, all the women come in bringing their food. That's really important to bring their food because they've been able to cook that and to share themselves. Part of their life went into cooking that food to be able to give that to someone else. That's the important part. It isn't all the dancing, and the singing, and the drumming. It's people being able to share.

"Most people never really tried to be themselves. They haven't been allowed to be themselves. There's always someone trying to take control of you. Your parents give you away to the school and the church and all that stuff, and they all have a set of rules and regulations for you to live by, so you never have been able to be yourself. And you never do what feels good to you. Now sometimes you say society has wounded you, or has forced you into a control area where you just follow that and stay in line. But it takes a lot to get to know oneself and really say what feels good to me, you know. Do I like to get up early in the morning or don't I? To take the time to find out whether you want to get up early in the morning or whether you want to lie in bed—that's a challenge in itself, if you got the balls to do it. Because that little thing there, that watch, that runs in the night, and you watch that all day. And you do the hop and jump and you do what that thing is telling you to do. You eat when you're not hungry because when that thing says twelve o'clock, you eat—you know what I mean?

"People go to school and learn how to do nothing for the rest of their lives and to be happy with it. They say, 'Look, I'm making money, and I ain't doing nothing.' And they think they're happy? Well, I don't know. That can be suicidal because it has no substance. You take that money away from him and what has he got? Nothing. So basically, one really needs to start focusing on himself and his own path, and that's not selfish. It's what's really feeling good to you. You need to incorporate that, and to get yourself on the road to being a human being, something that is worth its weight up here—to affect other lives in a good way, to make things work in a good way. Not just to be here and exist, and sit here and shuffle papers and throw them in a trash bin somewhere. That doesn't make sense. How can you be satisfied with your life and do nothing for nothing, you know? It doesn't amount to nothing. And I find that if you don't do something to try and prevent harm from coming to somebody, or something that helps other people, you aren't going to feel like you're helping out, like you're part of something worthwhile. Sure, you can retire after so many years—you've got a pension, you know. Great. But have you got a life?"

⫷⫷⫷THIRTEEN ⫸⫸⫸

When the Condor Flies with the Eagle
WILLARU HUAYTA

Willaru Huayta emphasizes that he is not a shaman, nor is he a priest, or even a teacher. He is a *chasqui*, a spiritual messenger in the tradition of the Inca. Specifically, he says, he is a messenger of the Sun, and the message of solar wisdom that he bears is a synthesis of wisdom from all the traditions of the world. "I am a child of the universe," Willaru explains, "and my mission is planetary, even though the specific lore I know is from the Incan and Gnostic traditions."

With the assistance of an American named Anderson Hewitt, Willaru has recently completed building the Circles of Light Center in Cuzco, Peru, to serve as the foundation for continuing his work there among the people of the Andes. He is also beginning to travel to share his message in North America and Europe.

Willaru was born in August 1949 in a Peruvian village deep in the jungle. His family is of the Quechua Nation, which is part of the ancient Inca confederation. Inca, he says, is a form of government, not an Indian nation or tribe. The Incas were a confederation of many tribes. The history of Peru as we know it, he says, was made up by anthropologists.

Along with his eight brothers and sisters, Willaru was raised in the Inca tradition, which he describes as a solar, cosmic, universal religion. The code of this tradition, he says, is simple: not to lie, not to steal, and not to be lazy. At the age of fourteen he began going into the jungle alone for long periods of fasting and meditation. He says the Amazon jungle, vibrating with life, is the final retreat and sanctuary of the golden secrets of the Incan Empire, waiting for those who know how to return, and for the world to awaken to a new age of spirit.

Willaru says he went into the jungle to meditate, to cleanse the patterns of his past lives. He believes that for many lifetimes he was a priest at the Temple of the Sun, but that he has not yet attained full self-realization of his soul. "I'm still cleansing my own darkness, too," he says.

In the Amazon, by a river, he was meditating one day in rapport with the spirit of some of the oldest trees when a spiritual master appeared. "The master was very radiant, and about two meters high. He was wearing a white robe with a dark cape. He said, 'Humanity should get itself naturalized.' He sent the message to my heart, planting light and awakening me. And then he sent me to Cuzco with a message, as a *chasqui.*"

"The essence of my message is simple: Humanity should cure itself and give help to the poor. Humanity should come back to the house of the inner mother and father. Heal yourself—your physical and spiritual bodies. Regenerate yourself with light, and then help those who have poverty of the soul. Return to the inner spirit, which we have abandoned while looking elsewhere for happiness."

We've Been Waiting Five Hundred Years

When he is before a group, Willaru talks with his eyes closed. He says he wants to be in touch with inner spirit. It is strange to sit and listen to him speak and not be able to contact him through his eyes. But when his eyes do open, they are wonderfully round and luminous, remarkably gentle and understanding.

"We have been waiting five hundred years," he says. "The Incan prophecies say that now, in this age, when the eagle of the North and the condor of the South fly together, the Earth will awaken. The eagles of the North cannot be free without the condors of the South. Now it's happening. Now is the time. The Aquarian Age is an era of light, an age of awakening, an age of returning to natural ways. Our generation is here to help begin this age, to prepare through different schools to understand the message of the heart, intuition, and nature.

"Native people speak with the Earth. When consciousness awakens, we can fly high like the eagle, or like the condor in "El Condor Pasa." Ultimately, you know, we are all native, because the word native comes from nature, and we are all part of Mother Nature. She is inside us, and we are inside her. We depend totally on the Earth, the Sun, and the water. We belong to the evolution of nature in our physical bodies. But we also have a spiritual body that comes from the Sun—not the Sun you can see with your two eyes, but another Sun that lies in another dimension, a golden Sun burning with the fire of spiritual light. The inner light of humans emanates from this spiritual source. We came to Earth from this Sun to have experiences on Earth, and eventually we will return to the Sun.

"Many early civilizations in the Americas were solar cultures, cultures of the spirit. We are the children of the fifth solar generation. We are now in the early stages of the Aquarian Age. The revolutionaries of the Piscean Age have done their work already. Now it is up to all of us.

"Planet Earth is now beginning a new solar race, a solar generation created by the sacred Sun. Like an arrow or a sacred knife, the energy comes to planet Earth, the solar fire. The fire is inside everyone. There are two serpents that reside in the coccyx at the base of the spine. When we know how to channel this serpent energy, it rises up the spine for enlightenment. Apes, chimps, and monkeys are our brothers. They just channel the serpent energy another way, and so sleep in consciousness."

The Illuminated Ones

"In the Incan culture, we understand that we came from Atlantis. Atlantis had avatars and masters who sacrificed for humanity. One of them was named Noah, who built the ark. Another was named Amadu Muru. He was a red man who departed Atlantis and came to South America, which was a different shape in those ancient days. He was a founder of the red nations of South America, just as Noah was a founder of the peoples in the Middle East.

"In the last cataclysm, Atlantis sank into the angry waters of the ocean. That continent, with its millions of inhabitants, went into the abyss with all of its advanced technologies. That time humanity was also warned, but they would not listen. Only a few with awakened consciousness had the awareness to evacuate.

"At that time, after the great cosmic cataclysm, when the Earth was still trembling and taking its new form, the enlightened ones were returned to Lake Titicaca and other sacred places of the Earth to begin the formation of new humanity. From these sacred places, groups went in different directions with the mission of founding a new solar culture in harmony with nature and the Creator. They traveled out to the different parts of the South American continent. They had help from the spiritual realms, as did the survivors all around the Earth.

"You see, many, many years ago the indigenous people of South America were in contact with our universal brothers—what you call the ETs. We are not only brothers here on Earth, but we are also brothers with people from other planets. There is only one true religion—the religion of the solar, cosmic light. The ETs come from an illuminated realm. They live on planets where everyone has liberated themselves from negativities of the ego. They are here to encourage us so that we can succeed in an authentic revolution of consciousness.

"The Incan priests announced the arrival of the Spanish. They said, 'The enemy of the Sun, the Earth, the plants, is coming. We have to take our wisdom into our hearts to try and change them, or we will die with our own laws.' Then Cortés came to Mexico, and Columbus came, too, trying to escape the illnesses and madness of Europe. Meanwhile, the Incas continued to go on interplanetary journeys with the Illuminated Ones.

"When humanity became corrupted in South America with the coming of the Europeans, the Illuminated Ones stopped coming. The cosmic or celestial navies from other planets stopped visiting. At that time a great moral and spiritual darkness fell across the people of the Americas. Our wisdom keepers were killed and the new religion of materialism spread across the continent. The priests of science cannot see beyond this. They cannot experience the multidimensional world of spirit. The people of Earth, dominated by the dogma of scientific materialism and greed, have pillaged and ravaged the Earth. With the development of weapons, horrible beyond the imagination, they have again brought us to the edge of the abyss. During this time of great darkness on Earth, contact has been lost with our universal brothers.

"Each person is a sacred temple. The altar of that temple is the heart. The fire of love, a reflection of the greater Light, burns upon this altar. This Light within must be acknowledged, cared for, and venerated. This is the religion of the sons of the Sun. It is the same religion we learned from the extraterrestrials—the universal cosmic, solar religion. This universal community is our sacred family from all other planets.

"Now many spaceships are arriving again. They are coming to help us into the Aquarian Age, and to help us make union with God. They know that if we do not find God within ourselves, we will not find God anywhere. This is the end of the Piscean Age and the start of the Aquarian Age. Now we would be wise to recall the teachings of our ancestors. Those teachings are within us, for we ourselves are the ancestors living new lives.

"Mental capacity is a bridging element. It can be used for good or ill. Mental capacity should be used to enhance the inner spirit, but when humanity abandoned the inner temple of the spirit, everything became mental. This was the beginning of decadence. When we are in the Light, wisdom comes from the spirit. The life of humanity is sacred and holy. It is our responsibility to live in an elevated state of consciousness, to listen to the voice of the heart and intuition. Start to listen to your heart. This is how to develop wisdom.

"The most important thing now is to reveal the inner temple of the soul with right thinking and right activity. Let go of envy, pride, lust, anger, greed, jealousy, and so forth. Clean out the garbage, the inner enemies that block the voice of intuition and of the inner life. This is the time of awakening to the inner father and the inner mother. Without this we will receive no high initiation; instead we get initiated into darkness. That's because any investigation or revolution without God leads, not to freedom, but to more slavery."

An Authentic Revolution of Consciousness

"In 1750, the Inca Shora Atahuallpa warned the soldiers of the Sun. He said, 'When humanity loses its connection to the natural forces, it will create more war, and people will become lost in darkness.' Most leaders of political and social movements claim to have peace, happiness, and freedom as their goal. But too often they look for it in war, aggression, and terror, and by creating hatred and jealousy. This simply doesn't work. We have only to look at history to understand this. We are entering a new era. It is time for a new way. But we cannot expect society to change until we change ourselves—from within. The darkness of our world—the wars and the pollution—is only a reflection of our personal lives of darkness and mental, physical, and spiritual pollution. If there is an Antichrist outside in the world, it's because there's an Antichrist inside in our souls.

"Our true enemies, as well as our true sources of strength, lie within. When enough of us have conquered that enemy, then the external world will change. When this happens there will be no need for political parties of the left or right; there will be no need for governments because each citizen will know how to govern himself.

"It is necessary for any religion, school, or profession to connect with the authentic revolution in consciousness and to eliminate the negative dimensions of our personality—the inner terrorists that cause us to eat, drink, consume drugs, and use our sexual power in the wrong way. Whenever we do too much of anything, we are going against the solar force.

"The first factor in the revolution of consciousness is the mystic death of the ego—the death of negative thinking, negative personalities. We must purify the soul of the inner enemies. Every time a defect manifests— envy, gluttony, anger, lust, whatever—take that impulse to the heart. Ask, 'Do I really need to invoke this?' And then honor the heart. If you have the desire to smoke a cigarette, take that to your heart and ask. But honor the answer that comes in your heart. Also ask your heart to purify and cleanse this defect and harmful desire. Ask also the help of the inner father and mother. Every time we eliminate a defect, we build our soul, our inner temple. We ascend, like going up a stairway.

"The second factor is the mystic marriage, the spiritual marriage. We should use our sexual power and energy to grow in the Light. When we recognize that this is the essence of Creation and use this energy in a sacred way, it can activate our potential for longevity; otherwise our life expectancy shortens. The sexual power needs to be channeled in the right way if we are to live in authentic peace and freedom. We can live many more years, eventually, with the proper regenerative practices. The mainstream civilization does not know how to conserve and channel this essence, so it has led to overpopulation and abortion. In the mystic marriage are the keys that can open the door to solar wisdom. With the mystic marriage we create more solar energy within us. The mystic marriage need not be between a man and a woman; it can be an inner marriage, of the inner father and the inner mother.

"Our souls are in pieces on the ground. We need to reveal the inner temple, the spiritual body. Then the mystic marriage can take place. The psychic, atomic energy of our sexuality can be good medicine when it is recognized as sacred and divine. The spirit of Quetzalcoatl is sleeping in the coccyx. When we regenerate, it opens the heart and our psychic faculties.

"The third factor in the revolution of consciousness is to make a sacrifice for humanity, to help humanity in some way by sacrificing our egos. We cannot be authentic revolutionaries by turning our backs on the hungry, the homeless, and those who are suffering. They are our brothers and sisters and they require our help. On planet Earth today we speak more than nine hundred languages, but we still don't understand each other. We need to learn to speak heart to heart, to connect with each other through telepathic intuition.

"What's the goal of the revolution of consciousness—the purpose? It's an invitation from the angelic realm to get out of the mechanical life so we do not have to come back and incarnate again. Our physical body belongs to Mother Earth, but the spirit is eternal, and we need to liberate it, to elevate it."

A Time of Illumination

Based on his Gnostic training and his intuitive perception, Willaru believes that the Aquarian Age began on February 4, 1962. "This is a time of illumination and hope, a time when we will again begin to listen to the inner voice and the voices of the angels and the archangels. February 1962 was the first opening of the door from the spirit dimension to humanity. Then Harmonic Convergence of August 16, 1987, was another door opening, the second step. Between 1962 and 1987 was the first stage of preparation. People began to receive messages, powers, and to activate the faculties of the spirit. After Harmonic Convergence, many people regained their soul powers so they could complete their mission on planet Earth."

Willaru believes that the ancient Inca prophecy of the condor and the eagle is being fulfilled. He cites as an example a meeting in Monterey, Mexico, that occurred on February 17, 1989. At this meeting, which took place over a week, he says the South met the North for a high spiritual purpose. Specifically, Willaru says, the meeting included representatives of the ancient Native American confederation of the Anahuac, which includes many of the Native American nations from Nicaragua north to the Arctic Circle, and representatives of the confederation of the Tiwantinsuyo, which includes the native nations from Nicaragua south to Tierra del Fuego.

Willaru says he does not wish to single himself out, but that he was there at the meeting. "We met as guardians of planet Earth, to recall the importance of the Sun. The Great Peacemaker called the elders together to begin their mission again between the Northern and Southern hemispheres, because North and South America are to be the focus of the new civilization. It's time to prepare for it. In America many races mingle, and from all of this mixing will come one race. The souls are the same now—we are the people of this land, but we are now in different color bodies. We are a rainbow.

"February 17, 1989, was the meeting of the confederations. Then on March 21 came the third step in opening the door from the realm of spirit to humanity: the Lighting of the Diamonds in Monterey and all across Mexico. This was a big ceremony to receive the cosmic light forces. More than five hundred people gathered from all over Mexico, and also from the spirit realm.

"Step four came August 16, 1989, when elders in remote places all over the world journeyed to sacred sites to reawaken them. Now we are waiting for the fifth step in this process of illumination."

How Much Light We Have Within Us

Willaru says that as we await the fifth step we are supported by brothers and sisters from other planets. "The ETs are around now. They come from a planet of higher consciousness. They know authentic peace and freedom for they have eliminated all their negativities. Everyone there is their own priest. There is only one planetary family; they know the authentic communion. They know that God is living in everyone, and they treat each other that way. True masters don't say, 'Follow me,' or 'Pray to me.' They teach by their example. Be wary of looking outside yourself for saviors or answers. This gives your power away.

"The world is at a critical point of transition, which is highlighted by the crisis in spiritual and moral principles. Nationality is no longer important, nor race, nor tribe, nor social class, nor religions. We are flowers of many colors in the Earth garden. Human truth is one. The most important thing now is to awaken the consciousness in a positive form.

"Our ancestors developed their psychic faculties, allowing them to be in tune with the great mysteries of nature. They did their scientific investigations in a conscious manner. There is evidence of this in the Incan temples in Peru, which were created with megalithic stones cut by those with an awakened consciousness who had learned to focus and control the natural forces.

"Cataclysm is coming now in this time of transition, but there's no need to worry about it. Get your consciousness together and you will transcend it. Mother Nature will purify with all four elements. The Earth will shake, the air will be filled with hurricanes and tornadoes, the ocean will have huge waves, and the Sun will have great heat.

"The year 2013 is the end of the Incan calendar. The cataclysm may come then. All I know is that according to the Incan prophecies a big asteroid will come close to the Earth, an asteroid three times larger than Jupiter, with high magnetic energy. It will have an attraction to the Earth. The magnetic energy will open the volcanoes, start the earthquakes, and begin the deep cleansing of the Earth. Then, when the asteroid has gone, the seed people will return and begin a new civilization with ecologic thinking.

"The fifth generation will disappear with the cataclysm. The sixth generation, the future generation, is seeding now. A new solar age begins with new people. We can be the seed of the new sixth generation. At the time of the cataclysm, the universal brothers and sisters will return and open their ships to those who have clear auras. They will look to see how much love we have, how much work we have done on ourselves, how much light we have within us. That is what will be important—not what kind of car we have or where we are living."

⟨⟨⟨⟨ FOURTEEN ⟩⟩⟩⟩

Reconsecrating the Earth
HUNBATZ MEN

At the age of one, Hunbatz Men was chosen. His uncle, don Beto, recognized something special in him. Hunbatz was taken aside and slowly, year by year, instructed in the mysteries of Mayan science and religion. As his uncle educated him in the ancient traditions of his people, he also showed him the massive ceremonial centers near his village, Uenkal, about one hour south of Chichén Itzá on Mexico's Yucatán peninsula. Hunbatz's family has lived there for many generations, keeping and passing on the elaborate traditions of the Maya. As he learned of the intricate Mayan mathematics and calendars, the great spiral of the Milky Way, the pyramids, and the prophecies, Hunbatz became filled with both understanding and wonder.

For a long time, he lived with this beautiful knowledge. Then, at the age of fifteen, he moved to Mexico City and set aside what his uncle had taught him. It just didn't seem relevant to modern life. During this period, for the first time in his life, he felt the racial discrimination against Indian people that has been a fact of life in the Americas since the arrival of Cortés. "Yes," he explains, "it's tough to be an Indian."

In the teeming streets of Mexico City, he found that the dominant Hispanic culture and religion were very different, and did not honor the sacred reality of the Sun, the trees, the stars, or the Moon. "When I do my rituals, I have to include all of these in my family," he explains. "In Mayan there is no separate image for God; it is a pure concept: Hunab K'u—the One Giver of Movement and Measure. It is in everything."

At age sixteen, Hunbatz began going with his first girlfriend. The girl's family invited him to church, where he had more problems. "The Catholic church was completely different. It is not Mayan to confess to a man [priest], but rather to confess to the Sun and the trees." The girl's family was not sympathetic to these differences. After a time, as the cultural differences became more and more apparent, Hunbatz became deeply troubled. He was young; he did not understand that what he had learned about his culture, and who he was as an Indian, would be consistently devalued. He was unsure whether he should be ashamed of who he was or whether he should try to live like the dominant Mexican culture.

After four years in the city, studying painting and sculpture at La Esmerelda Academy and the Academy of Fine Arts, he returned home and shared his concerns with his uncle. Don Beto told him, "You have another education, another responsibility. I have shared with you teachings that are thousands of years old and that have been hidden for five hundred years—since before the Spanish came. This gives you a different life. It's not an easy responsibility to have."

For many days Hunbatz sat and learned from his uncle, and then his interest was rekindled. He began again to study the ways of his ancestors. For hours he would watch the sky. Together with his uncle, he would revisit the ceremonial centers and sit, watching and waiting. Don Beto showed Hunbatz how to have patience, how to wait. Sometimes his uncle would say nothing about the knowledge; he would just make Hunbatz sit and watch. In the culture of the Maya, they do not use abstract points for teaching, but real things. His uncle gradually taught him everything through nature: fire, wind, fruits, trees, and so forth.

In addition to his work with don Beto, Hunbatz deepened his study of Mayan culture and philosophy at the Center for Pre-American Culture and the Pre-American Cultural and Scientific Council, both in Mexico City. As the years went by, he became learned and was recognized as a Mayan daykeeper—an authority on the history, chronology, calendars, and cosmic knowledge of Mayan civilization. He became a shaman in his tradition, and a ceremonial leader who journeyed to teach all over North and South America, earning wide respect among native spiritual leaders. He also founded the Mayan Indigenous Community near Mérida, Mexico, and authored several books, including *Secrets of Mayan Science/Religion*, and *Los Calendarios Astronomicos y Hunab K'u*.

A warm man who is both humble and generous of spirit, Hunbatz is now traveling widely to share the information he has learned because, as he sees it, we have complicated our lives. He says he is sure, most of the time, that this is the right time to share his understandings. As he sees it, his job is to wake people up to the energy of the Sun. "High knowledge is coming," he says. "We must prepare to receive it."

According to Hunbatz, we are now participating in a new cycle of the Mayan calendars, which synchronize the cycles of time with human beings. "This is the time when the Maya believe they must work with others to reopen the schools of ancient knowledge—to teach the first stage of under-standing," he says. "We can learn what each of the sacred centers of the world has to offer us, so that we may become the kinds of human beings needed for this new solar age." Hunbatz teaches that we began entering the New Itzá Age, analogous to the Age of Aquarius, around August 1987, at an event many people called Harmonic Convergence. He says that we will have fully entered it by the year 2013. "It is time to work into the deepest part of our beings to regain the information we have impressed there—in the spiral of our DNA. Only in this way," Hunbatz says, "will millennial information rise into our conscious awareness, reminding us of an ancient time when knowledge was unified and there was no separation between science and religion."

Beginnings of the Rainbow Nation

The indigenous people of the Americas say they have known for a long time that there were people in all Four Directions, and that many Indian people have visited other places to study and exchange culture. The native culture of the Americas, though, began to change drastically with the com-ing of Columbus, who proved to be the first of many brutal men as he senselessly murdered many hundreds of peaceful Indians on his voyages of discovery and exploitation.

In the South, the genocide of indigenous people in Mexico began in earnest when Hernando Cortés arrived in Veracruz, Mexico, on Good Fri-day in 1519 with a Roman Catholic priest at his side. The indigenous people knew that someone like Cortés would come, and thanks to their calendars they knew exactly when—to the day. They had, in fact, sent scouts to Veracruz to greet Cortés, for they hoped he would be the return of the great spiritual messenger, Quetzalcoatl, not the bringer of sorrows.

The Aztec emperor Montezuma II felt his power was threatened. He was frightened by omens and the legend that prophesied the return of Quetzalcoatl from the East. He did everything short of violence to prevent Cortés from advancing inland. But Cortés did advance, and the rest of the story is one of sorrow, bloodshed, and disease as the native people were systematically killed or enslaved. "The problem is that when the Spanish came to visit they did not respect anything that was already here," Hunbatz says. "The native people could have built more weapons when they became aware that the white men were coming, but the elders knew this was not the path of wisdom. They took another approach."

According to the Mayan calendars, just as Cortés was stepping ashore, a long cycle of thirteen heavens was coming to an end. For the Maya, it was the beginning of a dark cycle of pain, suffering, sadness, and death—the entrance of the reign of Xibalba, the world of the Nine Lords of Darkness, the Nine Bolontikus, the Nine Hells. Though in many respects the time of the Nine Hells has been a time of great darkness, the Maya also saw it as time to start cross-fertilization among the seeds of the Four Directions and races of the planet. This difficult task they saw as the beginning of a new nation of multicolored beings. The seeds of the Four Directions would be mixing together to create the first Rainbow People.

Prior to the arrival of the Spanish, the Maya and many other Native American groups entrusted certain families with sacred information and the responsibility to keep it secret, so it could not be destroyed or abused. Guidance to take this action came from a confederation of Native American nations, a council of elders that, Hunbatz says, had met for thousands of years before the Europeans came. The council is made up of representatives from many of the Indian nations from Nicaragua north to the Arctic Circle. It continues to meet to this day. From dreams, visions, and prophecies, the elders of the council had become aware that the newcomers would try to change their spiritual beliefs. So they kept the most profound parts of their religion and science in their hearts, and did not speak about them.

Over five hundred years ago, Hunbatz's family was entrusted with safekeeping part of this wisdom tradition. He is the contemporary holder of the lineage, although now, because it is time, he has begun to share the secrets. "The eyes of modern civilization see only a short span of time," he says. "To the European-American culture, five hundred years seems to be a lot of time. But five hundred years is nothing in the eyes of the Maya."

The Beauty of His Culture

Though archaeologists might not agree, Hunbatz says that over the course of history the Mayan people have lived not only in the Yucatán but in many locations on Earth. "Sometimes," he says, "they were in the country of India, where they were known as the Naga-Mayas. At other times they were in the country of Greece. In that country they were called Cara-Mayas. Also, they were in Egypt with the name Mayax. This happened because the Mayan people are very ancient, and as descendants of Atlantis they understood many secrets of the telluric forces [Earth energies]. They took advantage of them so they could travel where they wished, and at the distance they wished, and at the hour they wished. When the Maya went to these places they went to deposit culture, to share their wisdom and to partake of the wisdom of other cultures. They never journeyed to conquer other peoples."

Hunbatz offers many bits of evidence to support the claim that the Maya traveled the world in antiquity. He points out, for example, that the Maya have the word *kun-da-lini*, the same as the Tibetan *kundalini*, which describes the life force that is said to rise up the human spine when a person becomes enlightened. According to Hunbatz, this was a Mayan word before it became a Tibetan word.

It is doubtless that debate over the origins and history of the Maya will occupy scholars for decades to come. Perhaps at some point they will recognize the tradition that has been handed down among the Mayan people themselves. But one thing is beyond debate. As is evident in their architecture, art, sculpture, ethics, and language, the Maya developed a high civilization. This, they feel, was their mission. They say they were chosen by the Creator, Hunab K'u, to live this out. The Maya did not seek to create a personal culture, but rather to mirror or reflect life. A typical Mayan expression is *In Lak'ech Yelir*, which means "I am another yourself," or "I am you— we are the same." Implicit in this expression of spiritual unity is the recognition that if people do something bad to other people, they are ultimately doing something bad to themselves. "If I destroy you," Hunbatz says, "I destroy myself. If I honor you, I honor myself."

The Mayan language has three poetic traits. It is mantric, onomato-poeic, and reversible: each word can be intoned to invoke the sacred aspect of life it describes; each word sounds like what it describes; and each word can be reversed to give another word that deepens understanding of the original word. For example, the Mayan word *pal* means "children," but when the word is reversed to *lap* it gives another level of understand-ing: *lap* denotes a soul that is thousands of years old and has lived many incarnations.

The mantric quality of the Mayan language is evident in the word *lil*, which, when correctly intoned in front of the Sun, is said to heal the person who sounds it. "Say it three times and go deep with the sound," Hunbatz says. "It brings energy, like a vitamin, and can help to heal illness." Another word Maya intone is their word for the Sun, K'in—pronounced with a hard *k* and an elongated *in* sound. This word attunes them to the energy of the Sun when it is repeated seven times.

"The culture of the Maya teaches the great secrets Mother Nature holds," Hunbatz says. "The Maya understood, as modern science is dis-covering, that all matter is vibration. Therefore, human life is linked to the heavenly bodies by cosmobiological law. The Maya understood this and made it part of their lives and culture.

"It is written in time and in the memory of the Indian peoples that our Sun will rise again, that we will be able to reestablish our culture—its arts, sciences, mathematics, and religion. Mayan knowledge will come forward again. It is for this reason that we of the Amerindian communities are once again uniting to reestablish our entire culture."

This Is the Cosmic Law

Another facet that reveals the beauty of the Mayan culture is its elaborate system of calendars. The Maya employed sophisticated astronom-ical calendars, mathematics, and geometry to express the relationship of humanity to the cosmos. The complexity of the astronomical calculations of the Maya is evident, when one considers that some of the calculations cover millions of years.

Altogether the Maya have seventeen calendars. One calendar, the Tzolkin, corresponds to the eleven-year sunspot cycle. Haab is a calendar of cultural consummation, based on a cycle of fifty-two years. According to this calendar, every fifty-two years the frequency of human beings shifts. Another calendar of twenty-six thousand years, Tzek'er, is based on the Pleiades, a constellation known in Western folklore as the Seven Sisters. According to the Mayan tradition, our Sun is actually part of the Pleiades, and orbits in concert with the other stars of this constellation. The joint rotation of all the stars in the Pleiades, including our Sun, is but a minor motion within the huge, 400-billion-star spiral of our local galaxy, the Milky Way. The Maya have known about the Milky Way for thousands of years, and they make ceremonies to help hold the balance of the galaxy. Hunbatz says that, by contrast, modern science has yet to discover our Sun's connection with the Pleiades.

At this point in time, the twenty-six-thousand-year cycle may be coming to an end, or to a peak—a thirteen-thousand-year midway point. Hunbatz is not sure. But he does know that we are at a critical turning point in this cycle. "At this moment we don't understand time very well. But we know the changes in correspondence with this turning point are drastic, and we know the Sun is going to help us. This is the cosmic law. Under the terms of cosmic law, a fast car, big money, and a fancy education do nothing for the cosmos. With our technologies we think we are superior, but before the universe we are nothing. We have created in this time a personal culture, instead of a community."

"The calendar of twenty-six thousand years is new for the dominant civilization. It is based on the rotation of the Pleiades, the constellation of which our Sun is part. This calendar portends big changes, a new age. But before this big frequency change is complete, we need to work, to regain the consciousness of the Sun. We need to gain respect for all this cosmic knowledge. If the people don't do that, the change is going to come anyway because no one can stop it. It's not possible to stop. When the people begin to feel the big changes they may be confused. The Sun will wake up everything to life. It shines on all of us, not just some. Seeds become sprouts, then stalks, then they develop leaves and flowers. The same thing is going to happen in the minds of people. The Sun will give to everyone.

But how will people respond? Some could be very confused by these new frequencies.

"We can pray to the Sun for understanding of what is happening. The Sun will help us if we ask. The Sun is not God, but a part of God, God's eye, a reflection of the eyes of God, Hunab K'u. We are a reflection of Hunab K'u, too. We are Hunab K'u—as is all of creation. Everything is integrated. Nothing is separate. The Maya have known this always. When the Maya make rituals to the Sun, they regard it as father, and ask for help. The Earth is mother."

Years ago researchers discovered they could take a picture of the energy field around the human body with Kirlian photography. Hunbatz says this human energy field, or aura, is a reflection of solar energy. "We have a piece of the Sun in us, which gives us life. The Maya have worked on this base of knowledge for thousands of years—intoning mantric words to amplify and clarify that personal energy, and making rituals to balance the energy in the world at large."

Right now, Hunbatz counsels, we need to work with our energy bodies so they will be able to cope with the intensifying energy frequencies in the world, a trend that he says will continue into the foreseeable future. One way to strengthen and stabilize the energy body is through chants and mantras such as those the Maya use. Another important way is through pilgrimage to holy sites around the Earth.

Awakening the Centers

"For the Maya," Hunbatz teaches, "it is the new age—time to give away the knowledge again, to raise the frequency of the global mind. Now the world has a dark civilization, a dark culture. We need to reestablish a high culture." One important part of doing this, according to Hunbatz, is reopening the Mayan initiatic centers, the temples and pyramids of the Yucatán, Guatemala, and Honduras.

"As foretold in the Mayan sacred calendars," Hunbatz says, "now is the time to reconsecrate the sacred pyramids and temples, and all the other sacred sites of the Americas. In so doing, we can help bring about the respiritualization of the people and the healing of the Earth. Pilgrimages to the magnetic center of Mayan lands are necessary to assist in the enlightenment of the human race." According to Hunbatz, the magnetic energy of the Earth and the cosmos flows more fluidly in sacred sites. When humans make ceremony there, it helps the energy to flow even better.

Hunbatz works not only with the Maya, but also with native people all over the Americas—North and South. "Most of the elders," he says, "know about this—that it is time to reopen the old centers, to go there with respect, and to begin to receive information."

In 1988, with the support of other elders and shamans, Hunbatz led the first of a series of pilgrimages to cleanse the temples of the dust of several centuries—to reopen and reconsecrate them so they could be used for sacred work. Over one hundred men and women of all ages and many nations participated in the first historic journey to the Yucatán to begin the process foretold by the Mayan calendars. For the first time in five hundred years, the temples reverberated with the heat, light, and sound of ceremony performed in their grand plazas.

In 1989 they reopened Nah Chan, Etz Nah, Uxmal, Kabah, Lol Tun, and Chichén Itzá. Then in 1990 they reopened Tik'al, Quilghua, and Copan, completing the work of reactivating the Mayan initiatic centers. The pilgrimages, however, will continue each year until 2013, when, according to the Mayan calendars, the transition to the New Itzá Age will be complete.

"We must reopen these places where the knowledge of the great mysteries is deposited," Hunbatz urges, "because the spirits of the ancient teachers are awaiting the new mind of humanity in order that these sacred places might be revived and indicate the correct path to humanity." The pyramids of Mesoamerica are not tombs, Hunbatz explains, but places to work with other dimensions of consciousness, places to understand time. The Mayan word for the pyramids is k'u—part of the name of God, Hunab K'u. "We go to the pyramids because the energy flow in there makes for a different vibration. We can use this to help make subtle changes in the frequency of our brain waves. In there we can make a connection with the magnetic forces of the Earth and the cosmos. The geometrical form of the pyramids helps people to transform themselves, to raise their consciousness by raising the frequency of their brain waves. We hope something big is going to happen because of these ceremonies and all the other sacred activities around the world—that the frequency of the modern mind is going to change in a positive way.

"Now, I invite people to come and reopen the sacred centers. When thousands of people work like this, it will change the mind of all—even those who do not believe. You can't save the Earth by dictating laws—no one believes or cares. They will keep doing what they are doing to make money. We must change the frequency of the human mind."

The decision to open the Mayan initiatic centers came following some special gatherings. The first was the gathering of the Confederation of Tiwantinsuyo under rainbow banners in Machu Picchu during the spring of 1986. This confederation is a council of indigenous groups in South America, just as there is a confederation of indigenous groups extending from Nicaragua north. In 1987, at a gathering in Peru of spiritual leaders from many traditions, the actual decision to reopen the sacred ceremonial centers of the planet was taken. According to Hunbatz, this decision was reinforced by the worldwide event known as Harmonic Convergence in August 1987, as well as a later conference of indigenous elders held in the land of the Hopi during the summer of 1989. In these prophetic reunions, spiritual representatives came together from around the world to assist in the inauguration of the solar new age. They shared the sacred symbols and prophecies of their traditions and demonstrated the unification of ancestral knowledge that is one, on and with the Earth.

Hunbatz says the Mayan pilgrimages helped initiate a new cycle of thirteen heavens. "This is the first stage of understanding Mayan wisdom," he explains. "Following the opening of the centers, a congress will begin to study the development of the enigmatic Quiche Maya. This study will culminate in the year 2013. At that time many prophecies will have been completed, and the human race will begin to live in the second stage of happiness, which will last one *kaltun* [260 years]. After this *kaltun*, the destiny of humanity will be guided by the minds and hands of the new schools of solar initiation located in the sacred centers of the world."

The Rainbow Feathered Serpent

There are about twenty-one thousand temples, pyramids, and sacred centers in Mesoamerica. This elaborate network of sacred centers was used to keep balance on the Earth and to expand the consciousness of human beings. According to Hunbatz, there are more pyramids in Mesoamerica than anywhere else in the world. The culture of the pyramids was created here. The main temple, he says, is the one at Chichén Itzá.

"The ceremonies that culminated at Chichén Itzá were intended to help reprogram human DNA so that we humans can learn to exist on Earth in symbiosis with our light bodies—Sun bodies. Our DNA during the Mayan cycles of the last twenty-six thousand years has been encoded with a flaw that can, ultimately, become a source of deevolution. This flaw causes us to believe that we are separate from the Divine Source. For us to evolve identity, this flaw was required. But now it is time for us to move into communion with the Divine.

"Our Mayan teachers knew that with the passage of time people would return to this land to regain the knowledge of these stones. They are vibrating with the new era, to teach that which was written there. The prophecies say that thousands of people will come back there to try to rediscover the secrets and the philosophy of the Maya." Hunbatz says that since the early 1980s as many as thirty thousand to forty thousand people come each year as tourists. They began coming when the mainstream culture suddenly recognized that a dramatic insignia is formed on the side of one of the pyramids at special times of the year.

Indeed, at the vernal and autumnal equinoxes, a magnificent serpent of light and shadow forms on the north facade of the Pyramid of Kukulcan at Chichén Itzá. The body of the serpent consists of seven triangles of light and shadow that end at the stone serpent head at the bottom of the stairs. The solar angle that produces this spectacular phenomenon occurs only at the two equinoxes, on March 21 and September 22.

This phenomenon is known as the magical descent of the Rainbow Feathered Serpent, Kukulcan. Kukulcan was called Quetzalcoatl in the northern lands, and Gucumatz in the southern lands. The wavy lines that are used to symbolize the energy of electricity are symbolically representative of the pure energy of creative intelligence that is intended by the symbol of Kukulcan, the Feathered Serpent. The serpent represents the Earth, because it lives so close to the Earth and uses its whole being to go forward in life. The feathers are the feathers of an eagle, because the eagle, of all creatures, flies closest to the heavens. In the symbol of the Feathered Serpent, Earth and spirit are therefore brought together and integrated in a good way. The symbol of the rainbow suggests that all the colors and all the pathways of humanity are to be respected and honored. Quetzalcoatl, or Kukulcan, is said to be the embodiment of the serpent rainbow beam of cosmic intelligence, the sperm of the universe fertilizing the womb of the Earth.

"This teaching can be comprehended by any human being," Hunbatz says. "One has only to prostrate oneself in front of the pyramid and the information will begin to flow. The Maya designed it so that this temple of initiation would guard the ageless knowledge. We are working with our subconscious to be able to pierce and reclaim this information, which we have impregnated in the deepest part of our being. Only in this way will the ancient information rise again in our consciousness."

Before the first pilgrimage, Hunbatz said that "the Maya were going to move the Sun." That year, 1989, beginning with the New Moon eclipse of March 7, gigantic solar flares arose, so violent that astronomers called them solar hurricanes. This is when the pilgrimage was beginning. The culmination of the pilgrimage was a ceremony at Chichén Itzá that was held between the equinox and the Full Moon, prophesied as a time to "return Quetzalcoatl as fire in the sky." In fact, the Sun exploded with activity at just that time. Solar storms reached a phenomenal peak of intensity then, and the Aurora Borealis, or Northern Lights, became visible all across the United States, as far south as Florida, Texas, Cuba, and even the Yucatán Peninsula where the pilgrims had assembled in a circle around the pyramid at Chichén Itzá. The solar flares were of such intensity that they could not be measured by any scientific instruments on Earth.

Family-Based Democracy

Hunbatz had the vision and led the pilgrimages to open the Mayan initiatic centers in 1989 and 1990, but then he stepped back. He did not want to become an institutionalized leader, with everyone thinking they needed to listen to him to make ceremony and thereby abdicating their own intelligence, intuition, and free will. He says that in this new time everyone needs to learn to lead and to trust their own perceptions. While he will continue to teach, he has turned his focus primarily to establishing a new community based on ancient Mayan principles.

After Hunbatz received all the ancient, sacred information from his uncle, don Beto, he was asked to begin a group, and to try and live again in the old way. When Hunbatz tried to help people live in the old way in his village, he was thwarted by the local church. He would gather villagers to talk or make a ceremony to the Sun, but the local Catholic church would blast the Ave Maria over loudspeakers so that they could not converse among themselves.

Hunbatz went to the priest and told him about his attempt to restore the sacred culture of the Maya. The priest did not like his message, and continued to oppose him, using the sacred songs of Christendom as weapons, so Hunbatz left the village. He was able to acquire a large parcel of land—one square mile—near Mérida in the Yucatán, upon which he formed the Mayan Indigenous Community, Communidad Indigena Maya.

His vision is to establish an intentional community there. Twelve families are moving onto the land, where they will live the lifestyle of the Maya, not modern civilization: no televisions, no electricity. For four months a year the community will be open for people to come and study. The other eight months they will live a simple, sacred life. "We don't need very much help," Hunbatz says. "The land has twenty different fruit trees. We have no winter, so things grow fast. We have fresh food every day. It never gets cold, so we can sleep outdoors. We don't need anything more. When you work with the Earth Mother on the land, you learn to love her.

"Karl Marx committed a serious error in basing his social theory on Henry Morgan, who described the stages of development of 'primitive societies,' but was ignorant of the great pre-Columbian cultures. Since Morgan belonged culturally to European modes of thinking, his philosophy, religion, and ethics were necessarily based on the exaltation of private property. This is very different from the thinking in the highly complex earlier civilizations, which flourished with communalism and family-based democracy as the foundation of their social organization. This is what we seek to reestablish as a model for the times we are moving into.

"Wisdom does not belong to one person. Most of the time when we come back to Earth to live out another incarnation, we need to act in accord with wisdom. But it does not belong to anyone. It's the illumination of old and proven ideas through generation after generation of discovering natural law.

"Wisdom means a lot of things. In the dominant culture, a child is taught that money is important, and so his whole life he makes decisions based on money. But another child may be taught to love the trees and the water, and so the decisions he makes in his life will be very different. Both children are wise based on what they know. The child who grows up in the dominant society may make a lot of money acting out of his particular wisdom, but he may poison a river to do it. So is this, ultimately, wisdom? Is it wisdom to teach the children to love money? Society needs information on how to respect the Earth. In the Indian culture this is not a problem, because we have a different perspective."

Respect for High Knowledge

When Hunbatz presents a lecture, he carefully ties a hand-woven band around his head, and he asks the permission of the Creator to help him understand everything, especially the high knowledge and our connection with the Earth. Then he tries to explain everything that comes to his mind, even though sometimes he doesn't have words to match his insights or experiences.

As he looks about the modern world, he is particularly concerned about the burgeoning industry of biotechnology, which is based on the manipulation of genes, the biological structures that hold the code of life. Ancient Maya prophecies address the hazards of manipulating the stuff of life, he says. And he cautions all who are involved in biotechnology: "Don't play with sacred knowledge unless you have understanding, humility, and the permission of the Spirit as it is manifest in the life forms you wish to change. Otherwise, playing God will come to no good. You cannot anticipate all the effects when you make genetic alterations."

Hunbatz draws an analogy with Einstein, a scientist who, late in his life, was appalled when he saw his theories put to destructive use in the form of nuclear bombs. Likewise, he says, scientists who are changing genes will regret the day they applied their intelligence to this task without also considering the spirits of the plants, the animals, and the people.

As a lineage holder of traditional Mayan knowledge, Hunbatz explains that his people have appreciated the concept and reality of genes for thousands of years. In fact, he believes the word "gene" ultimately derives from the Mayan *ge ne*, which denotes the sacred spiral of life that is evident not only in the double helix of our genes, but also in the form of the Milky Way galaxy, of which our Sun is part.

"It took nature millions of years to develop the genes in a good way," he says. "Now scientists motivated by money think they can change it all in two years. That's not a good motivation when you are dealing with something sacred. Scientists should study the plants as they are, and find ways to make them healthier by working with the spirit of the plants. This is the way to help humanity.

"Who is going to change the frequency of the minds of those who are now working with genes? It's up to us. When one person meditates, the energy is so big and has so much power. But when many people meditate, the power of the energy is far greater. We need to work in concert on this to change the frequency of their minds."

Hunbatz likewise cautions that modern scientists are fooling with something they don't understand when they experiment with nuclear fusion. "Fusion is the power of the Sun. Scientists are now playing with this, but they do not know what they are doing. First they are destroying the basic harmony of the genetic structure in plants, and then the plants that have been altered will have a subtly different effect on other plants and the creatures who eat those plants, as well as on the people who eat those plants and animals. It's the same with fusion. Scientists are playing with something they just don't know about. Fusion is no good without respect and good conscience. To get there, they need to make rituals."

Big Changes Are Coming

Hunbatz says the Maya believe that the legendary continent of Atlantis was a real place, the place of their origins. They still have a word, *atlan ti ha,* meaning "Sun—big place—water." Their legend says they came from this place when "the waters took the big stone of knowledge." And they believe Atlantis will rise again sometime. According to the Maya, the Yucatán peninsula where they live has been under water four times previously, and when that has happened the people who lived there simply moved away. "We heard the warning and we moved, unlike the people who live in California. They hear the warnings and they stay because they live in houses that they think are worth $250,000. They are attached to the wealth they have and so they ignore the warnings. The Maya did not ignore the warnings when they came. We all just packed up and moved. Then when the flood waters receded, we moved back."

Hunbatz points out that the USSR took nearly eighty years to build up its governmental system, but that it seemed to crumble within two weeks as the Berlin wall came down. That, he said, is also what the Mayan prophecies suggest for the governments on this continent. "The prophecies say big changes are coming, and that the Sun is going to help us. We cannot say whether the change will be good or bad, but we can influence it. When we make ritual in front of the Sun, the frequency changes in a good way for everyone. We need a big change now.

"This culture, the mainstream culture, does not have a lot of time left. Cultures come and go unless they copy the laws of eternity as the Maya have tried to do. The Mayan culture attempts to mimic eternity in language and ritual practices. Before the Greeks, Romans and Spaniards, the Maya made rituals for the Sun. In the time of the dark age, over the last five hundred years, those rituals have been hidden. But now they are coming back."

"If thousands of people believe in disasters, then they will happen. But not just because of the thought, rather because those who think this way are taking harsh actions upon the skin of the Earth Mother: cutting trees, pumping out the oil that is the lifeblood of the planet, and setting off nuclear bombs. Earth is delicate, like a small child. Most people think that they can take everything, including the blood of the Earth [oil]. The contamination of the sky with pollution allows harsh solar energies to penetrate to the surface of the Earth. And as people cut trees, they weaken the skin of the Earth, making her vulnerable to these and other cosmic energies that can then penetrate the Earth and lead to further imbalances.

"The Maya do not see God as wreaking havoc, but rather the people, who are, after all, part of God, destroying their mother. If we continue, it will happen. Our mother has a blanket to protect her. If we peel it off, she will catch an illness. Then big problems will come."

According to the Mayan prophecies, in the year 2013 we may see big white circles in the sky. If so, that would be an ominous sign that we had failed to make a successful and harmonious transition to the New Itzá Age. "In the prophecies of X'nuck'in," Hunbatz explains, "it is said, 'When the leaders have disorder in their minds, they will throw heat that is enclosed within receptacles.' If that comes to pass it will mean that nuclear bombs have gone off, that nuclear war has started. But I hope that will not happen. We can change that; that's also clear from the prophecies. We are responsible for the condition of the Earth. We are the ones who are responsible, and we can change that. If we wake up it is possible to change the energy. It is possible to change everything."

⟨⟨⟨⟨ CONTACTS ⟩⟩⟩⟩

*M*any of the elders profiled in this book live private lives, and would not necessarily welcome contact from readers. Yet others are teachers who seek to reach out to the world with their understandings and traditions. The list below contains the names and addresses of those elders who are open to contacts from those who wish to learn more. Approach them with respect, and be patient.

Dhyani Ywahoo
Sunray Meditation Society
P.O. Box 308
Bristol, VT 05443

Brant Secunda
Dance of the Deer Foundation
P.O. Box 699
Soquel, CA 95073

Twylah Nitsch
Wolf Clan Teaching Lodge
12199 Brant Reservation Rd.
Brant, NY 14027-0136

Medicine Story
Mettanokit Community
c/o Another Place
Rt. 123
Greenville, NH 03048

Sun Bear
Bear Tribe Medicine Society
P.O. Box 9167
Spokane, WA 99209

Oh Shinnah
Four Directions Foundation and the
    Center for Grandfather Coyote
c/o P.O. Box 56-1685
Miami, FL 33256-6705

AmyLee
c/o Hawk Hollow
Tippecanoe, OH 44699-9612

Slow Turtle
Massachusetts Center for Native
    American Awareness
330 Washington Ave.
Chelsea, MA 02150

Willaru Huayata
c/o Anderson Hewitt
Circles of Light
1404 Gale Lane
Nashville, TN 37212

Hunbatz Men
Communidad Indigena Maya
APDO. Postal 7-013
Mérida 7
Yucatán, México

〈〈〈〈 ABOUT THE AUTHOR 〉〉〉〉

Steven McFadden writes, counsels, and gardens from his home in rural New Hampshire. As he has learned from both vision and experience, his work is not just to communicate a vision of a healthy future, but also to help others develop their innate capacity to make that future real.

In the process of interviewing native grandfathers and grandmothers for this book, he deepened his appreciation of the wisdom principles necessary to help build a world that works for everyone, no matter the color of their skin or the name of their religion. Through his work he helps to weave the rainbow path—integrating the best of the past with the emerging technologies and spiritual sensibilities of a sustainable future. He has worked with groups in both corporate and private settings since 1975, and he travels widely offering lectures and workshops.

Steven is coauthor of a book entitled *Farms of Tomorrow: Community Supported Farms, Farm Supported Communities*. He is also a contributing writer in *Ecologue: The Environmental Catalogue and Consumer's Guide for a Safe Earth*. He can be contacted at the following address:

Steven McFadden
Chiron Communications
P.O. Box 481
New Ipswich, NH 03071

BOOKS OF RELATED INTEREST
BY BEAR & COMPANY

ANCIENT VOICES, CURRENT AFFAIRS
The Legend of the Rainbow Warriors
by *Steven McFadden*

CRYING FOR A DREAM
The World Through Native American Eyes
by *Richard Erdoes*

GIFT OF POWER
The Life and Teachings of a Lakota Medicine Man
by *Archie Fire Lame Deer and Richard Erdoes*

THE PRAYING FLUTE
Song of the Earth Mother
by *Tony Shearer*

THE RETURN OF PAHANA
A Hopi Myth
by *Robert Boissière*

SACRED PLACES
How the Living Earth Seeks Our Friendship
by *James Swan*

Contact your local bookseller or write:
BEAR & COMPANY
P.O. Drawer 2860
Santa Fe, NM 87504